Fundamentals of Linux

Explore the essentials of the Linux command line

Oliver Pelz

BIRMINGHAM - MUMBAI

Fundamentals of Linux

Commissioning Editor: Vijin Boricha
Acquisition Editor: Prachi Bisht
Content Development Editor: Dattatraya More
Technical Editors: Aditya Khadye, Cymon Pereira, Sayli Thanekar
Copy Editors: Laxmi Subramanian, Safis Editing
Project Coordinator: Kinjal Bari
Proofreader: Safis Editing
Indexer: Aishwarya Gangawane
Graphics: Jisha Chirayil
Production Coordinator: Deepika Naik

First published: June 2018

Production reference: 1300618

Published by Packt Publishing Ltd.
Livery Place
35 Livery Street
Birmingham
B3 2PB, UK.

ISBN 978-1-78953-095-7

www.packtpub.com

`mapt.io`

Mapt is an online digital library that gives you full access to over 5,000 books and videos, as well as industry leading tools to help you plan your personal development and advance your career. For more information, please visit our website.

Why subscribe?

- Spend less time learning and more time coding with practical eBooks and Videos from over 4,000 industry professionals

- Improve your learning with Skill Plans built especially for you

- Get a free eBook or video every month

- Mapt is fully searchable

- Copy and paste, print, and bookmark content

PacktPub.com

Did you know that Packt offers eBook versions of every book published, with PDF and ePub files available? You can upgrade to the eBook version at `www.PacktPub.com` and as a print book customer, you are entitled to a discount on the eBook copy. Get in touch with us at `service@packtpub.com` for more details.

At `www.PacktPub.com`, you can also read a collection of free technical articles, sign up for a range of free newsletters, and receive exclusive discounts and offers on Packt books and eBooks.

Contributor

About the author

Oliver Pelz has more than 10 years' experience as a software developer and system administrator. He graduated with a diploma degree in bioinformatics and is currently working at the German Cancer Research Center in Heidelberg, where he has authored and co-authored several scientific publications in the field of bioinformatics. He loves coding and riding his mountain bike in the Black Forest of Germany. He develops web applications and biological databases for his department and scientists all over the world and administers a division-wide Linux-based datacenter.

Packt is searching for authors like you

If you're interested in becoming an author for Packt, please visit authors.packtpub.com and apply today. We have worked with thousands of developers and tech professionals, just like you, to help them share their insight with the global tech community. You can make a general application, apply for a specific hot topic that we are recruiting an author for, or submit your own idea.

Table of Contents

Preface

In this book, the goal is to build a solid foundation of learning all the essentials of the Linux command line to get you started. It has been designed to strongly focus on learning only the practical core skills and essential Linux knowledge, which is really important when beginning this wonderful OS in an easy way. All the examples shown in this course have been carefully chosen to be everyday and real-world tasks, use cases, and problems Linux beginners or system administrators will probably encounter when starting out from scratch. We begin our journey with the virtualization software and install CentOS 7 Linux as a VM. Then, we will gently introduce you to the most basic command-line operations, such as cursor movement, commands, options and arguments, history, quoting and globbing, file streams and pipes, and getting help, and then introduce you to the wonderful art of regular expressions and how to work with files. Then, the most essential everyday Linux commands are demonstrated and explained, and a compact introduction to Bash shell scripting provided. Finally, the reader is introduced to advanced topics such as networking, how to troubleshoot your system, advanced file permissions, ACL, setuid, setgid, and sticky bit. This is just the starting point and there is so much more you can learn about Linux.

Who this book is for

This book is for individuals looking to work as Linux system administrator.

What this book covers

Chapter 1, *Introduction to Linux*, introduces you to the general idea of Linux. Topics range from virtualization, and the installation of VirtualBox and CentOS, through to the working dynamics of VirtualBox, and SSH connectivity with VirtualBox.

Chapter 2, *The Linux Command Line*, sheds some light on a wide range of topics, including shell globbing, an introduction to command-line operations, the navigation of files and folders in the Linux filesystem, the central idea of different streams, regular expressions, and important commands such as grep, sed, and awk.

Chapter 3, *The Linux Filesystem*, focuses on the working dynamics of the system, including file links, users and groups, file permissions, text files, text editor, and an understanding of the Linux filesystem.

Chapter 4, *Working with the Command Line*, walks you through essential Linux commands, signals, additional programs, processes, and Bash shell scripting.

Chapter 5, *More Advanced Command Lines and Concepts*, provides an overview of basic networking concepts, services, ACL, troubleshooting, setuid, setgid, and sticky bit.

To get the most out of this book

You will need a basic lab setup and at least a system with 8 GB of RAM and a dual-core processor. If you are planning to create a virtual environment, then a system with the same memory and a quad-core processor is recommended.

A VirtualBox and a VMware workstation are the best options for Windows. For Mac systems, run the testing system on parallels.

Throughout the book, we have used CentOS 7 minimal as the operating system.

Download the color images

We also provide a PDF file that has color images of the screenshots/diagrams used in this book. You can download it here: https://www.packtpub.com/sites/default/files/downloads/FundamentalsofLinux_ColorImages.pdf.

Conventions used

There are a number of text conventions used throughout this book.

CodeInText: Indicates code words in text, database table names, folder names, filenames, file extensions, pathnames, dummy URLs, user input, and Twitter handles. Here is an example: "The first CentOS 7 VM server can now be accessed using the IP 127.0.0.1 with port 2222, the second at port 2223, and the third at port 2224."

Any command-line input or output is written as follows:

```
# yum update -y
```

Bold: Indicates a new term, an important word, or words that you see onscreen. For example, words in menus or dialog boxes appear in the text like this. Here is an example: "Select our **CentOS 7** server VM and click on the green **Start** button to start it."

 Warnings or important notes appear like this.

 Tips and tricks appear like this.

Get in touch

Feedback from our readers is always welcome.

General feedback: Email `feedback@packtpub.com` and mention the book title in the subject of your message. If you have questions about any aspect of this book, please email us at `questions@packtpub.com`.

Errata: Although we have taken every care to ensure the accuracy of our content, mistakes do happen. If you have found a mistake in this book, we would be grateful if you would report this to us. Please visit `www.packtpub.com/submit-errata`, selecting your book, clicking on the Errata Submission Form link, and entering the details.

Piracy: If you come across any illegal copies of our works in any form on the Internet, we would be grateful if you would provide us with the location address or website name. Please contact us at `copyright@packtpub.com` with a link to the material.

If you are interested in becoming an author: If there is a topic that you have expertise in and you are interested in either writing or contributing to a book, please visit `authors.packtpub.com`.

Reviews

Please leave a review. Once you have read and used this book, why not leave a review on the site that you purchased it from? Potential readers can then see and use your unbiased opinion to make purchase decisions, we at Packt can understand what you think about our products, and our authors can see your feedback on their book. Thank you!

For more information about Packt, please visit packtpub.com.

Introduction to Linux

1

An **operating system** (**OS**) is a special piece of software running on your computer to make it possible to start and run programs such as Microsoft Word and Excel. Besides that, it handles your computer's input and output for you and delivers filesystem and hardware control. Examples of operating systems you may already know are Windows, macOS, iOS, or Android.

In this chapter, we'll cover the following topics:

- An overview of the Linux system
- Virtualization
- Installing VirtualBox and CentOS
- Working with VirtualBox
- Connecting VMs through SSH

An overview of the Linux system

Linux is not the name of a specific and full working OS, but implements only the essential inner core of an OS, which is referred to as the kernel. Most types of Linux OS do not cost anything, but provide thousands of programs and software to use completely free of charge. Most of these programs are also open source, which means you can view the exact blueprint of how the program has been created and it can be changed by anyone. One very important area in which Linux is very popular and is used heavily is managing many network services. These are programs that run in the background of your Linux server, continuously waiting for external events to respond with some kind of action or information. Examples are popular internet services such as a web server, which presents websites to the user; main servers for email communications; and also database servers to store and deliver any kind of data. As mentioned before, Linux is only the name of the kernel part, not a full working OS. To make it complete, you need to bundle it together with all kinds of programs, which is then referred to as a **distribution**.

Nowadays, one can choose between an insane amount of different Linux distributions, all designed for a special purpose and all with their own pros and cons. The main difference between them is the software selected and bundled together with the Linux kernel. The most important Linux distribution families are Red Hat- and Debian-based Linux distributions. CentOS is one of the most important free Red Hat-based Linux server distributions out there at the moment. It's a very stable, secure, and reliable OS, which is why it's often used in running very critical networking services in enterprise environments. Also, it's good to know that the development of this OS is very strong and updates are well selected and suitably tested. The first chapter of this book is about installing Linux; here we will be starting easy by introducing you to the concepts of virtualization. Then, we will create a new CentOS 7 **virtual machine (VM)** using a free virtualization software called VirtualBox.

Virtualization

In this section, we will give you an overview of the concepts of virtualization. We will also show you how to work with VirtualBox, and afterward show you how you can install your first CentOS 7 virtual machine in VirtualBox. It is a very hot topic and the core IT skill at the moment is virtualization.

Simply put, it is a technology to run separate operating systems parallel to your main operating system on the same computer. For example, if you are currently working on a Windows computer, you can run another operating system such as Linux or macOS in parallel to a simple Windows application on your desktop. Modern virtualization software does not even limit you to run only one parallel OS, but you can run multiple systems in parallel. The limits are only defined by your own computer hardware. The applications for virtualization technology in modern IT are endless, and you will find them everywhere. The advantages can range from shifting IT infrastructure paradigms to undoing changes to your operating systems, which is quite ideal for beginners.

In cloud computing or modern data centers, powerful virtualization server clusters are running many different operating systems simultaneously, instead of using dedicated server hardware. If you wanted to use Linux before the age of virtualization, you needed access to dedicated physical computers. Also, most beginners will mess up their new Linux installation several times when starting out on Linux. Oftentimes, such system changes can be hard to reboot and the only efficient and useful consequence is to reinstall a complete system when getting stuck. Virtualization gets rid of all these problems. We will use it for conveniently working with all the examples throughout the entire chapter thanks to its powerful features such as cloning, taking snapshots, or creating images, which also eliminates the fear of breaking something. At the moment, there is a broad range of different virtualization products available for both desktop and non-graphical server environments to choose from, both in the commercial and open source sector.

At the core level, all of these different virtualization products have the same basic features and common definitions, which we need to make clear before we can dive deeper. When we talk about operating systems running in parallel to your physical machine's operating system, we will refer to them as VMs, or virtual machines, from this point forward. In the same context, our main operating system running our physical machine which runs the virtualization software is called the **host system** or **hypervisor**. The VMs running on this host are called the **guest systems** or **guests**. Copying and cloning is one of the most important features of virtualization. This can save you precious time, for example, if you need another identical machine or to make your work more portable. Just copy the image to your laptop or a different data center and you're done. The portable copy of a VM is also called an **image**. Another awesome feature is taking snapshots of your VM. Taking such a snapshot only takes a few seconds but will save the complete and current state of your VM at any given point in time. This is very useful if you want to preserve a given version of your VM you may later want to revert to. Another feature different virtualization products have in common are the types of supported network modes.

The different modes a VM can use to connect to a network can be as follows:

- **NAT**: All incoming and outgoing network traffic of your guest VM will go through the host network adapter. This means that the VM is not visible in the network we are currently on and we only see our host's MAC and IP addresses.
- **Bridged**: This network mode means the VM exposes itself and connects to the surrounding physical network as if it were a normal physical machine with its own unique MAC address. A DHCP server in this network will give the machine its own IP address that differs from the host machine.

- **Host-only**: This means that the VM can only communicate with and is visible to its host and not the rest of the network.
- **Specific virtual network**: This is a very great feature where you can define private and isolated subnet works, independent of the surrounding physical network, and then associate VMs to it. This can be useful so that only VMs can see and talk to other machines, which are in the same virtual network.

Installing VirtualBox and CentOS

In this section, we will show you how to install the free virtualization software called **VirtualBox**, before creating a new CentOS 7 VM. We will also finish very important post-installation tasks, which we will need to perform in the upcoming sections. Installation of VirtualBox is really straightforward. Executable installers are available for every major operating system. The following are the steps to install VirtualBox:

1. Open your favorite web browser and navigate to `https://www.virtualbox.org/`. Now, click on the download button that is clearly visible on the home page.
2. Select a target host OS of your choice. In our example, we will select Windows.
3. Click on **Windows hosts** to start the download. Also, don't forget to download the VirtualBox extension pack that you can find on the same **Downloads** page.

This is a package that will provide better USB support, among other useful features. After the download has finished, open the downloaded installer to run it and install it using the default settings.

Now, let's create a new CentOS 7 VM in VirtualBox. In order to do so, we first need to download the CentOS 7 Minimal ISO file version 1611 from the official CentOS website (`https://www.centos.org/`). This contains only the most important software packages needed to run a non-graphical Linux server, which is exactly what we want.

The following are the steps for creating a new CentOS 7 VM:

1. Open a web browser and navigate to `https://www.centos.org/`. Navigate to **Get CentOS Now | Minimal ISO**.
2. On the next screen, select the download URL near to your current location for fast download speed. I'm currently located in Germany, so my actual download URL will most likely be different than yours if you're somewhere else.

3. Wait until the download has finished.

On a modern and fast computer, you can install a fully working operating system such as CentOS 7 inside VirtualBox within a few minutes.

4. Run VirtualBox on your system. Now, let's reproduce the following steps to install our first CentOS 7 VM:

   1. Click on the **New** button to create a new VM. If you type the VM **Name** as CentOS 7, VirtualBox will recognize the two other fields, **Type** and **Version**, to be **Linux** and **Red Hat (64-bit)** correctly for you.
   2. Click on the **Next** button to proceed to the next step.
   3. Now, select how much memory or RAM your VM must have. If you don't want any performance issues for your host system, stay in the green area displayed to you in the **Memory size** window.
   4. For a basic headless server, which means a non-graphical server, at least 2 GB of RAM is recommended. Don't worry, you can change this setting later too.
   5. Click on the **Next** button and on the next screen leave the default settings as is. Now, click on **Create**.
   6. Select the **VDI** option and click on **Next**. Now, on this screen, stay with the **Dynamically allocated** option. Click on **Next**.
   7. On the next screen, double the virtual hard disk size to 16 GB, as 8 GB is way too little for our work.
   8. Finally, click on the **Create** button to create a fresh and empty VM ready for installation of CentOS 7.

Now, let's install CentOS 7 in our empty VM:

1. Select our **CentOS 7** server VM and click on the green **Start** button to start it. Here, our downloaded CentOS 7 ISO file will be used as a virtual CD-ROM by VirtualBox and this is where it can be booted or started from.
2. To do this, click on the small folder symbol and navigate the file browser to your downloaded CentOS 7 Minimal ISO file, and then click on the **Start** button.
3. Now, your VM will present you with a text-based start menu, where we will use the up arrow key on the keyboard to select **Install CentOS Linux 7** and then press *Enter* to start the installer.

4. After waiting for some time, you will be presented with the first graphical installation screen.

 Before we click or type something into the VM window for the first time, we need to know how we can switch back to our host system once we are in. If you click once on the guest window, a popup will show up telling you how you can switch controls back and forth.

5. Select the installer language. In our example, we used the default **English** language.

 This is not the language of your CentOS 7 installation. We will set this type of information on the next screen.

6. Click on **Continue**. Now, we are on the main installation screen, where we can customize our installation. You will need to wait until all the items have been loaded.

 Here, all the items which are marked with an exclamation mark need to be done before we can proceed with the installation, but you can also do optional settings here like setting your location information.

7. Next, we need to set the installation destination. Click on **INSTALLATION DESTINATION**. As we are using an empty VM, we will use the full hard disk for installation, which is the default, so just click on **Done** which is present at the top-left side of the screen.

8. Before we start the actual installation, let's quickly enable our Ethernet network card here, so we don't have to do this post installation using the command line. If you are behind a proxy, you can also add this kind of information here in this menu. Click on **Done** if you're ready.

9. Now, let's click on **Begin Installation**. While the installation is ongoing, set a strong and secure password for the administrator or root account, which is the account that has all the rights and control over a system. Click on **Done** after setting up the strong password.

10. Now, from the same screen, you can create a normal user account for your everyday work.

The first rule of any secure Linux system is never work with the root user unless you need to.

11. Click on **Done** after creating the new user account.
12. Now wait until the installation has finished. Once the installation is finished, click on the **Reboot** button to restart your system.
13. Pressing the *Enter* key on the start screen will always select and use the latest kernel.
14. Now, wait until you get a login screen in this window, which is also called our **Service Terminal**.
15. Log in using the `root` user and password you set during the installation.
16. Then, type the following command in the Terminal and press the *Enter* key:

```
# yum update -y
```

This command will install all the latest software updates available for your CentOS 7 installation, as the installer media does not have them included.

If you get a new error while this command is running, something must be wrong with your internet connection, so troubleshoot internet connectivity on your host system.

If the core of the CentOS 7 system, which is called the **kernel**, has been updated, we need to reboot the system. So, type `reboot` in the Terminal, and then press *Enter*. After rebooting again, press the *Enter* key then wait for the login screen to load and log in again.

Next, we type in another two commands, which will clear out all our free space so that we can create a smaller backup image of the system. Now, type the following command with administrative/root access in the Terminal:

```
dd if=/dev/zero of=/dd.img; rm -f /dd.img
```

```
CentOS Linux 7 (Core)
Kernel 3.10.0-862.3.3.el7.x86_64 on an x86_64

localhost login: root
Password:
Last login: Mon Jun 18 05:50:06 on tty1
[root@localhost ~]# dd if=/dev/zero of=/dd.img; rm -f /dd.img
dd: writing to '/dd.img': No space left on device
25806681+0 records in
25806680+0 records out
13213020160 bytes (13 GB) copied, 111.434 s, 119 MB/s
[root@localhost ~]# _
```

Now, press the *Enter* key. This command will override all the free space of your Linux filesystem by creating one big file containing only zeros until the disk is full. This will take some time, so you will need to be patient. If this command outputs some text, it has been finished. You can ignore the error output as this is the expected behavior.

Finally, for setting up SSH port forwarding, we need to write down the actual IP address of our VM's connected network adapter. Run the following command:

```
ip addr list
```

Press *Enter* and, in the output line type in the IP address, which is the value after the word inet. In our example, it's 10.0.2.15.

To shut down the VM, use the following command and then press the *Enter* key:

```
shutdown -h
```

Working with VirtualBox

In this section, we will learn the most important steps needed to properly work with the VirtualBox. Note that most of the settings discussed here can be directly translated from VirtualBox to any other desktop virtualization software such as KVM, VMware, Workstation, or Parallels Desktop.

Let's follow these steps to export the VM image:

1. Navigate your cursor to the top-left corner of the **Oracle VM VirtualBox Manager** screen. Here, click on the **File** menu and in the drop-down menu select **Export Appliance...**.

2. In the same drop-down menu, you'll find another menu item called **Import Appliance...**, which allows you to import an image file once it has been created.

3. Now, click on **Export Appliance...** to start the process.

4. In the **Export Virtual Appliance** screen, select the VM you want to create an image of and then click on **Next**.

5. Now, on the **Storage settings** screen leave the default settings as it is and then click on **Next** again.

6. Again, on the **Appliance settings** screen, we don't want to change anything, so click on the **Export** button to start the process. This will take some time, so you will need to be patient.

7. After the export process has been completed, let's examine what the resulting file will look like.

8. Go to the location where VirtualBox has exported your file (usually, you'll find it in the Documents folder) and then right-click and select the **Properties...** option to view the file's properties:

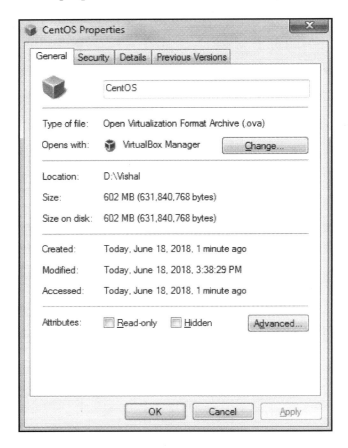

As you can see, the exported VM size is over 600 MB in size, which is pretty awesome. This image file could now be copied to a backup location or transferred to another machine or data center for running it. The next thing we should do before working with our VM is also make a snapshot from the current state right after installation, so we can revert to the status quo whenever we need to.

Follow these steps to create a snapshot of the VM:

1. Select the appropriate VM and then click on the **Snapshots** option for your marked VM. Give it a suitable name and an optional description.
2. The next thing we want to do here is create some exact copies of our VM so that we have multiple CentOS 7 servers. To do this, right-click on the VM and select the **Clone...** option. Give it a suitable name and mark the option named **Reinitialize the MAC address of all network cards**, so it will be seen as a unique machine in our network.
3. On the **Clone type** windows, select **Full clone** and click on **Next** to continue. Now, click on the **Clone** button while leaving the default option selected.
4. Repeat the previous steps to create another fully cloned VM.

Now, let's demonstrate the power of working with snapshots. A snapshot should always be taken before doing something risky. For example, start one of our CentOS 7 VMs and log in to the system. Now, let's imagine we want to work on the /boot directory, where the Linux kernels reside. This is a critical directory, so it's a good idea to create a snapshot of the current VM state before proceeding:

```
localhost login: root
Password:
Last login: Mon Jun 18 05:55:43 on tty1
[root@localhost ~]# cd /boot
[root@localhost boot]# ls
config-3.10.0-862.3.3.el7.x86_64
config-3.10.0-862.el7.x86_64
efi
grub
grub2
initramfs-0-rescue-e89f02001229438d95a7f046601cdef0.img
initramfs-3.10.0-862.3.3.el7.x86_64.img
initramfs-3.10.0-862.el7.x86_64.img
symvers-3.10.0-862.3.3.el7.x86_64.gz
symvers-3.10.0-862.el7.x86_64.gz
System.map-3.10.0-862.3.3.el7.x86_64
System.map-3.10.0-862.el7.x86_64
vmlinuz-0-rescue-e89f02001229438d95a7f046601cdef0
vmlinuz-3.10.0-862.3.3.el7.x86_64
vmlinuz-3.10.0-862.el7.x86_64
[root@localhost boot]# rm -rf *
[root@localhost boot]#
[root@localhost boot]#
[root@localhost boot]#
```

In the previous screenshot, you can see that I've made a severe mistake. I completely deleted the whole kernel directory, so the directory is now empty. What will happen if I restart the system now? Let's see:

```
error: file `/grub2/i386-pc/normal.mod' not found.
Entering rescue mode...
grub rescue> _
```

As you can see in the previous screenshot, I cannot boot without any kernel and the system is now completely unresponsive, and this gets really hard to fix. What is the best solution for this problem? Reverting to the state of your last snapshot.

Perform the following steps to revert the VM state to the previous snapshot:

1. First shut down your VM. Now, select the snapshot of your choice and then click on the **Restore** button. This will ask you if you want to create a snapshot of the current state. If we don't want to do this, then we click on the **Restore** button, as shown in the following screenshot:

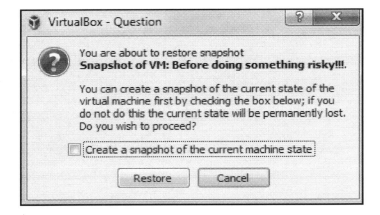

2. Now, you can start the VM. As you can see from the following screenshot, we are just about to execute the `delete` command:

```
CentOS Linux 7 (Core)
Kernel 3.10.0-862.3.3.el7.x86_64 on an x86_64

localhost login: root
Password:
Last login: Mon Jun 18 05:55:43 on tty1
[root@localhost ~]# cd /boot
[root@localhost boot]# ls
config-3.10.0-862.3.3.el7.x86_64
config-3.10.0-862.el7.x86_64
efi
grub
grub2
initramfs-0-rescue-e89f02001229438d95a7f046601cdef0.img
initramfs-3.10.0-862.3.3.el7.x86_64.img
initramfs-3.10.0-862.el7.x86_64.img
symvers-3.10.0-862.3.3.el7.x86_64.gz
symvers-3.10.0-862.el7.x86_64.gz
System.map-3.10.0-862.3.3.el7.x86_64
System.map-3.10.0-862.el7.x86_64
vmlinuz-0-rescue-e89f02001229438d95a7f046601cdef0
vmlinuz-3.10.0-862.3.3.el7.x86_64
vmlinuz-3.10.0-862.el7.x86_64
[root@localhost boot]# _
```

3. If we start the machine again, all the problems are gone and we are back where we were before deleting the kernel files. It is recommended to use the snapshot feature often since it can save your precious time.

4. Finally, we can easily adjust our VM's hardware parameters if we need to, as shown in the following screenshot:

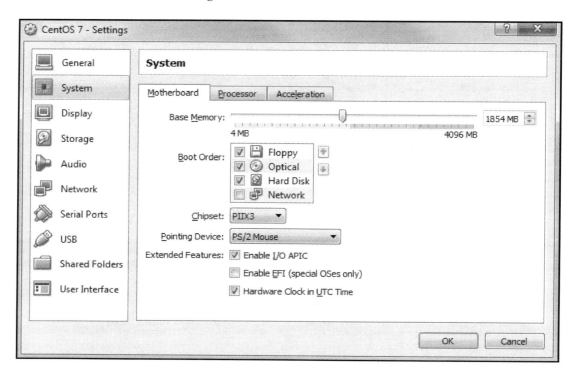

 Before making any hardware changes, ensure that you shut down the VM and then proceed.

You can only do this on a part of the machine. Select your VM of choice and click on **Settings** and then on **System**, where you can adjust your memory. Also, you can adjust your virtual process here. Click on **Display** to change the **Video Memory** settings. Under **Storage**, you can attach virtual hard disks or create new ones. Under **Network**, you can create new network adapters for your VM and choose between different network modes. Under USB, select **USB 2.0 (EHCI) Controller** so that we can connect a physical USB device to our VM properly if we want to.

Connecting VMs through SSH

Working with your new Linux OS using its Terminal window through the VirtualBox user interface will get you started and can be used for configuring the most basic settings of your new server. A more convenient, efficient, and professional way of accessing your server's command line is by using a terminal emulator program and SSH. A terminal emulator is an external program running outside VirtualBox in a separate window on your OS. It can be used exactly the same way as your server's main black and white Terminal:

```
$ netstat -an
Active Internet connections (servers and established)
Proto Recv-Q Send-Q Local Address           Foreign Address         State
tcp        0      0 10.93.118.246:39003     0.0.0.0:*               LISTEN
tcp        0      0 10.197.76.73:5060       0.0.0.0:*               LISTEN
tcp        0      0 10.93.118.246:42952     0.0.0.0:*               LISTEN
tcp        0      0 10.93.118.246:59899     10.56.84.12:5061        ESTABLISHED
tcp        0      0 10.93.118.246:57838     104.17.161.9:443        ESTABLISHED
tcp        0      0 10.93.118.246:50880     74.125.68.114:80        ESTABLISHED
tcp        0      0 10.93.118.246:58035     216.58.220.162:443      ESTABLISHED
udp        0      0 10.93.118.246:45067     0.0.0.0:*
udp        0      0 10.93.118.246:49656     216.58.220.162:443      ESTABLISHED
udp        0      0 10.197.76.73:5060       0.0.0.0:*
raw        0      0 0.0.0.0:1               0.0.0.0:*               1
Active UNIX domain sockets (servers and established)
Proto RefCnt Flags       Type       State         I-Node Path
unix  2      [ ACC ]     STREAM     LISTENING      9243 @mcdaemon
unix  2      [ ACC ]     STREAM     LISTENING      9287 /data/.socket_stream
unix  2      [ ACC ]     SEQPACKET  LISTENING     23565 /dev/socket/vpnclientd
unix  2      [ ACC ]     STREAM     LISTENING     12318 @imsd
unix  2      [ ACC ]     STREAM     LISTENING      5885 /data/app/rpmbd
unix  2      [ ACC ]     STREAM     LISTENING      5907 @epdgd2
unix  2      [ ACC ]     STREAM     LISTENING      8355 /data/.diagsocket_stream
unix  2      [ ACC ]     STREAM     LISTENING      8356 /data/.diag_stream
unix  2      [ ACC ]     STREAM     LISTENING      7433 /data/ss_kbservice_daemon
unix  2      [ ACC ]     STREAM     LISTENING      9297 /data/.mtp_stream
```

It has a lot of convenient features, such as easy copy and paste in clipboards from your OS window and customizing font size and colors. Also, it uses tabs for better navigation, but how can you communicate with such a terminal emulator from your server? This is done using a client-server connection. The terminal emulator running on your host machine will be declined; we will connect to the CentOS 7 server to execute commands on it. Such a connection can be done using SSH. This is a system for remotely accessing and using Linux servers. It uses strong encryption for secure connections. As SSH is one of the most fundamental core services for communication on any Linux server, it is already installed and enabled on CentOS 7. All we need to do is run an SSH client within our terminal emulator program, which can connect and communicate with any server running the SSH service on Linux and macOS, a terminal emulator program, and an open source, as a stage client is already installed by default and ready to use.

On Windows, you need to install the program PuTTY, which contains not only the SSH client program, but is also a fully operational terminal emulator. Before we can access the CentOS 7 SSH service, we need to make its correct network address available to the host system where our terminal emulator is running. A correct network connection for communicating between a client and server always consists of an IP address, or domain name, bundled together with a specific port number. The domain name or IP is like a house number, whereas the port number is like the exact apartment number in that house. We always need both values for the correct delivery of network packages. By default, the ports of any guest VM are not available to the outside host system, so we first need to create the link between the host and the guest by using a feature that is called **port forwarding**. SSH, by default, is running on port 22, but this low port number cannot be used for forwarding to by non admin users or route users. As we are running VirtualBox as a normal user, we need to forward port 22 to a user port higher than 1024.

In our example, we use port 2222. To do this, perform the following steps:

1. Select your VM of choice and navigate to the **Settings** option. Click on the **Network** tab.
2. Explore the **Advanced** option. Now, click on the **Port Forwarding** button to create a new port forwarding rule.
3. In the **Port Forwarding Rules** window, click on the **Adds new port forwarding rule** button. Now, use the 127.0.0.1 IP for the **Host IP** section, which is the IP of the localhost, then the **Host Port**, 2222. For the **Guest IP** section, type 10.0.2.15 and **Guest Port** 22, as illustrated in the following screenshot:

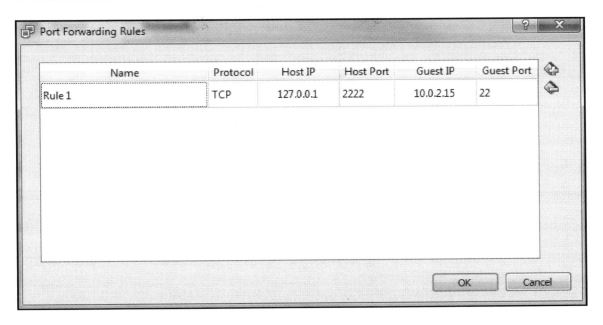

4. Click on **OK** to create this rule.
5. Repeat the same for the other two CentOS 7 VMs we cloned earlier. Make sure to use different host ports so that we can create distinct network endpoint connections for every host.
6. The first CentOS 7 VM server can now be accessed using the IP 127.0.0.1 with port 2222, the second at port 2223, and the third at port 2224. Now, start all three of your CentOS 7 VMs.
7. Open your favorite terminal emulator, for example, xterm, GNOME Terminal, or (as is in my example) the Xfce4 Terminal.
8. To log in to your first CentOS 7 server using the terminal emulator, use the root credentials. Type the following command in the Terminal window:

```
ssh -p space 2222 root@127.0.0.1.
```

9. Press the *Enter* key. This command will connect your local SSH client to the SSH server running at the IP address 127.0.0.1 on port 2222, which gets redirected to your VM's network address 10.0.2.15 at port 22.
10. When prompted, type yes in the Terminal, if you are logging into the server for the first time.
11. Now, enter the credentials of the root user you set during installation.

12. Here, we can now work and type commands as we would on the real Terminal screen. We can also log into the other two CentOS 7 VMs using the other two ports.

13. To exit the SSH session, type in `exit` and press *Enter*.

14. On a Windows system, you can use the free program named PuTTY to do exactly the same operations.

15. Just open the PuTTY graphical user interface, type in the SSH server's **IP address**, `127.0.0.1`, and use port `2222` for connection. Now, use the root account to access the VM.

16. After setting up port forwarding, the easiest way is to use the free SCP program available on Mac or Linux. On Windows, you need to download PSCP.

17. To download a file called `/etc/passwd` from the CentOS 7 VM guest to the host using the root user in the current directory, type the following command:

    scp -P 2222 root@127.0.0.1:/etc/passwd .

18. When asked, type in your root password. Now we can view the file locally:

19. The other way around to upload a local file called `my-local-file`, filled with some random data to the server, and type `scp -P 2222 my-local-file root@127.0.0.1:~`.

20. Press *Enter*, and type your root's password. The file has now been uploaded to the server into the `/home` folder, which is specified by the `~`.

Summary

In this chapter, we've covered the introductory concepts of Linux and VirtualBox. We started off by gaining an understanding of the working principle of an operating system and progressed towards virtualization. Next, we covered the installation of VirtualBox and CentOS. Then, we learned how to work with VirtualBox and connected it using SSH.

In the next chapter, we'll understand the workings of the command line.

The Linux Command Line

In this chapter, we will introduce you to the most fundamental concepts when starting to work with the Linux command line. It is a very powerful and efficient tool with which you can execute the various actions that you'll generally require when using Linux. A plethora of shortcuts and tricks will help you to navigate the command line more efficiently.

In this chapter, we'll walk you through the following:

- Shell globbing
- Redirecting and piping
- The `grep`, `sed`, and `awk` commands
- Navigating files and folders in a Linux system

Introducing the command line

In this section, you'll learn how to run Linux command-line programs and what the basic structure of the command line is. You will also learn what program options and arguments are and why they are important for customizing your commands.

When we say the Linux command line, what we really mean is the **shell**. It's important to know that the shell is not the same as a terminal emulator. A Terminal is a screen or window that lets you access a Linux server's input and output. A shell is just a program that runs on the server as does any other command and which awaits, interprets, processes, executes, and responds to commands typed in by the user.

First, open up a new terminal emulator and log in to your CentOS 7 server by using SSH, as we learned in the Chapter 1, *Introduction to Linux*. Log in using your normal user account, which you set up during installation, because, as we have said before, never work with the root user unless you have to. In my example, the username is olip:

```
olip@localhost:~
[root@localhost ~]# ssh -p 22 olip@127.0.0.1
olip@127.0.0.1's password:
Last login: Wed Jun 20 02:05:01 2018 from localhost
[olip@localhost ~]$ 
```

After successfully logging in to your server, an important program has been started automatically, which is called the shell, and which have been using this whole time. In fact, when we talk about the Linux Terminal, what we are really speaking of is the shell. There exist several shell variants; on CentOS 7 we are using **Bash**, or the **Bourne Again Shell**, by default. When the shell is started, the first thing you will notice is the line ending with the dollar sign ($), which is called the shell prompt.

In our example, it gives us some useful information: the login username and the current directory we're on. The tilde is a special character and it means home directory, which is the default directory when logging in. After the shell prompt comes the cursor, which is the underscore character, and this is where the user can type in the text that then gets processed and executed by the shell. But user input will only get processed and executed by the shell when the input has been ended with the *Enter* key. If you make any type of mistake, just hit the backspace key to delete the last character. The first useful command we will learn in this chapter is how to log out of the system.

On the Linux Terminal, this command logs out the current user and goes back to the login screen:

1. Open the Linux Terminal and type the logout command and after that press the *Enter* key.
2. However, if you perform the same operation while using an SSH connection, it has the same effect as the exit command that we learned about in the previous chapter.
3. Let's try to log in again to the CentOS server.
4. Let's try out a simple command; type date and press the *Enter* key. This is a command that prints out the current date-time value:

```
olip@localhost:~
[olip@localhost ~]$ ssh -p 2222 olip@127.0.0.1
ssh: connect to host 127.0.0.1 port 2222: Connection refused
[olip@localhost ~]$ logout
Connection to 127.0.0.1 closed.
[root@localhost ~]# clear
[root@localhost ~]# ssh -p 22 olip@127.0.0.1
olip@127.0.0.1's password:
Last login: Wed Jun 20 02:02:23 2018 from localhost
[olip@localhost ~]$ du -h --max-depth=1 /tmp
0       /tmp/.font-unix
0       /tmp/.Test-unix
0       /tmp/.XIM-unix
0       /tmp/.ICE-unix
0       /tmp/.X11-unix
du: cannot read directory '/tmp/systemd-private-711ef173c3d147df99f49b23b1a44e62-chronyd.service-VLcPWH':
0       /tmp/systemd-private-711ef173c3d147df99f49b23b1a44e62-chronyd.service-VLcPWH
4.0K    /tmp
[olip@localhost ~]$ whoami
olip
[olip@localhost ~]$ logout
Connection to 127.0.0.1 closed.
[root@localhost ~]# ssh -p 22 olip@127.0.0.1
olip@127.0.0.1's password:
Last login: Wed Jun 20 02:03:50 2018 from localhost
[olip@localhost ~]$ date
Wed Jun 20 02:05:05 EDT 2018
[olip@localhost ~]$ []
```

As you can see, if the shell has finished executing a specific command and is ready to accept new input by the user, a new shell prompt will appear in a new line marking its readiness. Now, type `cal` and press *Enter*. This command prints out a nice table view of the current month.

 If the first character of any command types is prepended in the shell with the hash key, the command will not be executed when pressing the *Enter* key.

A typical Linux system such as CentOS 7 contains hundreds of different commands included in the default installation. If you could only type in the pure commands and nothing more, our work in the shell would be very limited and static and you would not be able to work properly at all. So, we need a way to customize our commands or change the default behavior during execution, feeding them further information. But how can we do that?

Enter the power of command-line options and arguments. First, we need to discuss the general structure of a command in the shell, which in its most simple form is COMMANDNAME OPTIONS ARGUMENTS. The command name is the name of the command to be started. Be careful, in Linux command names are case sensitive. Type whoami and then press *Enter*. This command will print out the name of the current user working in the shell. As Linux is case sensitive, this command cannot be started using uppercase letters, such as each version refers to a different command. Here, we will also see why the shell is such a useful program. It not only listens and interprets commands, but it also shows you helpful error messages when something goes wrong, such as a command cannot be found in the system. Normally, on Linux all standard Bash script commands are written in lowercase. To get a list of some of the available commands, type ls /bin. Now, let's move on to one of the most fundamental commands available in the shell. Type ls and press the *Enter* key. This command lists files in a directory. If no further information is given, it prints out all the visible files in the directory that we are currently in at the moment:

```
olip@localhost ~
[olip@localhost ~]$ ls
file_1.txt   file_2.txt   file_3.txt   file_4.txt
[olip@localhost ~]$ []
```

As you can see, a shell command can also contain options and arguments that are appended to the command name and separated from it using spaces. This means if you want to provide at least one option or argument, then we need at least one space after the command name. First, let's talk about command-line options. Their aim is to influence the behavior of a command. They are also called **switches** or **flags**. There is no obligatory standard, but normally any single-character command-line option starts with a single dash, whereas longer option names have two dash symbols. Also, if you want to provide multiple single-character command-line options, for most standard Linux commands you can just write them in series. It is good to know that single-character command-line options are often abbreviations describing their meaning: −d could stand for directory, −x for exclude, and so on.

We already know that the ls command without any further options gives us a list of all the files in the current directory. If you type ls −a and press *Enter*, you just run your first command with the command-line option. The a switch stands for all and this influences the default behavior ls by giving you a list of all files, including the hidden ones, which in Linux start with the leading dash in the current directory. Now, let's type ls −alth and press the *Enter* key to see the result:

```
[olip@localhost ~]$ ls -alth
total 32K
drwx------. 2 olip olip 155 Jun 20 02:25 .
-rw-r--r--. 1 root root   2 Jun 20 02:25 file_4.txt
-rw-r--r--. 1 root root   2 Jun 20 02:25 file_3.txt
-rw-r--r--. 1 root root   2 Jun 20 02:25 file_2.txt
-rw-r--r--. 1 root root   2 Jun 20 02:25 file_1.txt
-rw-------. 1 olip olip 255 Jun 20 02:24 .bash_history
drwxr-xr-x. 3 root root  18 Jun 20 01:43 ..
-rw-r--r--. 1 olip olip  18 Apr 10 20:53 .bash_logout
-rw-r--r--. 1 olip olip 193 Apr 10 20:53 .bash_profile
-rw-r--r--. 1 olip olip 231 Apr 10 20:53 .bashrc
[olip@localhost ~]$
```

This influences the command's default behavior even more by using the −a flag that we just discussed, and also using the −l switch, which stands for **list**, and it prints all the files in a list format, including more detailed information, such as the creation date. The −t switch stands for **time** and it sorts the file list by modification date with the newest entries appearing first, and −h stands for **human readable** and it will print out the file size in a more readable form using **MB** instead of bytes for the file size.

 Often, command-line options can have arguments bound to them. In addition to options, we have command-line arguments, which are also called **parameters**. This is any dynamic or free-text piece of information that is not an option, and which gets fed into the command when it starts. Typical examples are filenames or directories that the command wants to process during execution. Arguments are also divided by *spaces*.

Type echo Hello and press *Enter*:

```
[olip@localhost ~]$ echo Hello
Hello
[olip@localhost ~]$
```

In the previous command, Hello is an argument for the echo command and not an option. The echo command is one of the most fundamental shell commands. It just prints the arguments given to it back to the command line. As we will see, this is ideal for testing shell features such as **globbing**, which we will learn more about later in this section. Now let's type ls -al /boot /var in the Terminal and press *Enter* to see a result similar to the following:

```
[olip@localhost ~]$ ls -al /boot /var
/boot:
total 146256
dr-xr-xr-x.  5 root root     4096 Jun 20 02:00 .
dr-xr-xr-x. 17 root root      224 Jun 20 01:58 ..
-rw-r--r--.  1 root root   147823 Jun 15 00:29 config-3.10.0-862.3.3.el7.x86_64
-rw-r--r--.  1 root root   147819 Apr 20 12:57 config-3.10.0-862.el7.x86_64
drwxr-xr-x.  3 root root       17 Jun 20 01:38 efi
drwxr-xr-x.  2 root root       27 Jun 20 01:39 grub
drwx------.  5 root root       97 Jun 20 01:49 grub2
-rw-------.  1 root root 55394321 Jun 20 01:42 initramfs-0-rescue-c829291fe54b45ac94048e60228bbbe4.img
-rw-------.  1 root root 20876330 Jun 20 01:49 initramfs-3.10.0-862.3.3.el7.x86_64.img
-rw-------.  1 root root 13090049 Jun 20 02:00 initramfs-3.10.0-862.3.3.el7.x86_64kdump.img
-rw-------.  1 root root 20876208 Jun 20 01:50 initramfs-3.10.0-862.el7.x86_64.img
-rw-------.  1 root root 13083880 Jun 20 01:46 initramfs-3.10.0-862.el7.x86_64kdump.img
-rw-r--r--.  1 root root   304943 Jun 15 00:31 symvers-3.10.0-862.3.3.el7.x86_64.gz
-rw-r--r--.  1 root root   304926 Apr 20 13:00 symvers-3.10.0-862.el7.x86_64.gz
-rw-------.  1 root root  3409952 Jun 15 00:29 System.map-3.10.0-862.3.3.el7.x86_64
-rw-------.  1 root root  3409143 Apr 20 12:57 System.map-3.10.0-862.el7.x86_64
-rwxr-xr-x.  1 root root  6224704 Jun 20 01:42 vmlinuz-0-rescue-c829291fe54b45ac94048e60228bbbe4
-rwxr-xr-x.  1 root root  6228896 Jun 15 00:29 vmlinuz-3.10.0-862.3.3.el7.x86_64
-rw-r--r--.  1 root root      170 Jun 15 00:29 .vmlinuz-3.10.0-862.3.3.el7.x86_64.hmac
-rwxr-xr-x.  1 root root  6224704 Apr 20 12:57 vmlinuz-3.10.0-862.el7.x86_64
-rw-r--r--.  1 root root      166 Apr 20 12:57 .vmlinuz-3.10.0-862.el7.x86_64.hmac

/var:
total 12
drwxr-xr-x. 19 root root  267 Jun 20 01:45 .
dr-xr-xr-x. 17 root root  224 Jun 20 01:58 ..
drwxr-xr-x.  2 root root    6 Apr 11 00:59 adm
drwxr-xr-x.  5 root root   44 Jun 20 01:40 cache
drwxr-xr-x.  2 root root    6 Apr 12 13:45 crash
drwxr-xr-x.  3 root root   34 Jun 20 01:40 db
drwxr-xr-x.  2 root root   18 Jun 20 01:40 empty
drwxr-xr-x.  2 root root    6 Apr 11 00:59 games
drwxr-xr-x.  2 root root    6 Apr 11 00:59 gopher
drwxr-xr-x.  3 root root   18 May  9 09:48 kerberos
drwxr-xr-x. 24 root root 4096 Jun 20 01:40 lib
drwxr-xr-x.  2 root root    6 Apr 11 00:59 local
lrwxrwxrwx.  1 root root   11 Jun 20 01:38 lock -> ../run/lock
drwxr-xr-x.  7 root root 4096 Jun 20 02:00 log
lrwxrwxrwx.  1 root root   10 Jun 20 01:38 mail -> spool/mail
drwxr-xr-x.  2 root root    6 Apr 11 00:59 nis
drwxr-xr-x.  2 root root    6 Apr 11 00:59 opt
drwxr-xr-x.  2 root root    6 Apr 11 00:59 preserve
```

In this example, for the first time we used command-line options and arguments. The command `ls` is executed with the `a` and `l` options, and the arguments are `/boot` and `/var`. This will print out all the files, including hidden ones, in a detailed list view in the `/boot` and `/var` directories. As mentioned before, oftentimes arguments are bound to specific options, for example, the `tar` command, which we will discuss later. When you need to process an input file, you have to specify directly after the `-f` option and nowhere else or, in short, the input file argument is bound to the `-f` option. This approach is incorrect and will produce errors.

File globbing

In this section, you will learn how shell expansion works and how we can use file globbing to make our lives easier when using commands that deal with a lot of input files. We will discuss all existing and available shell globbing character classes and show you important use cases and examples for each of them. When working with commands that use file or directory names as arguments, such as the `ls` command, it is very helpful to learn about file and directory globbing. These are special characters typed in the shell that behave differently than regular characters. All globbing characters are going to be replaced by the shell with a list of files matching the characters' pattern right before any command can use them as parameters. It's a notation to simplify working with files, especially when dealing with a large number of files that you need to type and process. Using file globbing can save you a lot of time, by not doing repetitive work, because multiple files can be addressed by a single-character. The concept of replacing such special characters with a group list of files by the shell is also called **shell expansion**. There are several globbing characters available and we can use them to create very sophisticated file list selections.

Globbing characters are the wildcard, the question mark, the exclamation mark, the square brackets, and the dash. Although they look and behave very similarly, shell globbing and regular expressions are not the same, and both concepts are not interchangeable. This means you cannot apply regular expressions for globbing files and vice versa. We will learn more about regular expressions in an upcoming section in this chapter. The most important globbing character is the wildcard character. It will match any number of any character filename available in a specific directory, with one exception, it does not match files beginning with a dot, which you may have already noticed when looking at hidden files in Linux. What happens if you use the wildcard character with a file beginning with a dot and press *Enter*? Let's look at an example. As we showed before, we can use the `echo` command to print out random text in the Terminal.

Let's first change to a different directory. Type `cd /etc` and press *Enter*. Now, type `echo *` and press *Enter*:

```
olip@localhost/etc
[olip@localhost ~]$ cd /etc
[olip@localhost etc]$ echo *
adjtime aliases aliases.db alternatives anacrontab asound.conf audisp audit bash_completion.d bashrc binfmt.d centos-release c
entos-release-upstream chkconfig.d chrony.conf chrony.keys cron.d cron.daily cron.deny cron.hourly cron.monthly crontab cron.w
eekly crypttab csh.cshrc csh.login dbus-1 default depmod.d dhcp DIR_COLORS DIR_COLORS.256color DIR_COLORS.lightbgcolor dracut.
conf dracut.conf.d e2fsck.conf environment ethertypes exports favicon.png filesystems firewalld fstab gcrypt GeoIP.conf GeoIP.
conf.default gnupg GREP_COLORS groff group group- grub2.cfg grub.d gshadow gshadow- gss host.conf hostname hosts hosts.allow h
osts.deny init.d inittab inputrc iproute2 issue issue.net kdump.conf kernel krb5.conf krb5.conf.d ld.so.cache ld.so.conf ld.so
.conf.d libaudit.conf libnl libuser.conf locale.conf localtime login.defs logrotate.conf logrotate.d lvm machine-id magic make
dumpfile.conf.sample man_db.conf mke2fs.conf modprobe.d modules-load.d motd mtab my.cnf my.cnf.d nanorc NetworkManager network
s nsswitch.conf nsswitch.conf.bak openldap opt os-release pam.d passwd passwd- pkcs11 pki plymouth pm polkit-1 popt.d postfix
ppp prelink.conf.d printcap profile profile.d protocols python rc0.d rc1.d rc2.d rc3.d rc4.d rc5.d rc6.d rc.d rc.local redhat-
release resolv.conf rpc rpm rsyslog.conf rsyslog.d rwtab rwtab.d sasl2 securetty security selinux services sestatus.conf shado
w shadow- shells skel ssh ssl statetab statetab.d subgid subuid sudo.conf sudoers sudoers.d sudo-ldap.conf sysconfig sysctl.co
nf sysctl.d systemd system-release system-release-cpe terminfo tmpfiles.d tuned udev vconsole.conf virc wpa_supplicant X11 xdg
 xinetd.d yum yum.conf yum.repos.d
[olip@localhost etc]$ []
```

In the previous command, in the first step, the shell replaces the wildcard character with a list of files in the current directory and prints them separated by whitespace that follows the rule, and then shows all files and directories that contain any character, but it doesn't show files that start with a dot. Using `echo` is the perfect way to test whether your globbing patterns match exactly what you want before applying them as real command-line arguments. You can mix the wildcard character with any other static character to make a file filter more stringent. Type `echo pa*` and press *Enter*. This will match all files starting with a lowercase p followed by a, followed by any other character. Or type `echo *.d` and press *Enter*. This example finds all files that have the `.d` filename extension:

```
olip@localhost/etc
[olip@localhost etc]$ echo pa*
pam.d passwd passwd-
[olip@localhost etc]$ echo *.d
bash_completion.d binfmt.d chkconfig.d cron.d depmod.d dracut.conf.d grub.d init.d krb5.conf.d ld.so.conf.d logrotate.d modpro
be.d modules-load.d my.cnf.d pam.d popt.d prelink.conf.d profile.d rc0.d rc1.d rc2.d rc3.d rc4.d rc5.d rc6.d rc.d rsyslog.d rw
tab.d statetab.d sudoers.d sysctl.d tmpfiles.d xinetd.d yum.repos.d
[olip@localhost etc]$ []
```

You can even define a more stringent pattern, for example, by typing `echo li*.conf` and pressing *Enter*. This globbing pattern will match all files in your current directory starting with a lowercase l, followed by i, followed by any other character, but only those that have a `.conf` filename extension. We can use file globbing with any command that accepts an option list of files as arguments, such as the `ls` command.

For example, using the globbing pattern, `li *.conf`, as a command-line argument for the `ls` command, gives us a detailed list of all the files matched by this pattern. Again, it's important to understand that we are not feeding the globbing pattern into the `ls` command and `ls` is not expanding files internally during the execution of the program. The truth is that a shell in the first step expands the wildcard character to a list of files and then feeds this list as arguments to the `ls` command.

> We will use the `ls -d` option to not show directory content, which it does by default; this is because shell globbing doesn't differentiate between files and directories.

Type `ls -d rc?.d` in the Terminal. This will get you a list of all the files that have only a random character as the third character. Next, type in the `ls -d krb5.conf??` command, as follows:

```
[olip@localhost etc]$ ls -d rc?.d
rc0.d   rc1.d   rc2.d   rc3.d   rc4.d   rc5.d   rc6.d
[olip@localhost etc]$ ls -d krb5.conf??
krb5.conf.d
[olip@localhost etc]$
```

As you can see, the question mark can also be used multiple times. This will get all files that have two random characters at the extension and only these files. The final globbing characters that we will learn about are the square brackets, which define ranges of allowed characters at a specific position, for example, type `ls -l sub[ug]id`. This will expand to a list of all the files starting with `sub` and having either u or g as the fourth character, followed by the word id:

```
[olip@localhost etc]$ ls -l sub[ug]id
-rw-r--r--. 1 root root 0 Apr 11 00:18 subgid
-rw-r--r--. 1 root root 0 Apr 11 00:18 subuid
[olip@localhost etc]$
```

As we will learn next, we can mix the brackets with other globbing characters. Type the following `ls` command argument:

```
ls /bin/[mM]ail*
```

This expands to a list of all the mail programs in the `bin` directory with and without capitalization. We will learn more about the `bin` directory later. You can also use numbers for ranges; type the `ls -d rc[01234].d` command in the Terminal:

```
[olip@localhost ~]$ ls /bin/[mM]ail*
/bin/mailq   /bin/mailq.postfix
[olip@localhost ~]$ ls -d rc[01234].d
ls: cannot access -d: No such file or directory
rc0.d   rc1.d   rc2.d   rc3.d   rc4.d
[olip@localhost ~]$ []
```

In our example, this would be expanded to `rc0.d`, `rc1.d`, and so on. If you have consecutive ranges of numbers or letters, as in the last example, you can also use the minus symbol to shorten your globbing expression even more. For example, type `ls /bin/m[a-z] [a-z]`. This would give us all the three-letter command names in the `bin` directory starting with `m`.

There's another helpful globbing character, which is the exclamation mark, and it can be used in brackets to define something that must not be in expansion results, for example, `ls -d rc[!256].d`:

```
[olip@localhost ~]$ ls /bin/m[a-z] [a-z]
ls: cannot access [a-z]: No such file or directory
/bin/mv
[olip@localhost ~]$ ls -d rc[!256].d
ls: cannot access -d: No such file or directory
rc0.d   rc1.d   rc3.d   rc4.d
[olip@localhost ~]$ []
```

This says that we don't want to expand files that have a 2, 5, or 6 as the third character. This also works for consecutive ranges within brackets, for example, `ls -d rc[!3-6].d`.

You have already learned three things about hidden files in Linux. They start with a dot in the filename, the wildcard globbing character ignores them, and `ls`, by default, doesn't show them; therefore, they're named hidden. To show all hidden files in your home directory, we use the `-a` option with the `ls` command. You see that there are several hidden files in your home directory, for example, the `.bashrc` file:

```
olip@localhost ~
[olip@localhost ~]$ cd ~
[olip@localhost ~]$ ls -a
.      .bash_history  .bash_profile  file_1.txt  file_3.txt  rc    rc1.d  rc3.d
..     .bash_logout   .bashrc        file_2.txt  file_4.txt  rc0.d  rc2.d  rc4.d
[olip@localhost ~]$
```

But there are also two other special files in your directory with the name [.] and [..], we will learn what these two special files are later on this chapter. What do you need to type if you want to display only the hidden files in the current directory without those two dot files? With all the knowledge you now have, this should be easy to accomplish, and the next line should now make sense to you. So, type `ls .[!.]*`. But this will also list directory contents. To not list directory contents, use the `ls -d` flag, so the command will be `ls -d .[!.]*`:

```
olip@localhost ~
[olip@localhost ~]$ ls .[!.]*
.bash_history  .bash_logout  .bash_profile  .bashrc
[olip@localhost ~]$ ls -d .[!.]*
ls: cannot access -d: No such file or directory
.bash_history  .bash_logout  .bash_profile  .bashrc
[olip@localhost ~]$
```

In this section, we discussed everything there is to know about Linux shell globbing. Remember, the wildcard character matches every filename character in any position. It's very important that there is one exception to this rule: it does not match filenames starting with a dot, which are called hidden files in Linux. The question mark does the same, but only in a single position; it also doesn't match filenames with the leading dot. The brackets match specific characters in a single position defined between the brackets. When having consecutive permitted characters, you can also use the dash symbol. To match everything except a set of characters at a specific position, use the exclamation mark in brackets.

Quoting commands

As we learned in the previous section, the shell has a list of special characters that have a special meaning in the shell and trigger some functionality, such as using the wildcard character as filenames. But there are even more special characters than the ones we showed you before. If you want to work with such special characters, for example, using filenames that contain question mark symbols, which are valid filenames, you have a problem, as the shell always first tries to apply special actions to special characters, so they will not work as normal filename characters. The solution here is to disable all special meanings of such characters using various approaches, such as quoting, so that we can treat them as any other normal literal character. As you now know, in the Linux Bash shell, there are some special characters, such as `* # [ ] . ~ ! $ { } < > | ? & - / , "` which have special meaning to the shell and get treated differently than normal characters. But what if you want to use a filename or directory as an argument that has one such special character in its name? Also, how do you treat filenames with spaces in the name, which can also be seen as special characters?

For example, if you have a file in your directory called `My private Documents.txt`, how can you use it as a command-line argument? If you use it with the `ls` command, since the space is the command-line argument delimiter, the shell is not able to see it as one distinct file. Rather, it thinks you provided three different files called `My`, `private`, and `Documents.txt`:

```
olip@localhost:~
[olip@localhost ~]$ nano "My private Documents.txt"
[olip@localhost ~]$ ls -l
total 40
-rw-r--r--. 1 root root 2 Jun 20 02:25 file_1.txt
-rw-r--r--. 1 root root 2 Jun 20 02:25 file_2.txt
-rw-r--r--. 1 root root 2 Jun 20 02:25 file_3.txt
-rw-r--r--. 1 root root 2 Jun 20 02:25 file_4.txt
-rw-rw-r--. 1 olip olip 2 Jun 20 03:44 My private Documents.txt
drwxrwxr-x. 2 olip olip 6 Jun 20 03:16 rc
-rw-rw-r--. 1 olip olip 2 Jun 20 03:15 rc0.d
-rw-rw-r--. 1 olip olip 2 Jun 20 03:15 rc1.d
-rw-rw-r--. 1 olip olip 2 Jun 20 03:15 rc2.d
-rw-rw-r--. 1 olip olip 2 Jun 20 03:15 rc3.d
-rw-rw-r--. 1 olip olip 2 Jun 20 03:15 rc4.d
[olip@localhost ~]$ ls My private Documents.txt
ls: cannot access My: No such file or directory
ls: cannot access private: No such file or directory
ls: cannot access Documents.txt: No such file or directory
[olip@localhost ~]$ 
```

Also, what happens if you want to use a file containing special characters such as the exclamation mark, for example, if you've got a file called !super!file!.txt, which is a valid filename in Linux? If we try to use this filename as a command-line argument parameter, it cannot find the file by this name because it contains special characters that are treated in a different way by the shell. Or what happens if you want to echo some text with more than one whitespace between the words? As we have learned, the space is also a special shell character that delimits command-line arguments:

```
olip@localhost:~
[olip@localhost ~]$ ls !super!file!.txt
-bash: !super!file!.txt: event not found
[olip@localhost ~]$ echo I like          Linux
I like Linux
[olip@localhost ~]$ 
```

In the examples just shown, we need to find a way to disable shell expansion and to stop the shell from processing special characters. There are two easy ways to disable shell expansion in arguments, and these are quoting and escaping. Putting special characters and space into single quotes will prevent shell expansion and treat all possible chars, including the special ones, as normal alphanumeric characters. In single quotes, nothing ever gets shell expanded; for most special characters, this also works in double quotes with a few exceptions to this rule.

In the following screenshot, two examples work, but others don't and they get special treatment:

```
olip@localhost:~
[olip@localhost ~]$ echo '$PATH'
$PATH
[olip@localhost ~]$ echo "* [a-z] ? / \ & %"
* [a-z] ? / \ & %
[olip@localhost ~]$ echo " I like            Linux."
 I like            Linux.
[olip@localhost ~]$ echo "*"
*
[olip@localhost ~]$ echo "/etc/krb?.conf"
/etc/krb?.conf
[olip@localhost ~]$ ls -l "!super!file!.txt"
-bash: !super!file!.txt: event not found
[olip@localhost ~]$ echo "`  `"

[olip@localhost ~]$ echo "$$"
17869
[olip@localhost ~]$ echo "$PATH"
/usr/local/bin:/usr/bin:/usr/local/sbin:/usr/sbin:/home/olip/.local/bin:/home/olip/bin
[olip@localhost ~]$ echo "* ! $SHELL"
* ! /bin/bash
[olip@localhost ~]$ echo "This is my home: $HOME"
This is my home: /home/olip
[olip@localhost ~]$ []
```

Also, as shown in previous screenshot, the dollar sign stays special as well, and this is often used if you need to shell expand environment variables while quoting. As said before, single quotes will disable all special characters. You can do the same by using the backslash key, which, in the shell, is also called the **escape character** and which does almost exactly the same as quotes, but will only disable shell expansion and every special meaning for the next, and only the next, immediate character after the backslash key:

```
[olip@localhost ~]$ echo \*
*
[olip@localhost ~]$ echo \! \* \[ \] \?
! * [ ] ?
[olip@localhost ~]$ echo I like \ \ \ \ \ Linux
I like        Linux
[olip@localhost ~]$ ls -l \!super\!file\!.txt
ls: cannot access !super!file!.txt: No such file or directory
[olip@localhost ~]$ ls -l My\ private\ Docuemnts.txt
ls: cannot access My private Docuemnts.txt: No such file or directory
[olip@localhost ~]$ ls -d -a -l -t -h /home /var /opt /etc /tmp
drwxrwxrwt.  8 root root  211 Jun 20 02:48 /tmp
drwxr-xr-x. 74 root root 8.0K Jun 20 02:25 /etc
drwxr-xr-x. 19 root root  267 Jun 20 01:45 /var
drwxr-xr-x.  3 root root   18 Jun 20 01:43 /home
drwxr-xr-x.  2 root root    6 Apr 11 00:59 /opt
[olip@localhost ~]$ ls \
> -d \
> -a \
> -l \
> -t \
> -h \
> /home \
> /var \
> /opt \
> /etc \
> /
drwxr-xr-x. 74 root root 8.0K Jun 20 02:25 /etc
dr-xr-xr-x. 17 root root  224 Jun 20 01:58 /
drwxr-xr-x. 19 root root  267 Jun 20 01:45 /var
drwxr-xr-x.  3 root root   18 Jun 20 01:43 /home
```

As you can see, it's basically the same. Often, the escape character is used to create clear multi-line command-line calls by escaping or disabling the new line character in each line. Another use case for the backslash character is to use it when working with arguments such as files starting with the dash, as this often confuses the shell because it interprets any dash symbol as an option.

For example, if we want to create an empty file named –dashy.txt, this will not work, as the command line is confused and thinks the filename is a list of single-character options. Here, we can use the escape character to get rid of the special meaning of the dash symbol. For arguments starting with the dash, some commands, such as ls or touch, also have another great feature, the double dash, which marks the end of the option list. So, to treat your dashy file as an argument instead of an option, we can also type the nano –dashy.txt or touch '-dashy.txt' command.

As you have learned, there exists a number of special characters in the shell that have a special meaning, for example, the shell globbing characters or the exclamation mark. What if you want to use these characters, not to shell expand the list of files, but in a filename or other literal command argument? You need to disable them. Using single quotes will disable all special characters and is the preferred way when working in the shell; it works for almost all everyday quoting use cases. When using double quotes, most special characters get disabled, but not all, such as the shell expansion of environment variables. So, this approach is very useful for text creation that contains normal characters and values of environment variables. The backslash or escaping character will disable any special meaning of the following character only.

Getting help

Before we can start teaching you how to get help using the various forms of documentation available for Linux commands, we first have to learn how to read the default command syntax documentation. Most of the provided standard shell commands in Linux follow a uniform format describing their usage. Afterward, we will show you how to get help.

When working with the Linux command line, getting help and looking up information and documentation is very important because the command line can be very complex and nobody knows and can remember everything. On every Linux system, there are several ways available to get help, depending on the kind of level of information you need to know. In this section, we will tap into the different sources of documentation.

In a previous section, you already learned the general structure of Bash shell commands and everything you need to know about command options and parameters in general, but oftentimes this is not enough. For a lot of shell commands, the specific structure of options and arguments are very complex. A post can be bound to a specific position, and some of them can be mandatory or optional. Also, options and arguments can be interdependent. In Linux, a description of a command's command-line format, including arguments and options, is called **command usage** or **syntax of a command**. Learning to read a command's usage is one of the most essential skills that a Linux beginner needs to learn when starting. The standard way to describe command usage in Linux is the command name, square brackets that contain text, dots, and text, for example, `CommandName [XXX]... TEXT`. Square brackets mean that the content within is optional. Three dots mean that the expression right before the dots can be repeated multiple times or only once. Any word without square brackets is mandatory.

Take, for example, the general syntax for the `ls` command, which you already know how to work with. From the official `ls` manual, it can be read as `ls [OPTION]... [FILE]...`; this means that the command to list files has the following usage. It starts with the `ls` command name, everything else is in brackets, so all the options and arguments are optional, which means you can also execute `ls` without providing any further information, just by pressing the *Enter* key. But you can also provide multiple options or only one. Also, we can see that the arguments are of the `FILE` type, which means a file or directory is needed here at this position. You can also provide multiple files or directories, or only one or zero, as shown in the following screenshot:

```
[olip@localhost ~]$ ls
-dashy.txt  file_2.txt  file_4.txt              rc    rc1.d  rc3.d  \!super\!file\!.txt
file_1.txt  file_3.txt  My private Documents.txt  rc0.d  rc2.d  rc4.d
[olip@localhost ~]$ ls -a -l -t -h
total 68K
drwx------. 3 olip olip 4.0K Jun 20 04:06 .
-rw-rw-r--. 1 olip olip    2 Jun 20 04:06 -dashy.txt
-rw-rw-r--. 1 olip olip    2 Jun 20 03:57 \!super\!file\!.txt
-rw-rw-r--. 1 olip olip    2 Jun 20 03:44 My private Documents.txt
drwxrwxr-x. 2 olip olip    6 Jun 20 03:16 rc
-rw-rw-r--. 1 olip olip    2 Jun 20 03:15 rc4.d
-rw-rw-r--. 1 olip olip    2 Jun 20 03:15 rc3.d
-rw-rw-r--. 1 olip olip    2 Jun 20 03:15 rc2.d
-rw-rw-r--. 1 olip olip    2 Jun 20 03:15 rc1.d
-rw-rw-r--. 1 olip olip    2 Jun 20 03:15 rc0.d
-rw-------. 1 olip olip  569 Jun 20 03:11 .bash_history
-rw-r--r--. 1 root root    2 Jun 20 02:25 file_4.txt
-rw-r--r--. 1 root root    2 Jun 20 02:25 file_3.txt
-rw-r--r--. 1 root root    2 Jun 20 02:25 file_2.txt
-rw-r--r--. 1 root root    2 Jun 20 02:25 file_1.txt
drwxr-xr-x. 3 root root   18 Jun 20 01:43 ..
-rw-r--r--. 1 olip olip   18 Apr 10 20:53 .bash_logout
-rw-r--r--. 1 olip olip  193 Apr 10 20:53 .bash_profile
-rw-r--r--. 1 olip olip  231 Apr 10 20:53 .bashrc
[olip@localhost ~]$ ls -a
.              .bash_history  .bash_profile  -dashy.txt  file_2.txt  file_4.txt              rc    rc1.d  rc3.d  \!super\!file\!.txt
..             .bash_logout   .bashrc         file_1.txt  file_3.txt  My private Documents.txt  rc0.d  rc2.d  rc4.d
[olip@localhost ~]$ ls /home
olip
[olip@localhost ~]$ ls -al /home
total 4
drwxr-xr-x.  3 root root   18 Jun 20 01:43 .
dr-xr-xr-x. 17 root root  224 Jun 20 01:58 ..
drwx------.  3 olip olip 4096 Jun 20 04:06 olip
[olip@localhost ~]$ ls -al /home /tmp /etc
/etc:
total 1064
drwxr-xr-x. 74 root root  8192 Jun 20 02:25 .
dr-xr-xr-x. 17 root root   224 Jun 20 01:58 ..
-rw-r--r--.  1 root root    16 Jun 20 01:43 adjtime
-rw-r--r--.  1 root root  1518 Jun  7  2013 aliases
-rw-r--r--.  1 root root 12288 Jun 20 01:45 aliases.db
drwxr-xr-x.  2 root root   236 Jun 20 01:48 alternatives
-rw-------.  1 root root   541 Apr 10 21:48 anacrontab
-rw-r--r--.  1 root root    55 Apr 10 16:38 asound.conf
```

As another example, the `copy` command can be run by using the `cp` command name followed by zero or multiple options. The syntax of the `cp` command is `cp [OPTION]...SOURCE... DEST_DIR`. You can completely skip option, but at least one or more source directory and exactly one destination directory are mandatory and denoted by the three dots, and you cannot run the command without them. For example, running just `cp` without at least two arguments produces the following error. Correct usage would be with all options:

```
olip@localhost ~
[olip@localhost ~]$ cp
cp: missing file operand
Try 'cp --help' for more information.
[olip@localhost ~]$ cp /etc/passwd /tmp
[olip@localhost ~]$ cp -r ~ /tmp
[olip@localhost ~]$ []
```

Now that we know how to read any standard command syntax or usage, how can we actually get help? As we said before, there are several ways available, which are command help options, man pages, and full program documentation. Normally, all of these three types of help are installed together with the command line or program, so it's a very good habit to first try to get help for shell commands locally on the same machine where the commands live. This is usually the most accurate, reliable, and up-to-date information for every command and should be favored before doing internet research or using documentation from another computer with a different Linux version or system.

 Often internet solutions found in blogs or forums are too unspecific or plain wrong for your specific Linux installation, and should always be used with caution. Don't ever blindly copy and paste command snippets from the internet.

Command parameters, options, and features can change over time depending on the version and implementation, and they can be very dangerous if applied incorrectly. There are hundreds of commands available on Linux and every one of them has a different syntax. No one can memorize everything, so first let's start with the easiest and fastest way to get quick help for any standard Linux program that you already know the name of. In fact, most programs do have a special command-line switch that prints out a quick summary of the usage of its options and arguments on screen, which in most cases is all you need to know. However, the help or usage flag is not standardized on Linux and some commands don't even have this flag at all, but most tool developers follow the rule to use the one-character flag –h, or the long option flag ––help.

 Not all shell commands have a help option, especially those very easy ones.

Now, if you need more help, you can check out the commands manual, which is often called **man pages** by Linux users. Most programs have such documentation. For the next few examples, you need to install some additional software using your root account's password, which you set up during installation. Man pages use lesser navigation, which we will talk about later when we learn how to view text files.

The following steps will help you to navigate the manual of any command in the Linux Terminal:

1. Open the Terminal and type man cp for the copy command.
2. Use the *Page Up* and *Page Down* keys to scroll the document up and down, and slash (/) can be used to search text; put any keywords after the slash to search for, and then press *Enter*. For example, /backup.
3. Press the *End* key to search for the next entry in the man page.
4. To quit the search option, use the *Esc* key.
5. Using lowercase *g*, you can scroll to the top of the page, whereas uppercase *G* scrolls to the bottom of the page.
6. You can press lowercase *q* to quit the man page.

When you go back to the top of the page, the man page of the `cp` command is divided into different topics and headings, as shown in the following screenshot:

```
olip@localhost:~

CP(1)                                                  User Commands

NAME
       cp - copy files and directories

SYNOPSIS
       cp [OPTION]... [-T] SOURCE DEST
       cp [OPTION]... SOURCE... DIRECTORY
       cp [OPTION]... -t DIRECTORY SOURCE...

DESCRIPTION
       Copy SOURCE to DEST, or multiple SOURCE(s) to DIRECTORY.

       Mandatory arguments to long options are mandatory for short options too.

       -a, --archive
              same as -dR --preserve=all

       --attributes-only
              don't copy the file data, just the attributes

       --backup[=CONTROL]
              make a backup of each existing destination file

       -b     like --backup but does not accept an argument

Manual page cp(1) line 1 (press h for help or q to quit)
```

Most standard Linux commands follow this type of structure. Also, you can see here that some commands can have different usage formats depending on the options and arguments given. Now, quit using the *q* key. The man command has a very useful option, type `man -k` and put any definition of interests as an argument afterward. This will search all man pages installed on your system for a certain keyword. For example, this is very useful if you forgot a specific command name or need general help with the topic or command to use or where to look first. If you type the `man -k copy` command, this will print out all the man pages for the commands that have something to do with copying:

```
[olip@localhost ~]$ man -k copy
btrfs-select-super (8) - overwrite primary superblock with a backup copy
cp (1)                 - copy files and directories
cpio (1)               - copy files to and from archives
dd (1)                 - convert and copy a file
install (1)            - copy files and set attributes
objcopy (1)            - copy and translate object files
scp (1)                - secure copy (remote file copy program)
ssh-copy-id (1)        - use locally available keys to authorise logins on a remote machine
xfs_copy (8)           - copy the contents of an XFS filesystem
xfs_metadump (8)       - copy XFS filesystem metadata to a file
xfs_rtcp (8)           - XFS realtime copy command
[olip@localhost ~]$ []
```

While using the −k flag, you also see that the search result writes some numbers in the brackets after the man name; these are man page sections, which is another very useful concept we need to know. A Linux shell definition, such as printf, can describe more than only a command-line program, and man pages not only describe command-line tools. In our example, printf is not only a command-line tool that can be started by the shell user, but also the name for a library function in the programming language C, which is used by this system. man now defines a system of section numbers for the type a specific man name is from. Typing man man will display the manual documentation for the man command, and search for the keyboard sections, as shown here:

```
[olip@localhost ~]$ man man
       man -w|-W [-C file] [-d] [-D] page ...
       man -c [-C file] [-d] [-D] page ...
       man [-?V]

DESCRIPTION
       man  is  the  system's  manual pager. Each page argument given to man is normally the name of a
       program, utility or function.  The manual page associated with each of these arguments is  then
       found  and  displayed.  A section, if provided, will direct man to look only in that section of
       the manual.  The default action is to search in all of the available sections, following a pre-
       defined order and to show only the first page found, even if page exists in several sections.

       The  table  below  shows  the section numbers of the manual followed by the types of pages they
       contain.

       1    Executable programs or shell commands
       2    System calls (functions provided by the kernel)
       3    Library calls (functions within program libraries)
       4    Special files (usually found in /dev)
       5    File formats and conventions eg /etc/passwd
       6    Games
       7    Miscellaneous (including macro packages and conventions), e.g. man(7), groff(7)
       8    System administration commands (usually only for root)
       9    Kernel routines [Non standard]

       A manual page consists of several sections.

       Conventional  section  names  include  NAME,  SYNOPSIS,  CONFIGURATION,  DESCRIPTION,  OPTIONS,
       EXIT STATUS,  RETURN VALUE,  ERRORS,  ENVIRONMENT, FILES, VERSIONS, CONFORMING TO, NOTES, BUGS,
       EXAMPLE, AUTHORS, and SEE ALSO.
```

As we can see in the previous screenshot, the man page of the man command has nine sections. The first one is the most important one for us in this section, as we are most likely the shell command users. But, as you can see, the third section is a library call. Type man printf, which prints the usage of the printf command. On the other hand, if you type man 3 printf, it will print the Linux programmers' manual for the C language.

Let's jump to the eighth section, which is the manual for the xfs_copy command written for the system administrators. Besides manual pages, a lot of commands that can be installed on Linux or that come right out of the box with the system, do have additional and advanced documentation available in a specific folder location in the filesystem on your hard disk. For some programs, additional documentation can also be installed using a special installation package, as we will learn later in this section. Sometimes, this additional documentation contains precious usage examples on how to use the program; information about the internal algorithms or approaches used; change log and license information; author contact information; history; a list of errors or limitations; or sample configuration files, which we will talk about later.

If you get stuck with the manual or it is just not enough for you, try to check out if a documentation folder exists for your command of interest in your CentOS 7 standard documentation path. Type, for example, the postfix documentation folder lives in. This is a good example. If you go into the directory, you will find a lot of additional documentation in text file format. Refer to the following screenshot for more information:

```
[olip@localhost ~]$ ls -l /usr/share/doc | grep postfix
drwxr-xr-x. 4 root root  211 Jun 20 01:40 postfix-2.10.1
[olip@localhost ~]$ cd /usr/share/doc/postfix-2*
[olip@localhost postfix-2.10.1]$ ls
bounce.cf.default  examples  main.cf.default  README-Postfix-SASL-RedHat.txt  TLS_LICENSE
COMPATIBILITY      LICENSE   README_FILES     TLS_ACKNOWLEDGEMENTS
[olip@localhost postfix-2.10.1]$ less README_FILES/OVERVIEW
[olip@localhost postfix-2.10.1]$ []
```

Use the less program to read the files. Use the same keyboard shortcuts to navigate the files as with the man pages, for example, type *q* to exit.

 If you need more or advanced documentation, look into the /usr/share/doc folder and see if there's something available for you.

Working with the Linux shell

In this section, we will learn how to work in the shell efficiently. We will introduce some important practices and techniques that will improve your productivity and make you a faster shell command hacker. This can make you a happier person because, eventually, you will be able to advance to feeling very comfortable working in the shell. Please note, in this section, we will show you a lot of keyboard shortcuts. Learning keyboard shortcuts is like learning any other craft, you begin slowly and gradually, because learning too many new skills at once can leave you overwhelmed and make you forget more quickly than learning in smaller chunks. My tip is to start by learning the first three to four command editing shortcuts and then incorporate more from day to day or week to week. We will start with the command editing shortcuts. Now, if you don't know any command editing shortcuts at all, let's recap what you probably know so far on how to type and edit text in the command line.

The first shortcut for moving the position of the cursor is that you can use the left and the right arrow keys, which are helpful to edit the text you wrote to insert or delete characters at a specific position. But if this were all that one could do in the shell, working in the shell would be very inefficient, because single-character cursor movement is very slow. Also, every time a command gets executed with a typo or the command needs to be rerun with a small difference, such as changing one option, the complete command needs to be retyped from beginning to end.

To be a lot more efficient, let's introduce some very important command editing shortcuts for your everyday work with Linux:

- To move the cursor to the end of the line, use *Ctrl + E.*
- To go back to the beginning, press *Ctrl + A, Ctrl + E, Ctrl + A* respectively.
- To move the cursor to the next word, which is defined by a space or special characters such as dot, semicolon, or point, use *Ctrl* and the right arrow key to move forward.
- To move backward one word, use the left arrow key while holding the *Ctrl* key. You can also use *meta + F* and *meta + B* to do the same.
- On most systems, like any normal PC keyboard, there is no meta key, so the meta key is mapped to the *Esc* or *Alt* key.

Using the *Alt* key in some terminal emulators such as the Xfce4 Terminal is reserved for menu accessibility. So, you first have to disable the *Alt* key as a menu shortcut in the preferences before you can use it as a shortcut.

- To toggle between the current position and the beginning of the line, press *Ctrl + XX* twice.
- Press *Ctrl + K* to delete the text from the cursor to the end of the command line.
- To delete the text from the cursor to the start of the command line, press *Ctrl + U*. Use *Alt + D* to delete to the end of the word.

All of the command editing keyboard shortcuts we just discussed here are only the most important and efficient ones for your everyday daily use, and there are many, many more.

In order to get a full list of all of the Bash keyboard shortcuts, do the following:

- Type man bash and then search for the section commands for moving
- In this man page, search for Killing
- In this man page, the C key is the *Ctrl* key, the M key is the meta key, and the dash means to combine or press and hold two keys, as we have shown you using the *Ctrl + A* shortcut earlier

For example, C-k stands for **kill-line**, which kills the text from the point to the end of the line. *Alt + T* is used to swap words, M-u to make words uppercase, and M-l to make words lowercase.

Now, let's move on to the command completion shortcuts. The most important command completion shortcut is the *Tab* key on your keyboard. It tries to guess and autocomplete the command you are about to type. It is very useful and speeds up typing commands tremendously, but don't overdo it when using this key, it can only print the full unique command name if there are no alternatives available. Type pass and press the *Tab* key; it will autocomplete the name passwd as there are no other programs with this full name available. Type pa and press the *Tab* key; this will give you several results as no unique name can be found. Type yp and press the *Tab* key; this will autocomplete to a long name as this is the only variant available. The *Tab* short key autocompletes commands by default; to autocomplete other things, such as filenames, use the *Alt + /* key. More can be found in the corresponding section in the Bash man page.

Now, let's look at to the command recall shortcuts. The Linux shell has a very nice feature available, which is the `history` command. This is a system for storing and retrieving all the commands typed into the shell. By default, on a CentOS 7 system, the last thousand commands are stored. This number can also be changed. The command-line history is a very useful feature to save time, by not doing repetitive typing, or to see how a specific command has been executed some time ago. To print out the current history, type `history` and press *Enter*. If you want to re-execute a command from this list use the exclamation mark and the corresponding number. Two exclamation marks run the last command from the history. Another exclamation mark notation can be used to extract specific arguments from history commands. This will extract the third argument from the `history` command, `166`, as shown in the following screenshot:

```
 olip@localhost:/usr/share/doc/postfix-2.10.1
  166  clear
  167  ls -l /usr/share/doc | grep postfix
  168  cd /usr/share/doc/postfix-2*
  169  ls
  170  less README_FILES/OVERVIEW
  171  clear
  172  man bash
  173  current history
  174  history
  175  clear
  176  history
[olip@localhost postfix-2.10.1]$ !166
clear
[olip@localhost postfix-2.10.1]$ []
```

Another very useful history feature is to recall the last command:

- To go through the previous history commands you executed, press the Up arrow key on your keyboard.
- To go back to the next history commands, use the Down arrow key.
- To search through the history for a command, press *Ctrl* + *R* and then enter the search keyword.
- To cycle through the results, press *Ctrl* + *R* again.
- To run a specific command that you have found, press the *Enter* key.

- To quickly insert the last argument of the previous command, use *Alt* + dot.
- Another very useful feature is to shell expand a line manually without actually having to execute the line, which can be useful to find out errors and boxes. This can be done using *Ctrl* + *Alt* + *E*.

Next, we need to know how to work with programs and processes. First, we will discuss how to abort any running program. This is important if you need to quit a command because it is unresponsive or you've made a mistake and want to stop it. For example, let's type the `cat` command, which will just run forever. Let's ignore what this command is doing at the moment. This leaves the shell unresponsive because `cat` never finishes running in the forefront of our shell and runs forever. To get back to the shell prompt so we can type in new commands and work again, we need to exit the command while it is running. To do so in the shell, we can use a special key combination that exits the current foreground process. Press *Ctrl* + *C*.

This is a very important key shortcut and it should be memorized: *Ctrl* + *C*.

You can also suspend a program, which is like pausing its processing and putting it into the background so you can work in the shell again. This can be done as follows:

1. Press *Ctrl* + *Z*. If you later want to continue the program running in the foreground, type `fg` and press *Enter*.
2. You can also put it in the background using the `bg` command while it is suspended. Now the program runs in the background and you can work in the foreground.
3. The easiest way to exit this program running in the background is to put it into the foreground and then use *Ctrl* + *C* to abort it.
4. The next very useful command is to press *Ctrl* + *L*, which clears the screen and has the same effect as the `clear` command.
5. The very last useful command we will learn here is to press *Ctrl* + *D*, which closes the Bash shell. This is similar to typing the `exit` command.

Understanding standard streams

In this section, you will learn why every command can use three standard streams for accessing its input and output. Also, you will learn how to work with those input and output streams and how to use redirection. Finally, we will learn how to use pipes and why they are so important. One philosophy of the Linux operating system is that every command has exactly one functionality in the system, nothing more, and nothing less. For example, there's one command to list files, another to sort text, and one to print the file's content, and so on.

Now, one of the most important features of the shell is to connect different commands to create custom tailored solutions and tools for all kinds of problems and workflows. But before we can show you how to concatenate different commands together to build something powerful, we first need to know how a command uses its input and output and what input and output redirection is. Most Linux commands follow a similar pattern when processing data. Most of the commands we are using do get some kind of input, for example, they read the content of a file and then they process this information, and afterward almost all of them do output some kind of results on the computer screen. Because every command uses some kind of input and returns some kind of output on Linux, three standard channels are defined and are available for every command. They are used for communication between the operating system and the command during execution. They are called **standard input** or stdin, **standard output** or stdout, and **standard error** or stderr.

Normal program output goes to the stdout channel, while stderr is also an output stream and it can be used for showing and processing any kind of error messages occurring while a command is executing. These are also called **standard streams**. They are called streams because the data is flowing continuously through a specific channel and gets processed or generated consecutively by the command, although they have an open end, which means the command working with them cannot predict when this flow of data will stop or finish. Now, we can change the stdin and stdout locations using certain files; this is called **redirection**.

Here, in this section, we will also explain the concept of pipes, which is one of the most fundamental concepts and major features of the Linux shell, and how to work with them. For example, if you type ls /var/lib/system/, the result random-seed will be printed to the screen because it is defined as an stdout device by default for every Linux command. But if you type cat /var/log/messages, an error message is printed to the same screen as both stdout and stderr are connected to the same output device, the screen.

On Linux, your physical input and output devices, such as your keyboard or screen, like any other hardware devices, are abstracted and represented by special system files. All of these special files reside in a system directory called /dev, which is also called the **system devices directory**. But what can we do with a system like that? Its beauty is that we can redirect the input and output of a command to another location other than the default keyboard and screen source or destinations, which also must be of the filetype. This is also very useful to separate stdout and stderr to two different locations, which especially helps to keep the overview of a command running if it produces a lot of output.

For output channel redirection, we use the greater than sign (>), for input redirection we use the smaller than sign (<). To address a specific channel, such as stdin, stdout, and stderr, we use the corresponding numbers 0, 1, and 2. When using output redirection, the stdout channel is expected, so we don't have to write it explicitly. For 99% of all cases you only redirect stdout and stderr, so let's focus on those examples.

To redirect the stdout stream output of a command to a file, use the greater than sign. As said before, the stdout channel is expected, so the last command can also be typed as follows:

```
ls /var/lib/systemd/ > /tmp/stdout-output.txt
ls /var/lib/systemd/ 1> /tmp/stdout-output.txt
```

Use the card command to print out the content of the file that we just created with the redirection to stdout. To redirect the stderr channel, use number 2 as the standard stream descriptor. The following screenshot shows the output of the previous commands:

```
[olip@localhost postfix-2.10.1]$ ls /var/lib/systemd/ > /tmp/stdout-output.txt
[olip@localhost postfix-2.10.1]$ ls /var/lib/systemd/ 1> /tmp/stdout-output.txt
[olip@localhost postfix-2.10.1]$ cat /tmp/stdout-output.txt
catalog
coredump
random-seed
[olip@localhost postfix-2.10.1]$ cat /var/log/messages 2> /tmp/stderr-output.txt
[olip@localhost postfix-2.10.1]$ cat /tmp/stderr-output.txt
cat: /var/log/messages: Permission denied
[olip@localhost postfix-2.10.1]$ []
```

As you can see, the error message has been redirected to a file. To redirect `stdout` and `stderr` to two different files, type the commands shown in the following screenshot:

```
[root@localhost bin]# ls /var/lib/systemd/ /boot/grub2 1>/tmp/stdout.txt 2>/tmp/stderr.txt
[root@localhost bin]# cat /tmp/stdout.txt
/boot/grub2:
device.map
fonts
grub.cfg
grubenv
i386-pc
locale

/var/lib/systemd/:
catalog
coredump
random-seed
[root@localhost bin]# cat /tmp/stderr.txt
[root@localhost bin]# []
```

Another notation, using the *ampersand* char allows the redirecting of one channel another one. To redirect `stderr` to the `stdout` channel, type the commands shown in the following screenshot:

```
[root@localhost bin]# ls /var/lib/systemd/ /boot/grub2 2>/tmp/channel-together2.txt 1>&2
[root@localhost bin]# cat /tmp/channel-together2.txt
/boot/grub2:
device.map
fonts
grub.cfg
grubenv
i386-pc
locale

/var/lib/systemd/:
catalog
coredump
random-seed
[root@localhost bin]# []
```

Sometimes, you are only interested in one output stream, therefore a special device file exists in any Linux system, which is called the `null` device, and it consumes and vanishes any kind of streaming data that gets redirected to it into the void. If you don't want any output at all for any command, for example, you can use the command shown in the following screenshot:

```
[root@localhost bin]# ls /dev/null
/dev/null
[root@localhost bin]# 
```

Finally, to redirect `stdin`, you use the smaller than sign [<]. For example, this can be very useful because some of the available shell commands can directly read a file's content as `stdin`, such as the `grep` command, which we will learn about later.

Now, let's discuss pipes. Besides redirecting a command's default input and output streams, `stdin`, `stdout`, and `stderr`, to files, we can also use the concept of shell pipes to get one command output as the input for another command. There are no limits to this system and it's very easy to build multi-command chains to answer very complex questions for you. As mentioned previously, this shell feature lets you create very powerful command pipelines and workflows for creating custom tailored solutions for all kinds of Linux command-line work, and to answer very complex questions for you.

To chain commands together, which means to use `stdout` from the first command as `stdin` to the next command, we use the vertical bar symbol [|] on our keyboard, which in Linux is called the **pipe** symbol. For example, if you've got a very long directory content list that you want to read without scrolling through the Terminal window forever, you can use the pipe to output the directory content from the `ls` command, not on the screen, but directly as input for the file viewer, as we learned before. Often, pipes are used to avoid intermediate result files and are more efficient without them. The use cases for this are endless, for example, if we got a file with unsorted names of people in it, we could sort them using `cat names.txt | sort`:

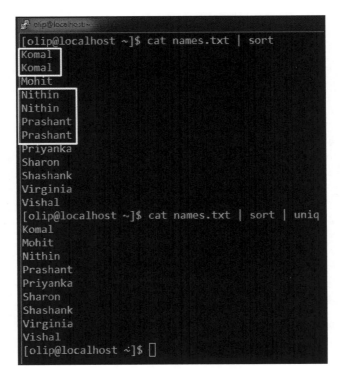

You can also get a list of all the unique names in this file. We will use the unique command to do so, which only works on a sorted list. So, we need to sort using `cat names.text | sort | uniq`:

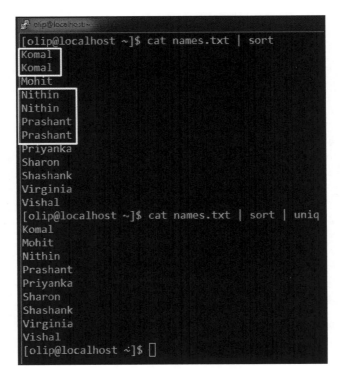

You can also count the number of unique lines using the word count command-line tool using `cat names.text | sort | uniq | wc`:

```
[olip@localhost ~]$ cat names.txt | sort | uniq | wc
      9       9      69
[olip@localhost ~]$ []
```

There are quite a few unique names in this file. The sky's the limit when it comes to pipe examples, and there are just too many examples. Ideally, this should be run with the `root` user account. Please ignore the errors. The following screenshot shows the core summary of the filesystem:

```
[olip@localhost ~]$ su -c 'du -h --max-depth=1 / | sort -h'
Password:
du: cannot access '/proc/18307/task/18307/fd/4': No such file or directory
du: cannot access '/proc/18307/task/18307/fdinfo/4': No such file or directory
du: cannot access '/proc/18307/fd/3': No such file or directory
du: cannot access '/proc/18307/fdinfo/3': No such file or directory
0       /dev
0       /media
0       /mnt
0       /opt
0       /proc
0       /srv
0       /sys
32K     /root
76K     /home
100K    /tmp
8.6M    /run
34M     /etc
135M    /var
151M    /boot
896M    /usr
1.2G    /
[olip@localhost ~]$ []
```

Also, another useful pipe command is to print out the used files in a directory. If you are using a Windows system, you may know of a utility called ZIP, which compresses files. On Linux, you can do something very similar, but here we need two tools to work together. For compression, we use the `gzip` tool. Because `gzip` can only work on single files, we first need to create an archive that will concatenate multiple files to a single file. For archiving, we use the `tar` command. So, to create a compressed archive of your home directory in the `/tmp` directory, first create an archive of your home directory using the `tar` command: `tar -cv /home/olip/ | gzip`. The archive will be output to the `stdout` stream, so we pipe it into the `gzip` command as `stdin`. As gzip itself outputs the compressed file to `stdout`, we will redirect it to a file. The result of the compression versus the uncompressed data amount is as follows:

```
olip@localhost:~
[olip@localhost ~]$ tar -cv /home/olip/ | gzip > /tmp/my-home-dir.tar.gz
tar: Removing leading `/' from member names
/home/olip/
/home/olip/.bash_logout
/home/olip/.bash_profile
/home/olip/.bashrc
/home/olip/.bash_history
/home/olip/file_1.txt
/home/olip/file_2.txt
/home/olip/file_3.txt
/home/olip/file_4.txt
/home/olip/rc0.d
/home/olip/rc1.d
/home/olip/rc2.d
/home/olip/rc3.d
/home/olip/rc4.d
/home/olip/rc/
/home/olip/My private Documents.txt
/home/olip/\\!super\\!file\\!.txt
/home/olip/-dashy.txt
/home/olip/.lesshst
/home/olip/names.txt
[olip@localhost ~]$ ls -alth /tmp/my-home-dir.tar.gz
-rw-rw-r--. 1 olip olip 1.9K Jun 21 00:49 /tmp/my-home-dir.tar.gz
[olip@localhost ~]$ du -h /home/olip/
0       /home/olip/rc
76K     /home/olip/
[olip@localhost ~]$ []
```

A lot more piping examples will be shown throughout this book. If you redirect `stdout` or `stderr` into a file, normally the file will be erased if it already exists, or a new file will be created before any content is written to it. So as not to delete a file, but append the content instead, use the greater than sign. For example, to create a new output file, execute the command shown in the following screenshot:

```
olip@localhost:~
[olip@localhost ~]$ ls /var/lib/systemd/ > /tmp/new-output-file.txt
[olip@localhost ~]$ echo 'Hello World' >> /tmp/new-output-file.txt
[olip@localhost ~]$ cat /tmp/new-output-file.txt
catalog
coredump
random-seed
Hello World
[olip@localhost ~]$ []
```

Now, to append the string, `Hello World`, to the output file, we will use the greater than sign. This will not delete the file's content when we start to redirect content to it. Instead, it will append the content to the end of the file. As said before, pipes are one of the most important concepts of the shell and it is so much fun working with them.

Understanding regular expressions

In this section, we will introduce the wonderful art of regular expressions. You will learn what they are and why they are so powerful. There are a lot of different regular expression characters available, and here we will introduce the most important ones. Afterward, you will learn how to apply regular expressions with the `grep` command to find, extract, and filter useful information out of text files. **Regular expressions**, or **regexps** for short, are a very powerful concept used to search through text using special patterns, describing the structure of the search term instead of a constant string of characters, which is also called **literal text search** in this context. Using regular expressions can save you a lot of time, by not doing repetitive work, and Linux system administrators use them quite heavily in their everyday work.

In the *File globbing* section, we learned a very similar concept when we used globbing characters to find patterns to address multiple filenames with some special characters. Regular expressions are an even more powerful tool; they contain a very broad set of all kinds of special characters for matching even the most complex text fragments completely or partially. In the Linux shell, we use regular expressions not for shell expansion or to group filenames, but rather to work on the content of text files or strings of text lines to parse and analyze their content or extract text features out of it. As said before, regular expressions are a very complex topic and we can only give you an overview here. Please note that there are several styles of regular expressions available, such as Perl regular expressions. In our examples, we'll use the POSIX, basic, and extended regular expressions, as used by most of the shell tools, such as `greb`, `sed`, and `awk`. There are a lot of different regular expression characters available, which are also called **meta characters**.

As some of these meta characters are extended POSIX characters, we need to start our regular expression processing commands in the extended mode.

Some of the extended expressions are as follows:

- n is used to match the end of the line.
- t matches space at the top.
- The caret ^ symbol matches the beginning of the line.
- The dollar $ symbol matches the end of the line.
- [x] is very similar to globbing brackets, which you have learned about before. This describes classes of characters to match within the brackets at a specific position. You can also define ranges of characters here.
- [^x] matches all characters that are not defined in the brackets.
- Parentheses are used for grouping; this will save the text within the parentheses for further referencing afterward.
- 1 for number is used for back referencing. This will get number *n* of the reference extracted from the parenthesis, which we showed you before.
- a|b means that at this position *a* or *b* are allowed.
- x* means to match zero or multiple occurrences of an *x* character at this position.
- y+ means to match one or more multiple occurrences of an *y* character at this position.
- Dot means to match any character at a specific position.

It's also very important to know that a lot of tools working with regular expressions, such as `sed` and `awk`, expect that the regular expressions are surrounded by slashes. Also, the scripting language Perl has adopted this style. In other tools such as `grep`, you don't need to use the slash notation.

Let's first experiment with our new regular expression concept using the command `grep`. We start grep in the extended mode using the `egrep` command-line tool. Instead of running the command `egrep`, you can also run the command `grep` with the capital `-E` option, which has the same effect. `grep` is a command that goes through a text file or input stream, line by line, and tries to match the search pattern argument given to it to every line. If a specific line matches the pattern, it will print out the complete line. This is very useful for all kinds of text extraction, and `grep` is one of the most important command-line tools available on Linux. In fact, I cannot remember a day working in the shell when I did not use it at all. Oftentimes, `grep` is used as a filter as part of a greater pipe command workflow to reduce huge output text that you want to process further.

First things first, as said before, we will use the POSIX `regex`. There exists a lot of different regular expression terms, too many to memorize, so every time you need to look up the syntax, type `man 7 regex`. In this manual, you will find everything you need to know about regular expressions.

Let's start extracting various information out of files. We will start by using the `grep` command without a regular expression, but rather searching for simple text literals, `grep root /etc/passwd`. This returns all lines in the `passwd` file that contain the word `root`. Any line in the output gives us information that groups the `root` user it belongs to. As you can see, grep goes through the complete file and finds all lines that contain the string `root` at any position. A very useful `grep` option is `-i`. This can be used to ignore case sensitiveness for the search term. For example, execute `grep -I root /etc/services`. This will find all occurrences of the word `root`, while ignoring the case. This will find all the other case permutations of the word `root` as well. When working with regular expressions as arguments for commands such as `grep`, `sed`, or `awk`, it is recommended to quote your meta characters with *single quotes*. This is because some of the regular expression characters are the same characters as the shell globbing characters, such as the wildcard character, and this would be bad. Shell expansion always takes place before any argument gets fed into any command, so using the correct command without a disabled wild card character would search for a string containing all the filenames in the specific file that you want to search for.

Instead, always put your regular expression meta characters in single quotes. Also, if you want to search for a literal special character in the file that is the same as the regular expression meta character, you need to escape the character, which is similar to what we learned in the *File globbing* section using the backslash key. The following screenshot illustrates one example for every meta character mentioned at the start of this section:

```
[olip@localhost ~]$ grep '\*' /etc/services
sql*net          66/tcp              # Oracle SQL*NET
sql*net          66/udp              # Oracle SQL*NET
exp1             1021/tcp            # RFC3692-style Experiment 1 (*)      [RFC4727]
exp1             1021/udp            # RFC3692-style Experiment 1 (*)      [RFC4727]
exp1             1021/sctp            # RFC3692-style Experiment 1 (*)      [RFC4727]
exp1             1021/dccp            # RFC3692-style Experiment 1 (*)      [RFC4727]
exp2             1022/tcp            # RFC3692-style Experiment 2 (*)      [RFC4727]
exp2             1022/udp            # RFC3692-style Experiment 2 (*)      [RFC4727]
exp2             1022/sctp            # RFC3692-style Experiment 2 (*)      [RFC4727]
exp2             1022/dccp            # RFC3692-style Experiment 2 (*)      [RFC4727]
pvsw-inet        2441/tcp            # Pervasive I*net Data Server
pvsw-inet        2441/udp            # Pervasive I*net Data Server
[olip@localhost ~]$ egrep 'data$' /etc/services
vpad             1516/tcp            # Virtual Places Audio data
vpad             1516/udp            # Virtual Places Audio data
vpvd             1518/tcp            # Virtual Places Video data
vpvd             1518/udp            # Virtual Places Video data
nsjtp-data       1688/tcp            # nsjtp-data
nsjtp-data       1688/udp            # nsjtp-data
tqdata           2700/tcp            # tqdata
tqdata           2700/udp            # tqdata
vat              3456/tcp            # VAT default data
vat              3456/udp            # VAT default data
topovista-data   3906/tcp            # TopoVista elevation data
topovista-data   3906/udp            # TopoVista elevation data
ampl-tableproxy  5196/tcp            # AMPL_Optimization - table data
pmip6-data       5437/udp            # pmip6-data
pcanywheredata   5631/tcp            # pcANYWHEREdata
pcanywheredata   5631/udp            # pcANYWHEREdata
prosharedata     5715/tcp            # proshare conf data
prosharedata     5715/udp            # proshare conf data
eor-game         8149/udp            # Edge of Reality game data
[olip@localhost ~]$ 
```

The dollar sign matches at the end of the line, so this will print out all the files ending with data in the services file. Similarly, we use the caret ^ symbol to match at the beginning of the line. The following command here matches all the lines starting with the word day:

```
[olip@localhost ~]$ egrep '^day' /etc/services
daytime        13/tcp
daytime        13/udp
dayliteserver  6113/tcp                    # Daylite Server
daylitetouch   6117/tcp                    # Daylite Touch Sync
[olip@localhost ~]$ 
```

A bracket expression is a list of characters enclosed in square brackets. It normally matches any single-character from the list at a specific position. You can also define ranges in square brackets using the dash symbol similar to the ones we have shown in the *File globbing* section. If the list in the brackets begins with the caret symbol, it matches any single-character not from the rest of this list. Normal brackets can be used to save a reference of the match within it. To back reference, we use /number of the bracket expression so that the regular expression matches all the lines starting with the first letter, for example, egrep 't(ac)1*s' /etc/services. The pipe symbol stands for *or*, so the next expression matches all the lines containing either **domain** or **gopher**. Dot matches any character at a specific position. Plus means to match zero or multiple occurrences of the character before, so that this regular expression matches all the lines containing at-, but not at the end of the line. The star meta character matches one or more occurrences of the character before, so that the egrep 'aa+' /etc/services expression here matches all the lines that contain at least two aa or more. The plus character matches one or multiple occurrences of the character before, so that this regular expression here matches all the lines.

As said before, the dot matches every character at a specific position, so that the regular expression matches all the lines containing exactly the number of characters corresponding to the number of dots in the expression. grep has a lot of useful options, for example, -v reverses the search match, which means print all the lines that do not contain the search pattern at all. I often use this option to remove all empty lines and command lines in a lot of configuration files that start with the hashtag in shell script files. For example, execute the command shown in the following screenshot:

```
olip@localhost:~
[olip@localhost ~]$ less /etc/services
# /etc/services:
# $Id: services,v 1.55 2013/04/14 ovasik Exp $
#
# Network services, Internet style
# IANA services version: last updated 2013-04-10
#
# Note that it is presently the policy of IANA to assign a single well-known
# port number for both TCP and UDP; hence, most entries here have two entries
# even if the protocol doesn't support UDP operations.
# Updated from RFC 1700, ``Assigned Numbers'' (October 1994).  Not all ports
# are included, only the more common ones.
#
# The latest IANA port assignments can be gotten from
#        http://www.iana.org/assignments/port-numbers
# The Well Known Ports are those from 0 through 1023.
# The Registered Ports are those from 1024 through 49151
# The Dynamic and/or Private Ports are those from 49152 through 65535
#
# Each line describes one service, and is of the form:
#
# service-name   port/protocol  [aliases ...]   [# comment]

tcpmux            1/tcp                          # TCP port service multiplexer
tcpmux            1/udp                          # TCP port service multiplexer
```

The manual contains a lot of command lines that start with the hashtag and empty lines. To filter out all these un-needed lines, use the grep -v option. Another useful feature is the grep -o option, which only prints the matched pattern and not a complete line. So, for example, egrep 'netbios-...' /etc/services prints out the full line, while the -o option only prints the pure NetBIOS name from the pattern.

Working with sed

In this section, we will learn about the sed command, the powerful stream editor. We will give you a brief introduction on how sed works and we'll be showing you the substitution mode for automatically replacing text and files, which is one of the most important modes available. Next, we will learn about the sed command. Let's first examine its syntax:

```
sed [OPTION] 'pattern rule' FILE
```

sed stands for **stream editor** and this command can edit files automatically without any user interaction. It processes input files on a line-by-line basis. Oftentimes, sed is used in shell scripts to transform any command's output to a desired form for further processing. Most everyday use cases for sed follow a similar pattern, which, in its most simple form, is first used with a regular expression or other pattern to define which lines to change in an input file or stream, and then provide a rule on how to change or transform the matched line. Similar to the grep command, always use single quotes when working with sed, unless you need to work with environment variables within the sed expressions, then you should use double quotes instead. Normally sed reads from stdin, processes the stream internally, and outputs the transformed version of the text to stdout. So, it's ideally being used in a pipe command, therefore it is often part of pipelines. sed can be used for a lot of different use cases.

A very easy example using address ranges would be the d option, to delete, which also helps you understand how sed does its processing on input and output streams. So again, cat /etc/services | sed '20,50 d' pipes the etc/services file stream using cat into sed. sed processes the input stream line by line, and, here, all the lines that are not between line number 20 to 50 get handled directly over to the stdout channel, while lines number 20 to 50 get suppressed completely. You can also use regular expressions with the d option. Remember to put any regular expressions in slashes when working with sed. The sed command ignores all the lines starting with the hash symbol, but it prints out all the others to stdout. There are a lot of different options and modes that can work, but there are too many to mention here.

The most important usage for sed is definitely the substitution mode, which can be used to automate file or text editing without any user interaction. Its general syntax is: sed 's/search_for_text/replace_with_text/' FILENAME. This will search for the pattern between the first slashes, which can be a regular or literal expression, in the file filename, and if and only if this pattern matches the text somewhere in the line in this file, will it be replaced by the text to be found between the other slash. This only works for the first occurrence in the file. If you need to replace all occurrences of the search text in the file, you have to use the g option at the end of the slash expression. For example, to replace the word root in the passwd file with the word King_of_the_Jungle, for every occurrence, execute the command shown in the following screenshot:

```
olip@localhost:~
[olip@localhost ~]$ cat /etc/passwd | sed 's/root/King_of_the_Jungle/g' | less

King_of_the_Jungle:x:0:0:King_of_the_Jungle:/King_of_the_Jungle:/bin/bash
bin:x:1:1:bin:/bin:/sbin/nologin
daemon:x:2:2:daemon:/sbin:/sbin/nologin
adm:x:3:4:adm:/var/adm:/sbin/nologin
lp:x:4:7:lp:/var/spool/lpd:/sbin/nologin
sync:x:5:0:sync:/sbin:/bin/sync
shutdown:x:6:0:shutdown:/sbin:/sbin/shutdown
halt:x:7:0:halt:/sbin:/sbin/halt
mail:x:8:12:mail:/var/spool/mail:/sbin/nologin
operator:x:11:0:operator:/King_of_the_Jungle:/sbin/nologin
games:x:12:100:games:/usr/games:/sbin/nologin
ftp:x:14:50:FTP User:/var/ftp:/sbin/nologin
nobody:x:99:99:Nobody:/:/sbin/nologin
systemd-network:x:192:192:systemd Network Management:/:/sbin/nologin
dbus:x:81:81:System message bus:/:/sbin/nologin
polkitd:x:999:998:User for polkitd:/:/sbin/nologin
sshd:x:74:74:Privilege-separated SSH:/var/empty/sshd:/sbin/nologin
postfix:x:89:89::/var/spool/postfix:/sbin/nologin
chrony:x:998:996::/var/lib/chrony:/sbin/nologin
olip:x:1000:1000:olip:/home/olip:/bin/bash
(END)
```

If you are searching for anything that contains slashes, you can escape the regular substitution usage using a different pattern delimiter, because otherwise you would need to escape the slash character that you want to search for or replace, which can look very complicated and unstructured. This can also be written as `sed 's:XX:YY:g' FILENAME`, or any other character of your choice. So for example, if you want to replace single slashes with double slashes in a file, instead of using `sed 's//////g' FILENAME`, it's cleaner to use `sed 's:/://:g' FILENAME`, or `sed 's#/#//#g' FILENAME`. Using the substitution mode without any `sed` option will always print the transformed text to `stdout`. Sometimes, it is useful to directly change the text in the input file. This can be done using the `sed -i` option, or inline option.

In the following example, we will work on a copy of the passwd file to show you how to do in-place editing. In order to do so, perform the following steps:

1. Create a copy of the passwd file in the /tmp directory, as shown in the following screenshot:

```
olip@localhost:~
[olip@localhost ~]$ cp /etc/passwd /tmp/test-passwd
[olip@localhost ~]$ grep root /tmp/test-passwd
root:x:0:0:root:/root:/bin/bash
operator:x:11:0:operator:/root:/sbin/nologin
[olip@localhost ~]$ []
```

2. Let's first show all the lines containing the word root.
3. Next, replace the word root in the file with random text on stdout only. Execute the following command:

   ```
   sed 's/root/RULER_OF_THE_WORLD/g' /tmp/test-passwd | less
   ```

4. Now to in-place edit the file, use the -i option:

   ```
   sed -i 's/root/RULER_OF_THE_WORLD/g' /tmp/test-passwd
   less /tmp/test-passwd
   ```

The file has been permanently changed. Please take care when using this option, because if you have not tested your substitution before and you have made a mistake, you cannot revert your changes. It is better to create a backup copy of the original file before applying in-place editing, which you can do using the sed -i option, for example, sed -i.bak 's/root/RULER_OF_THE_WORLD/g' /tmp/test-passwd. If you write a new extension such as .bak behind the -i option, it will create a backup copy with the extension bak before applying the regular expression to the original file. When working with these regular expressions in the substitution mode, the grouping and back referencing feature that we showed you before makes substitutions very powerful, because this gives you real control of the changes needed to be made for your input text, for example, the passwd file contains colons as field delimiters, one colon to separate one field. Using sed when back referencing, we can replace one colon with four:

```
olip@localhost:~
[olip@localhost ~]$ cat /etc/passwd
root:x:0:0:root:/root:/bin/bash
bin:x:1:1:bin:/bin:/sbin/nologin
daemon:x:2:2:daemon:/sbin:/sbin/nologin
adm:x:3:4:adm:/var/adm:/sbin/nologin
lp:x:4:7:lp:/var/spool/lpd:/sbin/nologin
sync:x:5:0:sync:/sbin:/bin/sync
shutdown:x:6:0:shutdown:/sbin:/sbin/shutdown
halt:x:7:0:halt:/sbin:/sbin/halt
mail:x:8:12:mail:/var/spool/mail:/sbin/nologin
operator:x:11:0:operator:/root:/sbin/nologin
games:x:12:100:games:/usr/games:/sbin/nologin
ftp:x:14:50:FTP User:/var/ftp:/sbin/nologin
nobody:x:99:99:Nobody:/:/sbin/nologin
systemd-network:x:192:192:systemd Network Management:/:/sbin/nologin
dbus:x:81:81:System message bus:/:/sbin/nologin
polkitd:x:999:998:User for polkitd:/:/sbin/nologin
sshd:x:74:74:Privilege-separated SSH:/var/empty/sshd:/sbin/nologin
postfix:x:89:89::/var/spool/postfix:/sbin/nologin
chrony:x:998:996::/var/lib/chrony:/sbin/nologin
olip:x:1000:1000:olip:/home/olip:/bin/bash
[olip@localhost ~]$ sed -r 's/(:)/\1\1\1\1/g' /etc/passwd
root::::x::::0::::0::::root::::/root::::/bin/bash
bin::::x::::1::::1::::bin::::/bin::::/sbin/nologin
daemon::::x::::2::::2::::daemon::::/sbin::::/sbin/nologin
adm::::x::::3::::4::::adm::::/var/adm::::/sbin/nologin
lp::::x::::4::::7::::lp::::/var/spool/lpd::::/sbin/nologin
```

POSIX extended regular expressions as used by grep, sed, and awk also define a number of very useful special character classes in brackets, which can be very useful in pattern matching. The general syntax is grep '[:digit:], [:space:], [:blank:]'. The digit bracket character class matches all digits at a specific position. Space matches all the spaces, and blank matches all the whitespaces, such as the *Tab* space, and blank matches all the whitespaces. To match all the lines containing digits in the etc/passwd file, use grep '[[:digit:]]' /etc/passwd. For a list of all special character classes, use the man 7 regex manual.

Working with awk

In this section, we will show you what the command awk is all about and why it can be important for us. We will also show you how to use it for text file manipulation and processing. awk is another very important tool for text processing and manipulation. It can be used as a complete scripting language to work on text files or streams. It contains some very powerful programming constructs, including variables: *if...else, while, do while* and *for* loops; arrays; functions; and mathematical operations. awk also works on a line-by-line basis, as sed does. One of the key features of awk and the main difference to sed is that it splits input lines into fields automatically. But how does it work and why is it so helpful?

awk enables you to create rule and action pairs, and, for each record that matches this rule or condition, the action will fire. The rules are also called **patterns** and are fairly powerful and can use **extended regular expressions**. The language for the actions is similar to the programming language C. Using the awk symbol paradigm to find a pattern in the input and then applying some kind of action often reduces complex and tedious data manipulation tasks to just a few lines of code, or even one-liners. awk also lets you create and execute powerful awk script files for automating challenging text transformation tasks but, in this section, we will only focus on using awk options and arguments on the command line. Please note that, as awk is a complete scripting language with a lot of features and options, we can only show you the most important use cases and examples here.

This is the basic structure of any awk command: awk [pattern] { action }...INPUTFILE. It's important to note that the actions must be surrounded by curly brackets. This can also be read as: go through the input file line by line and try to apply the pattern to each line. If, and only if, the pattern matches or the rule can be applied to the line and is true, the action between the curly brackets will be performed.

The simplest way to learn and understand the awk tool is to use it without any rule or pattern and just define a simple action. Without giving it a pattern, the action will be applied to any line of input. As said before, awk completely splits each input line into fields so we can directly access those fields in the action argument using the following notation. As always, actions and patterns should be put into single quotes:

```
awk '{print $1}' /etc/networks
```

This will print out field 1 of all the lines of the etc/networks file. As you can see, the action must be surrounded by curly brackets. $number is the number of the field and $0 is the complete line. As you will probably know now, awk splits on every whitespace position by default. You can use the -f option to change the field separator. For example, to split the passwd file correctly, which has colons as field separator, you would specify the field separator -f using colon. This will print out field one of the etc/passwd file and the username: awk -F: '{ print $1 }' /etc/passwd. You can also use the awk printf function, which prints out the text formatted, as you may know from other programming languages: awk -F: '{ print "user: %stgroup: %sn", S1, S3 }' /etc/passwd. The %s will be substituted by the field numbers. t makes a *Tab* character and n makes a new line character.

Now, it's time to test some patterns. As we've said before, if you define a pattern or rule that can also be an extended regular expression, it will be applied through every input line and only for those matching the rule will the action be executed.

The following command will print out field one of all the lines, and only the lines, starting with small t in the etc/services file. Here we will pipe it into the head command to reduce the output to only the first 10 lines:

```
[olip@localhost ~]$ awk '/^t/ {print $1}' /etc/services | head -10
tcpmux
tcpmux
telnet
telnet
time
time
tacacs
tacacs
tftp
tftp
[olip@localhost ~]$
```

Please remember to put any regular expressions into slashes when working with the awk command. One of the greatest features of awk is that the pattern can also be more than a simple regular expression. For example, you can also use string and mathematical comparison operators here. This will help you answer very complex text manipulation questions with just a few tiny expressions:

```
[olip@localhost ~]$ awk -F: '$3 > 500 {printf "user: %s\tgroup: %s\n",$1,$3}' /etc/passwd
user: systemd-bus-proxy group: 999
user: polkitd    group: 998
user: chrony     group: 997
user: olip       group: 1000
[olip@localhost ~]$
```

In the previous example, awk only outputs lines from users in the etc/passwd file, which have a group ID greater than 500. The greater than sign is the operator. There are lots of other operators available, but there are too many to mention here. For example, to match a regular expression, use awk '$1 ~ /netrjs/ {print $0}' /etc/services. The tilde is the regular expression match operator. To match string literals, use the equal sign twice instead, awk '$1 == "netrjs-4" {print $0}' /etc/services. To get a list of all the awk operators, search for operators in the man page. Also, awk has two special patterns, which are called **BEGIN** and **END**. As any other pattern, you can define an action for the begin and for the end pattern, and this will fire only once, at the beginning or at the end of the file. We can use this to print out the total number of bytes in a directory:

```
[olip@localhost ~]$ ls -l
total 52
-rw-rw-r--. 1 olip olip  2 Jun 20 04:06 -dashy.txt
-rw-r--r--. 1 root root  2 Jun 20 02:25 file_1.txt
-rw-r--r--. 1 root root  2 Jun 20 02:25 file_2.txt
-rw-r--r--. 1 root root  2 Jun 20 02:25 file_3.txt
-rw-r--r--. 1 root root  2 Jun 20 02:25 file_4.txt
-rw-rw-r--. 1 olip olip  2 Jun 20 03:44 My private Documents.txt
-rw-rw-r--. 1 olip olip 91 Jun 20 08:16 names.txt
drwxrwxr-x. 2 olip olip  6 Jun 20 03:16 rc
-rw-rw-r--. 1 olip olip  2 Jun 20 03:15 rc0.d
-rw-rw-r--. 1 olip olip  2 Jun 20 03:15 rc1.d
-rw-rw-r--. 1 olip olip  2 Jun 20 03:15 rc2.d
-rw-rw-r--. 1 olip olip  2 Jun 20 03:15 rc3.d
-rw-rw-r--. 1 olip olip  2 Jun 20 03:15 rc4.d
-rw-rw-r--. 1 olip olip  2 Jun 20 03:57 \!super\!file\!.txt
[olip@localhost ~]$ ls -l | awk '{SUM+= $5} {print $0} END {printf "total: %s\n",SUM}'
total 52
-rw-rw-r--. 1 olip olip  2 Jun 20 04:06 -dashy.txt
-rw-r--r--. 1 root root  2 Jun 20 02:25 file_1.txt
-rw-r--r--. 1 root root  2 Jun 20 02:25 file_2.txt
-rw-r--r--. 1 root root  2 Jun 20 02:25 file_3.txt
-rw-r--r--. 1 root root  2 Jun 20 02:25 file_4.txt
-rw-rw-r--. 1 olip olip  2 Jun 20 03:44 My private Documents.txt
-rw-rw-r--. 1 olip olip 91 Jun 20 08:16 names.txt
drwxrwxr-x. 2 olip olip  6 Jun 20 03:16 rc
-rw-rw-r--. 1 olip olip  2 Jun 20 03:15 rc0.d
-rw-rw-r--. 1 olip olip  2 Jun 20 03:15 rc1.d
-rw-rw-r--. 1 olip olip  2 Jun 20 03:15 rc2.d
-rw-rw-r--. 1 olip olip  2 Jun 20 03:15 rc3.d
-rw-rw-r--. 1 olip olip  2 Jun 20 03:15 rc4.d
-rw-rw-r--. 1 olip olip  2 Jun 20 03:57 \!super\!file\!.txt
total: 121
[olip@localhost ~]$
```

This awk command works this way: first it uses a variable called SUM that acts like a container for our number counting. The += is a mathematical operator that adds field number 5 to our container SUM, so that this action counts the number of total bytes from the single byte number in field 5 on each line. Also, on each line we print out the whole line content, and, once we reach the end of the file, the end pattern will fired, which will print out the content of our SUM variable, which holds the total number of bytes in this directory. As you just saw, we can define custom variables to hold values that we want to have and work with. There are also a number of predefined variable names available in awk, which contain very useful information. For example, the NR variable name contains the current line number. This can be useful in the following awk command:

```
awk '{printf "Line number: %st%sn", NR, $0}' /etc/passwd
```

This will prepend the line number to each line of the output using the NR variable, which contains the current line number in each line. For a list of all the special awk built-in variables, use the manual and search for variables.

awk contains a number of very useful predefined functions to use, such as the print or printf functions that we already know from the action statements. To execute more than one function in one action block you can use the semicolon. For example, awk contains a number of very useful string manipulation functions, such as the toupper (argument) function. Functions in awk work like functions in most other programming languages. You call it using the function name and then, in brackets, you add the argument or arguments. For example, we use this with the print and printf function in the awk action. For example, in awk there exists a string function called toupper, which converts every string argument to uppercase letters.

The following is a complete `awk` command-line example that uses the `toupper` function:

```
[olip@localhost ~]$ awk -F: '{print $1, toupper($1)}' /etc/passwd
root ROOT
bin BIN
daemon DAEMON
adm ADM
lp LP
sync SYNC
shutdown SHUTDOWN
halt HALT
mail MAIL
operator OPERATOR
games GAMES
ftp FTP
nobody NOBODY
systemd-network SYSTEMD-NETWORK
dbus DBUS
polkitd POLKITD
sshd SSHD
postfix POSTFIX
chrony CHRONY
olip OLIP
[olip@localhost ~]$
```

This prints out the first field in the `passwd` file normally, and then again with all letters in uppercase. Our final example will show you how to execute more than one expression or function in one action statement using the semicolon as an expression delimiter:

```
[olip@localhost ~]$ awk -F: '{A=toupper($1); print A,$1}' /etc/passwd
ROOT root
BIN bin
DAEMON daemon
ADM adm
LP lp
SYNC sync
SHUTDOWN shutdown
HALT halt
MAIL mail
OPERATOR operator
GAMES games
FTP ftp
NOBODY nobody
SYSTEMD-NETWORK systemd-network
DBUS dbus
POLKITD polkitd
SSHD sshd
POSTFIX postfix
CHRONY chrony
OLIP olip
[olip@localhost ~]$ 
```

Also, you can see here that you can assign the return value of any function to a variable name, and then reference this variable name later, so that this example is very similar to the example before by first printing out the uppercase version, and then the normal lowercase version, and then the normal field value version. For all the available awk functions, we use the manual and search for functions, numeric functions, string functions, time functions, and so on.

Navigating the Linux filesystem

In this section, you will learn how to navigate the Linux filesystem. You will also learn how the Linux filesystem is structured. If we print out the folder structure of the top-level directories beneath the root directory by executing the tree -d -L 1 / command, you will see a list of strange-sounding directory names. These directory names are the same on any Linux distribution and they follow a standard called the **filesystem hierarchy standard (FHS)**. Each of these standard directories in the Linux filesystem has a specific purpose, and the user can expect certain files in certain locations, and it also means that a program can predict where the files are located, and it also means that any program working with those system directories can predict where the files are located. The following are the directories:

- The / slash is the primary hierarchy root.
- /bin contains essential commands needed for the system, for example, so that a user can work in recovery mode of the system when something breaks or, for example, executables needed when a user boots into recovery mode.
- /boot contains files needed for booting, such as the kernel files.
- /dev contains the device files of the system, for example /dev/null, which we have used before. This directory is very important and you will use it a lot when you are working as a system administrator. It contains the system-wide configuration files of all your applications that you have installed on your system.
- /home contains the user's home directories, as we have learned in this section.
- /lib contains the libraries essential for the binaries in /bin and /sbin, as we will see next. /lib64 contains alternate format essential libraries for the 64-bit architecture.
- /media contains the mount points for removable media such as CD-ROMs.
- /mnt contains temporarily mounted filesystems.
- /opt contains optional application software packages.
- /proc contains the virtual filesystem providing process and kernel information as files, for example, this is where all the environment variables of the current sessions are stored.
- /root contains the home directory for the root user. The root user's home directory is not in /home.

- /run contains runtime variable data; this is information about the running system since last boot.
- /sbin contains essential system binaries.
- /srv contains all the data that should be served by the system, for example, data and scripts for web servers or data offered by FTP servers that are running as services on the system.
- /sys contains information about the devices connected to the system.
- /tmp contains temporary files. Every user has full access to this directory.
- /usr contains the majority of all the user utilities and applications, for example, all the applications installed by a user go in here. It's also called a **secondary hierarchy** for read-only user data; because it has a similar structure as the root directories, top-level directories. For example, you also have a /usr/bin directory, a /usr/lib directory, a /usr/sbin directory, and so on.
- /var directory is for all the files that are expected to continually change during normal operation of the system, for example, log files, spool files, and temporary email files.

First, let's introduce the concept of Linux home directories. Every user known to a Linux system has their own private place in the filesystem, where they can manage their own data and have full access to everything, for example, creating directories or new files, deleting things, or changing permissions. For security reasons, most places in the Linux filesystem, with a few exceptions, such as the system /tmp directory, are restricted in one way or the other, and normally a logged-in user does not have full access to it only the root user has full access to everything. Every logged in user has the property of a current directory, which is the directory you're currently at. When a user logs in to the Linux system, their specific home directory will be set as the current directory by default, so they will start in this directory.

To display the name of your current directory, which means where you are at the moment, type pwd, and then press the *Enter* key. pwd stands for **print working directory**. This is a very useful command because when you are browsing directories, it is easy to get lost. A directory is a concept to structure data. Often, it is used to categorize all files belonging to the same project or of the same type, such as all configuration files. As you can see, the output of the pwd command contains a string containing slash symbols that are used to separate directory names, and this is also called the **directory separator symbol**. The leftmost slash has a special name and it is also called **root directory**. The last directory name of the current directory can also be seen at the shell prompt. In a Linux filesystem, every directory can have files in it and can contain further directories that are then called subdirectories. These subdirectories can also include files and folders and so on. The directory containing a subdirectory is also called the parent directory, while the subdirectory is called the **child directory**. Here, in our example, the home directory is the parent of the olip directory, which is also called the child directory. These type of files and folders can be visualized using a tree-like structure, and also this can be called a hierarchical filesystem because every directory in this structure has a specific position and some are higher in the hierarchy and others are lower. The highest directory is the / directory, or root directory. We need to remember to visualize this hierarchical tree structure. We can use the tree command, which we need to install, because it is not available in the standard installation. To install it, use your root password that you set up during installation.

After installing, you can use the tree command to get a first overview of your system. At the top level we have the / directory, which is the highest directory in the tree. Directly beneath it we have a number of system directories. When we customize the tree command to show us two levels of directories in the tree by executing tree -d -L 2 / | less, we can see where the home directory in the tree is and how we can get to it from the root directory, which is the parent of all the other directories. Now, to create a new directory in your home directory, you can use the mkdir command. The mkdir command takes the name of the folder you want to create as an argument. To remove an empty directory, use the mrdir command. To create a new empty file, use the touch command. To remove a file, use the rm command.

Now, let's recreate the folder and the filename again. To change to a directory, you can use the cd command, which stands for **change directory**. The change directory command will change your current directory to the new directory, which you used as an argument for the cd command. Use pwd to test this again. The following screenshot illustrates this:

```
olip@localhost ~/test/FolderA
[olip@localhost test]$ mkdir FolderA
[olip@localhost test]$ rmdir FolderA/
[olip@localhost test]$ touch FileA
[olip@localhost test]$ rm FileA
[olip@localhost test]$ mkdir FolderA
[olip@localhost test]$ touch FileA
[olip@localhost test]$ ls
FileA   FolderA
[olip@localhost test]$ cd FolderA/
[olip@localhost FolderA]$ pwd
/home/olip/test/FolderA
[olip@localhost FolderA]$ []
```

In Linux, when we say to go to a directory, what we really mean is to make another directory our current one by using the cd command. As mentioned before, every directory contains two special shorthand links that you can't change and you can't remove, the . and the . ., which is the name of the directory we are currently in. Every directory contains the name . ., which is the name of the unique parent directory of the directory in which we are currently in. Also, every subdirectory contains exactly one parent directory, while one parent directory can contain multiple subdirectories. These dots are very useful for traveling through directories fast. To go back to the preceding directory, which in our case is the home directory, we can use the . . notation. To create a subdirectory in a subdirectory in a subdirectory, we can use the following approach:

```
olip@localhost ~/FolderA/FolderB/FolderC/FolderD
[olip@localhost ~]$ cd FolderA/
[olip@localhost FolderA]$ mkdir FolderB
[olip@localhost FolderA]$ cd FolderB/
[olip@localhost FolderB]$ mkdir FolderC
[olip@localhost FolderB]$ cd FolderC/
[olip@localhost FolderC]$ mkdir FolderD
[olip@localhost FolderC]$ cd FolderD/
[olip@localhost FolderD]$ []
```

To view the folder structure that we have just created, we can use the `pwd` command again. To go up one directory level, we can use `cd. ..` To go back down, use `cd FolderD`. Now, to go up two levels of directories, you can use the folder separator slash symbol-`cd ../ ../`. To go back two levels in our subdirectory structure, we can also use the folder separator slash symbol as well. When traversing directories there are always many ways to do this. To go back to the home directory quickly, we can use several different ways. To go back to the home directory first, you can use some shortcuts. As we have mentioned before, the tilde symbol stands for the home directory, so we can easily go back to the home directory `cd ~`. The tilde symbol works from everywhere, so you can go back to your home directory from any directory you are at. Also, a very helpful shortcut is `cd -`, which lets you toggle between the current directory and the directory you were at before.

There even exists a shorter way to go back to your home directory from every location, using only the `cd` command without any arguments. Another way to go to your home directory from every location is to use the path outputted from the `pwd` command directly. In order to delete a directory structure that contains subdirectories or files, you cannot use the `rmdir` command. To delete a directory subtree that contains files and directories, instead, we need to use the `rm -rf` option, but please use it with caution as this will delete everything without asking, which is completely irreversible.

To recreate the same subdirectory structure, as we showed you before in a much simpler form we can use the directory separator symbol with the `mkdir -p` option. So far, all our operations and actions on files and folders, such as `ls`, `mkdir`, or `mrdir`, were always in relation to the current directory, which means the description on how to go to the directory or file of choice was always in relation to the current directory. For example, we used commands to work with files and directories that are within our current directory. For referencing files and folders outside of our current directory, we use the `..` and a slash directory separator.

If we wanted to work on files and directories in the same directory, we just need the name of the resource. If we want to access a resource outside of our current directory, we can do this using the directory separator and the `..` notation to travel to the right file or directory. Now, let's again execute the `pwd` command. The output of the `pwd` command is called **absolute** or **full path**. An absolute path is easily recognized from the leading forward slash, which is called the root directory, as you now know. The slash symbol means that you start at the top-level directory, or root directory, and continue down. An absolute path is literally a path of names throughout the hierarchy. A pathname specifies and describes how to traverse or navigate the hierarchical directory names in the filesystem to reach some destination object starting from the highest root directory, which can be a file or directory. The full path always contains complete information on how to go from the root directory to any destination in the filesystem. In other words, to go to the current directory, which is called `/home/olip/FolderA`, you have to traverse, from the `/root` directory, to the `home` directory, to the `olip` directory, and to the `FolderA` directory. To visualize this in a tree-like structure, use the `tree` command with the subdirectory **L 3**:

```
[olip@localhost ~]$ tree /home/olip/FolderA/
/home/olip/FolderA/
└── FolderB
    └── FolderC
        └── FolderD

3 directories, 0 files
[olip@localhost ~]$ 
```

It's important to remember that the absolute path works from everywhere. A relative path doesn't have a preceding slash. Using a relative path, for example, changing to `FolderA`, is always dependent on where you are at the moment in the filesystem. So, `cd FolderA` only works in your current position. If you re-execute the command somewhere else, it doesn't work. When using any Linux command that works with files or directories, you always have the option to either use a local path relative to your current directory, or to use the full and absolute path relative to the root directory. Oftentimes, the relative path is faster to use and often it is also convenient to change to the directory of the files you want to work with directly. But the absolute path is important for scripts or if a command needs to work from every directory.

Summary

In this chapter, we started off with an introduction to the command line, file globbing, and quoting commands. We progressed towards practical execution by working with the shell, standard streams, and regular expressions. We also covered functionalities of `sed`, `awk`, and the Linux filesystem.

In the next chapter, we'll cover concepts pertaining to files.

The Linux Filesystem

3

In the previous chapter, we introduced you to Linux files and folders by navigating the filesystem. In this chapter, we will learn how to work with, find, and change permissions and access to reading and editing files. We will expand our knowledge on this topic, define what a filesystem is, and show you important commands for working with files, such as copying and moving.

We'll walk you through the following concepts:

- Understanding the filesystem
- Working with file links
- Searching for files
- Working with users and groups
- Working with file permissions
- Working with text files
- Working with VIM text editor

Understanding the filesystem

A filesystem is not only a tree of files and folders exposed to the Linux user, but it's also the structure and management to access and save data, and keep everything consistent. As already mentioned, you often hear the phrase that in Linux, everything is a file, and this is true. This means that a lot of different things in Linux get abstracted as files. For example, a directory is a file, hardware devices get represented by special system files, or ,useful, such as a random number generator, is also a file.

Let's quickly recap and summarize what we already know about working with files from the last two chapters. `ls` lists and displays files, `touch` creates a file, files are case sensitive, and . files are hidden files and are excluded from normal command execution, such as the `ls` command, and also from shell expansion using file globbing characters. Next, you should also already know `mkdir` creates a directory, `rmdir` deletes an empty directory, `rm` deletes a file, and `mkdir -p` creates a full subdirectory structure. `rmdir` cannot be applied on nonempty directories; in our example, it contained subfolders. `rm -rf` deletes a directory with all the subdirectories, but handle it with caution. When you use the `rm -rf` option to delete a whole directory structure, the `r` option stands for recursive, `f` for force. The recursive option is an important option you will often encounter when working with commands that do something for a whole subdirectory tree.

Now, let's learn some other important new file-based commands. If you need to copy a file, you can use the `cp` command. We already saw the general usage of `cp`in the previous chapter. If you go to the man page of the `cp` command, there are three different usage formats: `cp [option]... [-T] SOURCE DEST`, `cp [option]... SOURCE...` `DIRECTORY`, and `cp [option]... -t DIRECTORY SOURCE...` It's important to remember that there can be multiple source directories, but only one target directory. You have to memorize this. To copy one single file to one destination file, you can use the first usage form. To copy several files to one destination folder, you can use the second usage form. The third usage form is like the second usage form, but with mixed source and directory arguments.

For example, to create a copy of a file with a different filename, use `cp firstfile` `secondfile`; you can also do the same using local pathnames. As we have learned from the manual, you can also copy files to directories leaving the original filename. As shown in the manual, you can also do this for multiple source files. Note that you cannot copy complete directories out of the box using the `cp` command. In order to do so, you need to provide the `-R` option:

```
[root@localhost olip]# cp /etc/passwd/ /etc/services /home/olip/.bashrc /tmp
cp: omitting directory '/etc/passwd/'
cp: overwrite '/tmp/services'? y
cp: omitting directory '/home/olip/.bashrc'
[root@localhost olip]# cp /home/olip /tmp
cp: omitting directory '/home/olip'
[root@localhost olip]# cp -R /home/olip /tmp
[root@localhost olip]# ls /tmp/olip
fileC  file_new  fileX  fileXX  folderA  NeW-CaMelcAsE-File
```

As you can see, the complete `olip` home directory has been copied to the `/tmp` directory with all subdirectories and files. Please memorize that the `cp -R` option stands for recursive, again. To move files and folders on the command line you can use the move command, which implicitly copies and deletes the source files. The move command `mv` is often used to rename files and folders. Note that you can move or rename not only files, but also folders.

Now, again if you have a look at the `ls -l` option, for example, in the `/etc` directory, you will notice some things. You will be presented with a lot of useful information. The first character in the `-l` listing here is a d, or –, or l, and this represents the type of the file. A d stands for directory, a – is a normal file, and l is a link. The first character in the `ls -l` output is also called the file type flag. Besides the shown d, –, and l flags, there are a number of other available file types. To get a full list of all the available file type flags, use `man find`, search for `type`, then search for `type c`. You will get a full list of all the available file type flags in Linux:

```
-type c
         File is of type c:

         b        block (buffered) special

         c        character (unbuffered) special

         d        directory

         p        named pipe (FIFO)

         f        regular file

         l        symbolic link; this is never true if the -L option or the
                  -follow option is in effect, unless the symbolic link  is
                  broken.  If you want to search for symbolic links when -L
                  is in effect, use -xtype.

         s        socket

         D        door (Solaris)

    -uid n File's numeric user ID is n.
Manual page find(1) line 639 (press h for help or q to quit)
```

Also, there is another very useful piece of information given in the column adjacent to the permissions column. The number presented is the number of links a file contains:

```
drwxr-xr-x. 2 root root    27 Jun 19 14:14 plymouth
drwxr-xr-x. 5 root root    52 Mar 19 14:18 pm
drwxr-xr-x. 5 root root    72 Mar  2 14:19 polkit-1
[root@localhost ~]# _
```

File links tell us how many references exist on any given file or directory. Every normal file by default has one link and every directory has two links. There are hard links and soft links, which we'll discuss shortly.

Working with file links

In this section, we take a look at what Linux file links are and how to work with them. As you already might know, files are stored on the hard disk. In a Linux filesystem, the file's filename and the data are two separate concepts and are not stored together. A general structure is shown in the following diagram:

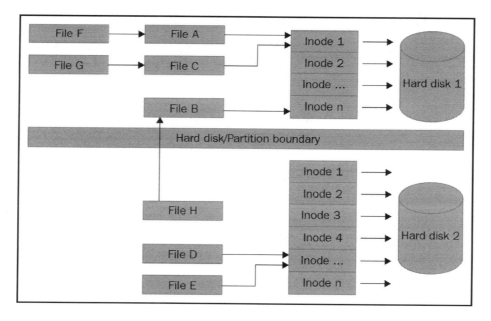

Connecting a filename to the actual data is managed by the filesystem using a table or database data structure, which is called a title allocation table. In the Linux filesystem, an Inode is the actual entry point or starting point to the beginning of a specific file's data on the hard disk. To simplify, we can just say that the Inode represents the actual data of a file. The filesystem management now takes care that every normal file, upon creation, has one link entry in its allocation table to connect the actual filename to the Inode or data on the hard disk. Such a link is also called **hard link**. The original filename to Inode relationship is also linked using a hard link, that's why in the last section the `ls -l` command gave us the number 1 for most of the files in the column adjacent to the permissions. Now, the cool thing about the Linux filesystem is that you can create additional hard links to an existing Inode, which is like having alternative names for a file.

One of the drawbacks of a hard link are that you cannot differentiate a hard link from the original filename or the Inode. This can cause problems and side effects, because if you change the original file's content the hard link's content will be changed as well. Another limitation of hard links is that you can only define them for Inodes, which are on the same partition as the hard link should go. Also, you cannot create hard links on directories. You can only create them on normal files. To solve these limitations of hard links, you can use **soft links**, also known as symbolic links. These are the type of links that you will use almost all the time in your everyday work as a Linux system administrator. Hard links also have their special use cases, for example, for creating backups of files, but are only used very rarely by the Linux user.

A symbolic link is a link to the filename and not to the Inode. Symbolic links also don't have the boundary that they must be on the same partition or hard disk as the original file. You can also create symbolic links on a directory. The main drawback is that if you delete or move the original file, you will have a broken symbolic link without further warning, which can also create some bad side effects. The main use cases and power of symbolic links are referencing configuration files or dynamic library versions in the Linux filesystem. Using links can save a lot of disk space because no actual data must be copied and they are very effective for quickly testing out such things as alternate configuration files for services.

File links are managed by the `ln` command. The basic syntax is `ln [OPTION]`, then the filename you want to create a link on, and finally the link name. To create a hard link to a file called `fileX` in your `home` directory, use the following code:

```
[root@localhost ~]# ls -l
total 16
-rw-------.  1 root root 1161 Jun 26 11:31 anaconda-ks.cfg
-rw-r--r--.  1 root root  153 Jun 27 05:45 edit
-rwxrwxrwx.  1 root root    0 Jun 27 02:09 file-to-delete
-rw-r--r--.  1 root root    0 Jun 27 05:46 fileX
drwx------.  3 olip olip   74 Jun 27 01:40 list
-rw-r--r--.  1 root root   34 Jun 27 04:31 my-source-file.source
drwxr-xr-x.  2 root root   75 Jun 27 05:31 scripts
drwxr-xr-x.  2 root root   66 Jun 27 05:24 stuff
drwxr-xr-x.  6 root root 4096 Jun 27 01:31 test_files
[root@localhost ~]# ln fileX fileX_link
[root@localhost ~]# ls -l
total 16
-rw-------.  1 root root 1161 Jun 26 11:31 anaconda-ks.cfg
-rw-r--r--.  1 root root  153 Jun 27 05:45 edit
-rwxrwxrwx.  1 root root    0 Jun 27 02:09 file-to-delete
-rw-r--r--.  2 root root    0 Jun 27 05:46 fileX
-rw-r--r--.  2 root root    0 Jun 27 05:46 fileX_link
drwx------.  3 olip olip   74 Jun 27 01:40 list
-rw-r--r--.  1 root root   34 Jun 27 04:31 my-source-file.source
drwxr-xr-x.  2 root root   75 Jun 27 05:31 scripts
drwxr-xr-x.  2 root root   66 Jun 27 05:24 stuff
drwxr-xr-x.  6 root root 4096 Jun 27 01:31 test_files
[root@localhost ~]# 
[root@localhost ~]# rm fileX_link2
rm: remove regular empty file 'fileX_link2'? y
[root@localhost ~]# df -i
Filesystem                 Inodes  IUsed   IFree IUse% Mounted on
/dev/mapper/centos-root   6991872  58516 6933356    1% /
devtmpfs                   124544    356  124188    1% /dev
tmpfs                      127107      1  127106    1% /dev/shm
tmpfs                      127107    412  126695    1% /run
tmpfs                      127107     13  127094    1% /sys/fs/cgroup
/dev/sda1                  512000    330  511670    1% /boot
tmpfs                      127107      1  127106    1% /run/user/0
[root@localhost ~]# mount_
```

As you can see, there's no way to differentiate the additional hard link from the original one. You can also create multiple links on the same file. To delete a hard link, use the `rm` command. There's a maximum number of Inodes on every filesystem, or we can just simply say files, which you can display using `df -i`. If you use the `mount` command, you will see that the `tmp` filesystem for the user is on a different partition than the `home` directory, which is in turn, on the root partition as shown in the following screenshot:

```
cgroup on /sys/fs/cgroup/cpu,cpuacct type cgroup (rw,nosuid,nodev,noexec,relatim
e,cpuacct,cpu)
cgroup on /sys/fs/cgroup/cpuset type cgroup (rw,nosuid,nodev,noexec,relatime,cpu
set)
cgroup on /sys/fs/cgroup/freezer type cgroup (rw,nosuid,nodev,noexec,relatime,fr
eezer)
cgroup on /sys/fs/cgroup/net_cls type cgroup (rw,nosuid,nodev,noexec,relatime,ne
t_cls)
cgroup on /sys/fs/cgroup/blkio type cgroup (rw,nosuid,nodev,noexec,relatime,blki
o)
cgroup on /sys/fs/cgroup/devices type cgroup (rw,nosuid,nodev,noexec,relatime,de
vices)
configfs on /sys/kernel/config type configfs (rw,relatime)
/dev/mapper/centos-root on / type xfs (rw,relatime,seclabel,attr2,inode64,noquot
a)
selinuxfs on /sys/fs/selinux type selinuxfs (rw,relatime)
systemd-1 on /proc/sys/fs/binfmt_misc type autofs (rw,relatime,fd=31,pgrp=1,time
out=300,minproto=5,maxproto=5,direct)
debugfs on /sys/kernel/debug type debugfs (rw,relatime)
mqueue on /dev/mqueue type mqueue (rw,relatime,seclabel)
hugetlbfs on /dev/hugepages type hugetlbfs (rw,relatime,seclabel)
/dev/sda1 on /boot type xfs (rw,relatime,seclabel,attr2,inode64,noquota)
tmpfs on /run/user/0 type tmpfs (rw,nosuid,nodev,relatime,seclabel,size=101688k,
mode=700)
[root@localhost ~]#
```

So the next command `ln ~/folderABC ~/folderABC_link` will fail because it is not allowed to create hard links between partitions. Also, you cannot create a hard link on a directory, and changing the origin of the file's content will change the hard link's file content as well. This can create some bad side effects. To create a symbolic link, use the `ln -s` option:

```
[root@localhost ~]# ln -s fileX fileX_sym_link
[root@localhost ~]# ls -l
total 16
-rw-------. 1 root root 1161 Jun 26 11:31 anaconda-ks.cfg
-rw-r--r--. 1 root root  153 Jun 27 05:45 edit
-rwxrwxrwx. 1 root root    0 Jun 27 02:09 file-to-delete
-rw-r--r--. 2 root root    0 Jun 27 05:46 fileX
-rw-r--r--. 2 root root    0 Jun 27 05:46 fileX_link
lrwxrwxrwx. 1 root root    5 Jun 27 05:56 fileX_sym_link -> fileX
drwx------. 3 olip olip   74 Jun 27 01:40 list
-rw-r--r--. 1 root root   34 Jun 27 04:31 my-source-file.source
drwxr-xr-x. 2 root root   75 Jun 27 05:31 scripts
drwxr-xr-x. 2 root root   66 Jun 27 05:24 stuff
drwxr-xr-x. 6 root root 4096 Jun 27 01:31 test_files
[root@localhost ~]#
```

As you can see, it's easy to show if a file as a symbolic link marked with the arrow. To create a symbolic link of a file in another directory, preserving the original file's name, you can use `ln -s /etc/passwd`. This created a symbolic link of the `/etc/passwd` file in the current directory under the same name, `passwd`. To delete a symbolic link, use the `rm` command; the original file will not be touched. You can also create a symbolic link on a directory. If you delete the original file that the symbolic link is pointing to, that is `fileX` here the symbolic link will broke. This can get problematic, which is denoted here with the blue color:

```
[root@localhost ~]# rm fileX
rm: remove regular empty file 'fileX'? y
[root@localhost ~]# ls -l
total 4
-rw-------. 1 0 root 1169 Jun 26 11:40 anaconda-ks.cfg
-rw-r--r--. 1 0 root    0 Jun 26 18:03 fileX_link
drwxr-xr-x. 2 0 root    6 Jun 26 18:30 folderABC
[root@localhost ~]#
```

Searching for files

In this section, we will learn how to search for files in Linux. The `man find` command, as the name implies, can find files based on versatile criteria. But more than that, you can even apply actions on every search result during execution of the program, which is a very useful feature. Find can take some options to change its default behavior, for example, how to treat files, which are symbolic links during execution of the program. The first few arguments are a list of directories or starting points to start your search in, all the other arguments are search expressions or conditions to find in your search. It's important to discuss what search expressions are. A search expression typically is a test and an action. Tests are typically separated by logical operators. If no operator is given, the end operator is assumed. If the expression contains no action by the user, then the `print` action will be performed for all the files in the search result.

Before we start using the man find command, it's important to know how the man find command processes the search results. For every file in the list of search paths, all the expressions get evaluated from left to right. By default, only if all the expressions are correct, the man find command marks the file as a hit. You can change this logical end behavior if you like using an OR expression as well, as we will see later in one of our examples. The man find command lets you create very sophisticated search queries using a broad range of very useful file test expressions. If you search for tests in the manual page of the man find command, you will get a full list of all the available test operators. For example, you can search for files that have been modified or accessed at specific time in the past, or which have a certain size. As mentioned earlier, the default action is the print action on every file match. Another very useful action is the exec expression, which lets you execute a specific command for every file match. The man find command is a very complex command and we cannot show you everything here. Thus, for the rest of this section we will show you some very useful use cases. You can use the find command without any options or arguments. This is the same as writing because without any options and arguments the search path is the current directory and the default action is the print action. This command goes through your current directory and prints out all the files and directories, including all subdirectories and files beneath the subdirectories, recursively. It does so because you have not provided any test expression, so it will just match any file or directory in your current directory and apply the print action to it. As mentioned earlier, what makes the find command so powerful is its huge list of different test expressions to locate files based on a variety of useful conditions. Such file search tests can be anything imaginable, such as timestamps, user permissions, users, groups, file type, date, size, or any other possible search criteria.

For the following examples, we will use the root user account set up during installation, because in the example shown here, we search a lot in the system directories, which need special privileges. To search for only files and not directories in the /etc directory for the filename logrotate.conf use the following:

```
find /etc -type f -name logrotate.conf
```

If the file is found, you won't encounter any errors. What this command does in the background is it goes through the /etc directory and picks up all the files and subdirectories included in the /etc directory and it processes them recursively one by one. Then, for every file, it checks whether the file is the actual file, and whether the name is equal to the filename. You can also use multiple directories as search starting points, as well as use the -type d to search only directories, this will print out all subdirectory names beginning with the /etc and /var directories and starting with the letter y:

```
[root@localhost ~]# find /etc /var -type d -name 'y*'
/etc/yum.repos.d
/etc/yum
/var/lib/yum
/var/lib/yum/yumdb
/var/lib/yum/yumdb/y
/var/cache/yum
/var/yp
[root@localhost ~]#
```

Here, the name expression takes normal POSIX 5 globbing characters, not regular expressions. If you want to use regular expressions for file search use the -regex expression instead. Note that if you use -iname expression instead, it will search case-insensitive. You can also search for files using file size as a criteria:

```
/etc/GREP_COLORS
/etc/security/group.conf
/etc/gdbinit
/etc/abrt/gpg_keys.conf
/etc/selinux/targeted/contexts/users/guest_u
/etc/selinux/targeted/modules/active/modules/games.pp
/etc/selinux/targeted/modules/active/modules/gdomap.pp
/etc/selinux/targeted/modules/active/modules/gear.pp
/etc/selinux/targeted/modules/active/modules/geoclue.pp
/etc/selinux/targeted/modules/active/modules/getty.pp
/etc/selinux/targeted/modules/active/modules/git.pp
/etc/selinux/targeted/modules/active/modules/gitosis.pp
/etc/selinux/targeted/modules/active/modules/glance.pp
/etc/selinux/targeted/modules/active/modules/glusterd.pp
/etc/selinux/targeted/modules/active/modules/gnome.pp
/etc/selinux/targeted/modules/active/modules/gpg.pp
/etc/selinux/targeted/modules/active/modules/gpm.pp
/etc/selinux/targeted/modules/active/modules/gpsd.pp
/etc/selinux/targeted/modules/active/modules/gssproxy.pp
/etc/selinux/targeted/modules/active/modules/guest.pp
/etc/postfix/generic
/etc/latrace.d/headers/getopt.h
/etc/GeoIP.conf
/etc/GeoIP.conf.default
[root@localhost ~]#
```

The `find / -type f -size +4M -name '1*'` searches for all the files equal to or larger than 4 MB starting with the name `1` and only files and not directories starting in the `root` directory, which means it will recursively search in the whole filesystem tree. As you see, only two files match all of these conditions. By the way, the + stands for greater or equals, if you use a – symbol it stands for less than. You can also search for specific file permissions. File permissions in general are discussed in later sections. To get a list of all the very dangerous directories with read, write, execute permissions for everybody searching in the whole filesystem, we use the following command:

```
find / -type d -perm 777
```

Note that if the user doesn't provide any action for the `find` command itself the default `print` action is assumed, so the command will print out every matched file to the `stdout` command line. We can change that using the `-exec` action expression, which will apply a command after the `-exec` expression for every matched file:

```
find / -type d -perm 777 chmod 755 {} ;
```

In our example, the `chmod 755` command will be applied for every matched file using the placeholder `{}`, which stands for matched. The `find` command here will search for all the files having a very dangerous file permission, `777`, and changes it back to a more moderate permission, `755`. So if we search again for the dangerous permission, the result will be empty. Why do we have to escape the semicolon? This is because normally a semicolon in the Bash shell delimits commands, so we have to disable its special meaning here. In all the examples shown so far, all the tests and expressions of a single `find` command must be true that the file can be counted as match.

For example command `find / -type f -size +4M -name '1*'` only files are matched and printed out if they are of type file and have a size of 4 MB or more and have a name starting with `1`. All of these three test expressions have to be `true` and are connected via a logical and. By default, the logical AND operator is connecting all the test expressions, which means only if all test expressions are true, the file can be matched as a hit. You can easily change a logical AND to a logical OR using the `-or` expression, like:

```
find / -type f -name p*.conf -or -name 'p*.d'
```

This will match all files starting with a p and having the extension conf or .d in the /etc directory, and having the type file. There are also some very useful test expressions based on the time of a file. For example, find /var —mtime 10| head will output all the files, which have been modified in the last three days, outputting only the first 10 hits before the last three days or longer. Using time-based test expressions is very useful and is often needed in your daily work as a system administrator. For example, if you would need to delete all the files uploaded by users of a web application running on your server, which are older than 30 days, you could do something like the following:

```
find /var/www/webapp-uploads —mtime +30 —exec rm {} ;
```

This command could also be easily put into a script running each day, such as in a Cron job, to automate deleting of all the files which are older than 30 days, so you don't have to take care of this manually anymore. To search for all the files in the entire filesystem, which start with the l and r and has a size between 1 and 4 MB use:

```
find / —type f —size +1M —size —4M —name 'l*'
```

You can also quickly search for files using the locate command instead of using find. You first need to install using the package and locate. The locate command does not do a live search in the filesystem, but rather uses a snapshot of the filesystem using a specific time point. This database gets updated every day at a certain point in time, but you can also regenerate the snapshot database by yourself using the following:

```
updatedb
```

Now if you use the locate command, it will search the database you just generated for all the files matching the name logrotate. This will only search for literal text. If you want to use for regular expressions, use the --regex option.

As we are searching a database, this is usually faster than doing a live search using the find command, but always remember this is not a live state of the current filesystem. Hence, you can run into problems especially when searching for files, which are newer than the search database.

Working with users and groups

In this section, we will learn how to create and remove users and groups, and how to add groups to users. Also, we will see how Linux internally stores user information and passwords, and how to retrieve user information programmatically. Finally, we will learn how to substitute user accounts while staying logged in. Linux is a multiuser system, which means more than one user can work with the system simultaneously. Therefore, a system is needed, which guarantees common access to Linux objects such as files using measurements of excess protection. For example, all files which have been created by one user should not be allowed to be erased by another user. Every Linux user is defined and identified by a unique user ID, as humans more easily can work with names than numbers. There also exists a literal username connected to each user ID, but Linux internally works with the **user ID (UID)** number when managing control on Linux objects such as files. There are two types of users accounts, login users which need a password to authenticate, and nonlogin users, which are useful for attaching user IDs to running programs or processes, as we will see later. Also there's one special account on every Linux system, the root user account, or administrator account, which we set up a password for during installation. This account on every system has access and is the owner to all objects, such as files presented in the Linux system, and this account can do anything to the system. If in Linux we have the username to control access files, it will be very limiting and time-consuming to grant or revoke permissions. Therefore, Linux also has the concept of groups to access control. Using groups can drastically simplify permission management by assigning permissions on a shared resource to a group, rather than to individual users. Assigning permissions to a group assigns the same access to the resource to all members of that group. Linux groups are also represented by a group ID, which is a number, but can also be referenced by its name, the group name. Every user in Linux has exactly one UID, but can belong to multiple groups or group IDs. One group is the primary group, which will be used when new files are created by that user.

Let's start by creating some new user accounts for our tests. Only root can do this. So first, let's log in as root. The useradd command adds a new user with the username given as an argument. This command creates a new user in the system and also creates the corresponding home directories. To make our new login accounts functional, we need to set passwords as well; we can do this with the passwd command. You can also use this command to change your own password. To set or change a password for other users, we type passwd username-this can only be done using the root user account. To delete a user, use the userdel command. By default, the userdel command will not delete the user's home directory, so you have to do it yourself. To delete a user, it's better to use the userdel -r flag, which not only deletes the user but also deletes the associated home directory and mailbox. Let's recreate the user. Let's log out the root user. You can use the su command, or substitute user command, to switch the user while you are logged in. When you call the su command without any argument, the root user is assumed to be switched. To switch a substitute to a different user, you use the username as the first argument. You can recheck who is logged in using the whoami command. Using the su command, will preserve the original environment of the user who has executed the su command, and will not switch to the home user of the substituted user account.

Now, let's exit the substituted user and switch to another user. Using the su command with a dash symbol as an argument, we create a more login shell-like environment, which means it behaves more like a user who would login to the shell for real. By executing pwd, you can see that the home directory has been changed to the substituted user's home directory. Now, exit the substituted user again. You can also directly execute a single command with another user account using su -c flag; su username -c. This is useful if you want to quickly start a script or a command using a different user account without completely switching the user.

 Only the root user is allowed to substitute users using the su command without providing a password. Any other user who wants to use the su command needs to know the password of the substituted user.

The useradd and passwd commands are making changes to the etc/passwd and etc/shadow files, which are the most important files to store authentication and user information in the entire Linux system. The passwd file stores a list of all the user accounts known to the system, all the login users and all the system users. Login users are typical physical persons who can log into a shell such as the Bash shell using a password for authentication. System users typically cannot log into a shell and are often associated to system services and processes.

For example, to get a list of all the usernames available in the Linux system use:

```
awk -F: '{print $1}' /etc/passwd
```

The passwd file stores a lot of useful information such as the user's home directory, the default shell, or the user ID number. Refer to the manual page of the passwd command to find out more. The /etc/shadow file contains all the password information for all the users in an encrypted format. You need the root user account in order to view this file. To create a new group, use the groupadd command and to delete a group, use the groupdel command. The groupadd and groupdel commands internally work with the /etc/group file. This file shows you all groups available in the system as well as all the user IDs associated to these groups. Instead of reading the /etc/group or /etc/passwd file for getting information about a user, you can also use the id command. This will tell you the user ID, the group ID, and all the associated groups a user has. To add existing groups to a user, you can use the usermod -G command. -G overrides all the secondary groups a user has, leaving the primary group as it is. You can also define a comma-separated list of group names to be added to a username. It's important to remember that the -G always overrides the existing group names a user has.

Now, let's examine the permission string, which specifies what the file owner, group owner, or any other user is allowed to do or not, based on who he is:

```
[root@localhost ~]# ls -l
total 4
-rw-------. 1 0 root 1169 Jun 26 11:40 anaconda-ks.cfg
-rw-r--r--. 1 0 root    0 Jun 26 18:03 fileX_link
drwxr-xr-x. 2 0 root    6 Jun 26 18:30 folderABC
[root@localhost ~]#
```

-l outputs the file owner in the third column. Here, it is root, and for this file it is olip. In the fourth column, the ls -l outputs the group owner of the file. Also, here it is root and here it is olip. You already know that the first character in the ls -l output is the file type. Now, the nine bits afterward l and d define the file's permission string. The first three characters of the permission string define the permissions for the file owner. The second three bits of the permission string define the permissions for the group owner. The last three bits in the permission string define the permissions for all the other users. In this example, folderABC has the file owner olip, the group owner olip. Furthermore, the file owner olip has full permissions on the directory, the group owner olip has full permissions on the directory, and all the other users have read and execute permissions on this directory.

Perform the following steps:

1. First, let's create a directory. We'll put in some files to work with and then change to the directory:

```
-rw-r--r--. 1 peter root  83 Jun 27 06:00 file1
-rw-r--r--. 1 root  root 140 Jun 27 06:00 file2
-rw-r--r--. 1 paul  root  19 Jun 27 06:00 file3
-rw-r--r--. 1 root  root 140 Jun 27 06:01 file4
---x--x---. 1 root  root  23 Jun 27 06:01 file5
drwxr-xr-x. 2 root  root   6 Jun 27 01:18 folder*
drwxr-xr-x. 2 root  root   6 Jun 27 01:18 folderA
d---r-x---. 2 root  root  31 Jun 27 01:27 folderB
drwxr-xr-x. 2 root  root   6 Jun 27 01:18 folderC
[root@localhost test_files]# chown peter file1
[root@localhost test_files]# chown paul file2
[root@localhost test_files]# ls-l
-bash: ls-l: command not found
[root@localhost test_files]#  ls -l
total 20
-rw-r--r--. 1 peter root  83 Jun 27 06:00 file1
-rw-r--r--. 1 paul  root 140 Jun 27 06:00 file2
-rw-r--r--. 1 paul  root  19 Jun 27 06:00 file3
-rw-r--r--. 1 root  root 140 Jun 27 06:01 file4
---x--x---. 1 root  root  23 Jun 27 06:01 file5
drwxr-xr-x. 2 root  root   6 Jun 27 01:18 folder*
drwxr-xr-x. 2 root  root   6 Jun 27 01:18 folderA
d---r-x---. 2 root  root  31 Jun 27 01:27 folderB
drwxr-xr-x. 2 root  root   6 Jun 27 01:18 folderC
[root@localhost test_files]# _
[root@localhost ~]# mkdir test_files
mkdir: cannot create directory 'test_files': File exists
[root@localhost ~]# cd test_files
[root@localhost test_files]# touch file1
[root@localhost test_files]# touch file2
[root@localhost test_files]# echo 'my_secret_pa$$worD' > file3
[root@localhost test_files]# touch file4
[root@localhost test_files]# printf '#!/bin/bash\necho "EXEC"' > file5
[root@localhost test_files]# ls -l
total 20
-rw-r--r--. 1 peter root  83 Jun 27 06:00 file1
-rw-r--r--. 1 root  root 140 Jun 27 06:00 file2
-rw-r--r--. 1 paul  root  19 Jun 27 06:00 file3
-rw-r--r--. 1 root  root 140 Jun 27 06:01 file4
---x--x---. 1 root  root  23 Jun 27 06:01 file5
drwxr-xr-x. 2 root  root   6 Jun 27 01:18 folder*
drwxr-xr-x. 2 root  root   6 Jun 27 01:18 folderA
d---r-x---. 2 root  root  31 Jun 27 01:27 folderB
drwxr-xr-x. 2 root  root   6 Jun 27 01:18 folderC
[root@localhost test_files]# _
```

2. Now, let's create some files to play around.

3. Let's look at the file permissions of the files we have just created.

4. As you can see in the preceding screenshot, the root user has created all these files. Hence, the file ownership and the group ownership are both `root` for all the files.

5. Now, to change the file ownership and group ownership information you can use the `chown` or `chgrp` commands.

6. Instead of using the `chgrp` command, you can also use the `chown` command using a different notation.

7. For example, to change a file's group, you can modify both the file owner and group ownership.

8. Let's also create some subfolders as well for testing directory permissions.

9. Put some files into these folders as well.

10. Next, let us use some very dangerous `test` directories so that everyone is able to work with the files properly during our tests. This is not meant to be for production.

11. Next, create some common permissions for our files.

12. Create some unusual permissions, also create some permissions for directory tests.

13. Change some file ownership permissions on files and group ownership permissions on a directory.

Now, let's work with our new files and change permissions. Let's first review the output of the `ls -l` command:

```
[root@localhost test_files]# chown peter file1
[root@localhost test_files]# chown paul file3
[root@localhost test_files]# ls -l
total 16
-rw-r--r--. 1 peter root    0 Jun 27 01:31 file1
-rw-r--r--. 1 root  root  122 Jun 27 00:31 file2
-rw-r--r--. 1 paul  root   22 Jun 27 00:29 file3
-rw-r--r--. 1 root  root  119 Jun 27 01:09 file4
-r-xr-x---. 1 root  root    1 Jun 27 01:07 file5
drwxr-xr-x. 2 root  root    6 Jun 27 01:18 folderA
drwxr-xr-x. 2 root  root    6 Jun 27 01:18 folderA
d----wx---. 2 root  root   31 Jun 27 01:27 folderB
drwxr-xr-x. 2 root  root    6 Jun 27 01:18 folderC
[root@localhost test_files]#
```

File one is a file which has full read, write, and execute permissions for anyone. For example, any user known to the system can modify this file. The next file has the standard permission every file gets upon creation on a CentOS 7 machine. File owners have read and write access, whereas the group and all the other users only have read access. Let's find out what this means if different users want to modify the file:

```
[root@localhost test_files]# ls -l file2
-rw-r--r--. 1 paul root 224 Jun 27 06:06 file2
[root@localhost test_files]# echo "just bla" >> file2
[root@localhost test_files]# su paul -c "echo 'a new line from paul' >> file2"
[root@localhost test_files]# su paul -c "echo 'a new line from peter' >> file2"
[root@localhost test_files]# cat file2
justbla
 a new line from peter
 even another line from paul
 just bla
 a new line from peter
 even another line from paul
just bla
just bla
just bla
a new line from peter
a new line from peter
just bla
a new line from peter
just bla
a new line from paul
a new line from peter
[root@localhost test_files]# _
```

Here we can see some interesting things. The `root` user has read, write, and execute permissions to any file despite what has been set in the permission string for the `root` user. `Peter` is the file owner, so he can write to this file. `Paul` is neither the file owner nor the group owner, so he has no write permissions at all. The next file has a permission often used for confidential files such as password files. Often this is done for services running a filesystem user account to protect others from reading credentials:

```
[root@localhost test_files]# echo " just bla" >> file2
[root@localhost test_files]# su -c "echo ' a new line from peter' >> file2"
[root@localhost test_files]# su -c "echo ' even another line from paul' >> file2
"
[root@localhost test_files]# cat file2
justbla
 a new line from peter
 even another line from paul
 just bla
 a new line from peter
 even another line from paul
[root@localhost test_files]# ls -l file3
-rw-r--r--. 1 root root 22 Jun 27 00:29 file3
[root@localhost test_files]# cat file3
 my_secret_pa2474word
[root@localhost test_files]# ls -l file4
-rw-r--r--. 1 root root 14 Jun 27 00:30 file4
[root@localhost test_files]#
```

In this example, only the `root` user has the ability to read the file, nobody else. The next file
has a common permission set used if not only the file owner but also members of the group
that owns the file's owning group should have full control over the file. As you see, `Peter`
and `Paul` don't have access to write to this file because they are neither the file owner nor
the group owner. To change this, let us add `Peter` to the group that owns this file, and then
test again:

```
[root@localhost test_files]# ls -l file4
-rw-r--r--. 1 root root 77 Jun 27 01:06 file4
[root@localhost test_files]# su -c 'echo "i can edit this file" >> file4'
[root@localhost test_files]# su peter -c 'echo "i can edit this file" >> file4'
bash: file4: Permission denied
[root@localhost test_files]# su paul -c 'echo "i can edit this file" >> file4'
bash: file4: Permission denied
[root@localhost test_files]# su -c 'echo "i can edit this file" >> file4'
[root@localhost test_files]# cat file4
 olip project
i can edit this file
i can edit this file
i can edit this file
i can edit this file
i can edit this file
[root@localhost test_files]# ls -l file5
-rw-r--r--. 1 root root 1 Jun 27 01:07 file5
[root@localhost test_files]# # ./file5
[root@localhost test_files]# su peter -c './file5'
bash: ./file5: Permission denied
[root@localhost test_files]# su paul -c './file5'
bash: ./file5: Permission denied
[root@localhost test_files]#
```

Now, `file5` has some unusual permissions, which are valid. `file5` is a script file, which prints something out. As you can see, only the `root` user can execute the file. To let `Peter` execute the script, add one of the groups that is associated with it to the file. This still does not work because now `Peter` can execute this file, but cannot read it. To change this, add read permissions for the group ownership of the file as well. Now, `Peter` is finally able to run the script:

```
[root@localhost test_files]# su peter -c './file5'
bash: ./file5: Permission denied
[root@localhost test_files]# ls -l file5
-r-xr-x---. 1 root root 1 Jun 27 01:07 file5
[root@localhost test_files]# chmod 550 file5
[root@localhost test_files]# ls -l file5
-r-xr-x---. 1 root root 1 Jun 27 01:07 file5
[root@localhost test_files]# su -c './file5'
[root@localhost test_files]#
```

Finally, a common misconception is to delete a file you need to set the file's write permission flag correctly for the user, but this is not true, as we can see. Why can't `Peter` delete this file even though we've assigned full permissions to everyone here? This is because file deletion is completely dependent on the write permission of the directory the file you want to delete is in, and not on any file permission. The following screenshot is where the user `Peter` is denied permission to delete the file:

```
[root@localhost test_files]# cd
[root@localhost ~]# touch file-to-delete
[root@localhost ~]# rm -f file-to-delete
[root@localhost ~]# touch file-to-delete
[root@localhost ~]# chmod 777 file-to-delete
[root@localhost ~]# su peter -c 'rm -f file-to-delete'
rm: cannot remove 'file-to-delete': Permission denied
[root@localhost ~]#
```

Finally, let's discuss directory permissions. The following screenshot is an example:

```
[root@localhost ~]# cd test_files/
[root@localhost test_files]# ls -l -d folder*
drwxr-xr-x. 2 root root 6 Jun 27 01:18 folder*
drwxr-xr-x. 2 root root 6 Jun 27 01:18 folderA
drwxr-xr-x. 2 root root 6 Jun 27 01:18 folderB
drwxr-xr-x. 2 root root 6 Jun 27 01:18 folderC
[root@localhost test_files]# su paul -c 'ls folderA'
[root@localhost test_files]# su peter -c 'cd folderA'
[root@localhost test_files]# su peter -c 'ls folderA'
[root@localhost test_files]#
```

`folderA` has read permissions for the file owner, so he's the only one who is able to see what's in the folder but cannot change into the directory. `folderB` has only read permissions for the group owner, which means only members of the `projectAa` group can change into this directory, but `Peter` cannot do anything in this folder other than entering it using the `cd` command:

```
[root@localhost test_files]# id paul
uid=1002(paul) gid=1002(paul) groups=1002(paul)
[root@localhost test_files]# id peter
uid=1001(peter) gid=1001(peter) groups=1001(peter)
[root@localhost test_files]# su paul -c 'cd folderB'
[root@localhost test_files]# su peter -c 'cd folderB'
[root@localhost test_files]# su peter -c 'ls folderB'
[root@localhost test_files]# su peter -c 'touch folderB/file'
touch: cannot touch 'folderB/file': Permission denied
[root@localhost test_files]# _
```

In order to list files in this directory, let's order the read permissions to the group owner:

```
[root@localhost test_files]# chmod 050 folderB
[root@localhost test_files]# ls -ld folderB
d---r-x---. 2 root root 17 Jun 27 01:24 folderB
[root@localhost test_files]# su -c 'ls folderB'
file
[root@localhost test_files]# chmod 020 folderB
[root@localhost test_files]# ls -ld folderB
d----w----. 2 root root 17 Jun 27 01:24 folderB
[root@localhost test_files]# su peter -c 'touch folderB/my_file'
touch: cannot touch 'folderB/my_file': Permission denied
[root@localhost test_files]# chmod 030 folderB
[root@localhost test_files]# ls -ld folderB
d----wx---. 2 root root 17 Jun 27 01:24 folderB
[root@localhost test_files]# su -c 'touch folderB/my_file'
[root@localhost test_files]#
```

As we have learned before, we need to enable the `write` flag on a directory in order to create or delete new files in it. But why is this not working here? It's because we also need to enable execute permissions on a directory, which makes sense because in order to create or delete a file in the directory, we need to have access to this directory. What can we do if we want to change permissions on a lot of files, for example, a whole subdirectory tree? Using the `ls -1R` flag, we can list all the subdirectories and files included. Now, to change the permission string for all the files in a subdirectory, you can use the `chmod -R` flag:

```
ls -1Rchmod 775 -R ../test_files
```

As always, be careful with the recursive flag as you easily can change the file permissions for your whole filesystem to an unsecure permission irreversible.

Working with file permissions

In this section, we will learn about the concept of file access control in Linux. We will also learn and understand how to read file permissions. Finally, we will learn how to change file ownership as well as file permissions and show you practical file permission examples. If you print out the file's details using `ls -l`, you will see a list of different important file attributes we need to learn about so as to understand file permissions. A typical `ls -l` output looks like `-lrwxr-xr-x olip administrator my-awsome-file.txt`. Every file in the system is associated to exactly one username, which is also called the file owner.

Every file is also associated to exactly one group name, which is also called the group owner. The file ownership of a file can be changed by the root user only. The group ownership can also be changed by the file owner. When a user creates a new file or directory, the file's ownership will be set to the user's UID who created the file. We already know that a user can belong to multiple groups, but one needs to be set as the primary group. This is why every new user that is created has a group with the same name as the username. Now, every Linux user who wants to access a file can be categorized into one of these groups. The user is the file owner if the user ID matches the ID of the file owner whose file we want to access. The user is the group owner if one of the groups he is associated with matches the group owner of the file he wants to access. If the user is not the file or group owner he falls into the other users category. These three permission categories are also called permission groups. Finally, all these permission groups, the file owner, the group owner, and the others group, have exactly three permission types each, read, write, and execute. These permission types manage the actual action a user belonging to one of these groups can or cannot do with the file.

Now, since we are working with a lot of different information for every file, the user owner, the group owner, the permission categories, and the permission types, some Linux commands such as the `ls` command use a very compact form for viewing, which use 9-bits to fully map all permissions for all the permission groups. This 9-bit information is also called the permission string. If a permission is granted a read/write/execute or `rwx` flag is put at a fixed permission in the string. If a permission is revoked, a dash symbol can be found at a specific position in the string. From left to right in the permission string the first three bits are the read/write/execute permissions for the file owner. The next three bits are for the group owner, and the last three bits are for all the other users. The 9-bit permission string is a very dense notation to fit the screen and coming from a time when space and memory were expensive in computer hardware. Changes to permission types or 9-bit permission string can be set or removed by the root user only. Read, write, and execute permissions are defined differently on files and on directories.

Let's first discuss what read, write, and execute means in a file context. If the r, or read, flag is set on a file, the corresponding permission categories, file owner, group owner, or other user can open a file and read its content. The w, or write, flag is to modify or truncate an existing file, but it's a common misconception and important fact to know that the write flag does not allow for new file creation or deleting of existing files. This is not a property of a file, but rather of the parent directory, as we will soon see. The x, or execute flag allows files to be executed. This is important for running script files or commands on the command line.

In order to execute a file to run it as a script or command, the read flag needs to also be set because the shell needs to read the content of a file in order to execute its instructions. In a directory context, read, write, and execute permissions mean something completely different than working on files, which every Linux user must be aware of.

Let's first start with the x, or execute, permissions, as this is the most essential permission for folders. x, or execute, permissions in a directory context means something completely different than in the file context. If an execute flag is set on a folder, it means that the corresponding user group or other is allowed to enter that directory or path into a directory, for example, using the cd command. But the x flag is not only important for the cd command, it's also mandatory if you need to rename, delete, or create new files using the write flag. The execute flag has to be set as well here. It's also mandatory if you need to rename, delete, or create new files using the write flag. As a rule of thumb, if you need to set some standard permissions on the folder, never miss the execute permission for the permission group you want to work with or otherwise you will run into problems, as you always need to change into a directory if you want to perform some actions. r, or read, is the permission to read the content of a directory, for example, using the ls command.

The w, or write, flag creates new files or deletes existing files in a directory. As we've seen before, deleting or creating new files is not a property of a file permission, but always a property of the directory permission the files you want to create or delete are in, so the write flag has to be set if you want to be able to create or delete files in it. In order to use the write flag for creating, deleting, or removing files, we also need to set the execute flag for commands such as touch or rm, because they need access to a directory in order to perform the actions.

Now, each actual user who wants to perform an action, that is, read, write, or execute on a file or directory is now being checked by the operating system based on whether the attempt access is legal or not. This is a hierarchical process. The first check which is being done is whether the user ID of the user who wants to work on a file matches the file's user owner. If this is not the case, all the user's group IDs get checked if one matches the file's group ownership. If no user group matches at all, the other user is assumed and will be used. Now, every user in the system matches one of these three permission categories. If the right category has been found, the corresponding three permission types, read, write, and execute will be checked to see whether they are allowed or not and whether they match the user's attempt read, write, or execute action.

Changing values in the 9-bit permission string is best done using a shortcut method based on the octal numbering system counting. Note that there is also another notation available which uses short options such as −, +, r, w, and e, which we will not discuss in this section. You can look it up using man chmod. Using a number between 0 and 7, which are eight different states, and therefore can be called octal notation, we can define every possible combination of read, write, and execute for every permission category, user owner, group owner, or other users uniquely.

The following are the chmod octal notations:

- 0: Using 0, no read, write, or execute permissions are allowed
- 1: It means execute permission only
- 2: It means write permission only
- 4: It means read permission only
- 3: It means the combination of execute and write permissions
- 5: It means the combination of execute and read comments only
- 6: It means a combination of write permissions and read permissions only
- 7: It means full permission or read, write, and execute permissions

So we can easily express the permission types of all three permission categories using three numbers only. The first digit represents the read, write, and execute permissions for the file's user owner. The second digit represents all the file permissions for the group owner, and the third digit represents all the read, write, and execute permissions available for all the other users in the system. So for example, the octal permission 777 means read, write, and execute permissions for all the users available in a system. A permission of 775 means read, write, and execute permissions for the user owner of a file, read, write, and execute permissions for the group owner of a file, and read and execute permissions only for all the other users in the system. A permission of 660 means read and write permissions for the user owner of a file, read/write permissions for the group owner of a file, and no permissions at all for all the other users in the system, meaning that they cannot read, write, or execute this file.

Since we have created some new users, Peter and Paul and associated groups project_a and project_b in the previous section, let's now work and experiment with the actual file permissions:

1. As we are working on permissions on the time in this chapter first login as root user.

2. Now, let's first create a directory where we put in some files to work with:

   ```
   mkdir test_files
   ```

3. Then change to this directory:

   ```
   cd test_files
   ```

4. Now, let's create some files to play with:

   ```
   touch file1
   touch file2
   echo "my_secret_pa$$worD" > file3
   touch file4
   printf '#!/bin/bashnecho "EXEC"' > file5
   ```

5. Let's have a look at the file permissions using ls-l.

As we now know, every file has a file owner, which can be seen in the ls -l output in the third column. Every file also has a group owner in the fourth column. The first character in the ls -l output is the file type, followed by the 9-bit permission string.

First, let's learn how to change the file's user owner. You can use the chown command to change the user owner of a file. You can use the chgrp command to change a file's user group. Let's use ls -l again to see what has been changed:

```
[root@localhost test_files]# chown peter file1
[root@localhost test_files]# chown paul file3
[root@localhost test_files]# ls -l
total 20
-rw-r--r--. 1 peter root  83 Jun 27 06:00 file1
-rw-r--r--. 1 paul  root 276 Jun 27 06:06 file2
-rw-r--r--. 1 paul  root  19 Jun 27 06:00 file3
-rw-r--r--. 1 root  root 140 Jun 27 06:01 file4
---x--x---. 1 root  root  23 Jun 27 06:01 file5
drwxr-xr-x. 2 root  root   6 Jun 27 01:18 folderA
drwxr-xr-x. 2 root  root   6 Jun 27 01:18 folderA
d---r-x---. 2 root  root  31 Jun 27 01:27 folderB
drwxr-xr-x. 2 root  root   6 Jun 27 01:18 folderC
[root@localhost test_files]# _
```

As you see, file1 and file3 have changed the user owner, file4 has a new group owner. Instead of using the chgrp command, there is an alternate way to define group membership of a file, which system admins often use. It has the following notation:

```
chown [username]:[groupname] [file]
```

This uses a colon to specify the user owner or group owner of a file. For example, to change only the group owner of a file use:

```
chown :project_b file 4
```

Or to change both the username and group use:

```
chgrp project_a file 4
```

Let's also create some subfolders as well for testing directory permissions later. Put some files in our newly created subfolders as well. Next, let's use some very dangerous permissions for the test directory so that everyone is able to work with the files properly during our tests. This is not meant to be for production.

As we have learned before, we will use the chmod octal notation for changing the 9-bit permission string file permissions. Next, let's create some common permissions for our new test files. Also, for showing things, create some unusual permissions. Also, change the permissions of our test directories:

```
total 16
-rw-r--r--. 1 peter root    0 Jun 27 01:31 file1
-rw-r--r--. 1 root  root  122 Jun 27 00:31 file2
-rw-r--r--. 1 paul  root   22 Jun 27 00:29 file3
-rw-r--r--. 1 root  root  119 Jun 27 01:09 file4
-r-xr-x---. 1 root  root    1 Jun 27 01:07 file5
drwxr-xr-x. 2 root  root    6 Jun 27 01:18 folder*
drwxr-xr-x. 2 root  root    6 Jun 27 01:18 folderA
d----wx---. 2 root  root   31 Jun 27 01:27 folderB
drwxr-xr-x. 2 root  root    6 Jun 27 01:18 folderC
[root@localhost test_files]# ls -l file5
-r-xr-x---. 1 root root 1 Jun 27 01:07 file5
[root@localhost test_files]# chmod 110 file5
[root@localhost test_files]# ls -l
total 16
-rw-r--r--. 1 peter root    0 Jun 27 01:31 file1
-rw-r--r--. 1 root  root  122 Jun 27 00:31 file2
-rw-r--r--. 1 paul  root   22 Jun 27 00:29 file3
-rw-r--r--. 1 root  root  119 Jun 27 01:09 file4
---x--x---. 1 root  root    1 Jun 27 01:07 file5
drwxr-xr-x. 2 root  root    6 Jun 27 01:18 folder*
drwxr-xr-x. 2 root  root    6 Jun 27 01:18 folderA
d----wx---. 2 root  root   31 Jun 27 01:27 folderB
drwxr-xr-x. 2 root  root    6 Jun 27 01:18 folderC
[root@localhost test_files]#
```

Finally, in order to prepare our tests, we also need to change some user ownership permissions and group ownership permissions on some of the directories. Now, let's play around with our new files' and folders' permissions. file1 is a file, which has full read, write, and execute permissions for anyone. This is a very dangerous permission and is never recommended in any scenario because anyone can modify this file:

```
[root@localhost test_files]# ls -l file1
-rw-r--r--. 1 peter root 31 Jun 27 01:36 file1
[root@localhost test_files]# echo "just bla" >> file1
[root@localhost test_files]# su peter -c "echo 'a new line from peter' >> file1"
[root@localhost test_files]# su -c "echo 'a new line from paul' >> file1"
[root@localhost test_files]#
```

As you can see, peter and paul can modify this file and have full access on it. The next file1, file2, has a permission, has the standard permission every file gets upon creation. The file owner can read and write, the group and all the other users can only read and execute, but not modify.

Let's see what happens if various users try to write to this file:

```
[root@localhost test_files]# ls -l file2
-rw-r--r--. 1 root root 122 Jun 27 00:31 file2
[root@localhost test_files]# echo "just bla" >> file2
[root@localhost test_files]# su peter -c "echo 'a new line from peter' >> file2"
bash: file2: Permission denied
[root@localhost test_files]# su paul -c "echo 'a new line from peter' >> file2"
bash: file2: Permission denied
[root@localhost test_files]# _
```

As you can see, only the file owner can write to this file; all the other users have no write access. The next file has a permission often used for protecting confidential data, such as password files.

```
[root@localhost test_files]# ls -l file3
-rw-r--r--. 1 paul root 22 Jun 27 00:29 file3
[root@localhost test_files]# echo "i hacked your password" >> file3
[root@localhost test_files]# su peter -c "cat file3"
 my_secret_pa2474word
i hacked your password
[root@localhost test_files]# _
```

As you can see, only the file owner can read the file and no one else can perform any other action on the file. The file owner is paul. If you try to read this file using various usernames, you will learn two things. First, despite which permission has been set to a file the root user always has full access to the file. Second, other than the root user, who has full access to a file anyways, in this example only paul, who has read access, can read this file, and no one else.

The next file has the common permission set used. Not only the file owner, but also members of the file's only group, should have full control over the file:

```
[root@localhost test_files]# ls -l file4
-rw-r--r--. 1 root root 140 Jun 27 06:01 file4
[root@localhost test_files]# su -c 'echo "i can edit this file" >> file4'
[root@localhost test_files]# su paul -c 'echo "i can edit this file" >> file4'
bash: file4: Permission denied
[root@localhost test_files]# id peter
uid=1001(peter) gid=1001(peter) groups=1001(peter)
[root@localhost test_files]#
```

As you can see, both `olip` and `peter` have write access to the file, `paul` doesn't have access to that file. `olip` has write access to the file because he is the file owner. `peter` has access to the file because the group owner also has access to the file, and Peter is member of the `project_a` group and also of the file's group owner group.

Now, `file5` has some unusual permissions, which are valid. `file5` is a script file, which prints something out:

```
[root@localhost test_files]# ls -l file5
---x--x---. 1 root root 1 Jun 27 01:07 file5
[root@localhost test_files]# ./file5
[root@localhost test_files]# su olip -c './file5'
bash: ./file5: Permission denied
[root@localhost test_files]# su peter -c './file5'
bash: ./file5: Permission denied
[root@localhost test_files]# su paul -c './file5'
bash: ./file5: Permission denied
[root@localhost test_files]#
[root@localhost test_files]# ls -l file5
---x--x---. 1 root root 1 Jun 27 01:07 file5
[root@localhost test_files]# su peter -c './file5'
bash: ./file5: Permission denied
[root@localhost test_files]#
[root@localhost test_files]# ls -l file5
---x--x---. 1 root root 1 Jun 27 01:07 file5
[root@localhost test_files]# su\ -c './file5'
-bash: su -c: command not found
[root@localhost test_files]# su -c './file5'
[root@localhost test_files]#
```

As we can see, only the root user has permissions to execute this file. To execute a script, we will use the `./` notation, as we will see later in another section. In order to make `peter` available to execute a script, we can just add the `project_a` group to `file5` because we know that `peter` is a member of this group. But wait, why do we get a permission denied error when `peter` is a member of the `project_a` group and `project_a` has permission to execute the script? This is because in order for the shell to run a script, it also needs access to read the script file's content. So, let's change the file's permission to also include the read flag. Now, the user `peter` is able to execute the script. For the `root` user, you don't need to set the read permissions because the `root` user has all the permissions on every file regardless what is said in the permission string.

Finally, a common misconception is that in order to delete a file, you need to set the file's write permission flag correctly for the user who wants to delete the file, but this is not true:

```
[root@localhost test_files]# cd ~
[root@localhost ~]# ls -ld ~
dr-xr-x---. 3 root root 4096 Jun 27 01:16 /root
[root@localhost ~]# touch file-to-delete
[root@localhost ~]# ls -l file-to-delete
-rwxrwxrwx. 1 root root 0 Jun 27 02:09 file-to-delete
[root@localhost ~]# su peter -c ' rm file-to-delete'
rm: cannot remove 'file-to-delete': Permission denied
[root@localhost ~]#
```

If this would be true, why can't Peter delete this file as we assigned full permissions to everyone here? The reason for this is because file deletion is completely dependent on the write permissions of the directory the file you want to delete is in, and never ever on any file permissions at all. So, in this example, the file we want to delete is in the root directory, which has no write permissions for the user Peter at all. So Peter is not able to delete or create any file in the /root directory.

Finally, let's discuss directory permissions. Let's first review our test folder's directory permissions. In order to do so, let's change to the test folder's directory. Let's first test out permissions on folderA:

```
[root@localhost ~]# cd ~/test_files
[root@localhost test_files]# ls -ld folder*
drwxr-xr-x. 2 root root  6 Jun 27 01:18 folder*
drwxr-xr-x. 2 root root  6 Jun 27 01:18 folderA
d----wx---. 2 root root 31 Jun 27 01:27 folderB
drwxr-xr-x. 2 root root  6 Jun 27 01:18 folderC
[root@localhost test_files]# su olip -c 'ls folderA'
[root@localhost test_files]# su peter -c 'ls folderA'
[root@localhost test_files]# su paul -c 'ls folderA'
[root@localhost test_files]# su paul -c 'ls folderA'
[root@localhost test_files]#
[root@localhost test_files]#
```

As you see, folderA has read permissions for the file owner only, so Peter is the only one who is able to read all the files and subfolders in folderA; no one else can do this. You can also see because there is no execute flag set on a directory; nobody's able to change into this directory.

Now, let's have a look at the folderB:

```
[root@localhost test_files]# ls -ld folderB
d----wx---. 2 root root 31 Jun 27 01:27 folderB
[root@localhost test_files]# su olip -c 'cd folderB'
bash: line 0: cd: folderB: Permission denied
[root@localhost test_files]# su -c 'cd folderB'
[root@localhost test_files]# su paul -c 'cd folderB'
bash: line 0: cd: folderB: Permission denied
[root@localhost test_files]#
[root@localhost test_files]# chmod 050 folderB
[root@localhost test_files]# su peter -c 'ls folderB'
ls: cannot open directory folderB: Permission denied
[root@localhost test_files]# su -c 'ls folderB'
file  my_file
[root@localhost test_files]# ls -ld folderB
d---r-x---. 2 root root 31 Jun 27 01:27 folderB
[root@localhost test_files]# ls -ld folderC
drwxr-xr-x. 2 root root 6 Jun 27 01:18 folderC
[root@localhost test_files]#
```

As only execute permissions are set on the project_a folder, and only execute permissions are set for the group owner project_a group, only Peter who is part of the project_a group can cd into this directory, but you cannot list files. So, it's always a good idea to always combine the execute flag on a directory with the read flag. The same is true for folderC. First, let's try out if someone is able to write a file in this directory:

```
su peter -c 'touch folderC/a-new-file'
```

As you can see no one can. If you review folder permissions, this is because none of our users has ownership permissions on that file.

So, let's set user ownership to the user `olip`. Still no luck to create a new file in the `folderC` with the user `olip`. This is because in order to create a new file in a directory, not only the write permission has to be set on the directory, but also the execute permission. This is also true if you want to delete a file in a directory. Finally, how can we change file and folder permissions for a whole subdirectory tree recursively for all entries? In order to change all the files and folders included in `folderA` recursively with only one command, use the `chmod -R` flag, which stands for recursive, and changes all the files and folder entries in a directory given as an argument. You can also use the `-R` flag for the change owner command as well. As always, be very careful with the recursive flag as you might change files to a permission. When it comes to understanding permissions in Linux, there are three things you need to memorize. Each of these three concepts have to be used from left to right. First, every file has a set of permission states for the user owner, group owner, and all the other users, for short, `u`, `g`, and `o`. For each of these categories, there exists three possible permission states, read, write, and execute, or `r`, `w`, and `x`. Read, write, and execute can be represented by the octal numbers 4, 2, and 1, for `r`, `w`, and `x`, respectively. Every combination of read, write, and execute you want to allow can be represented by a sum of the read, write, and execute corresponding octal number values.

Working with text files

In this section, we will learn all the important tools to print out text file content on the command line. We'll also learn how to view text files using a text file viewer. In Linux, there exists two different basic file types, text files and binary files. Text files are configuration files, while binary files can be image files or compressed data files. The files' encoding defines whether a file should be treated as a text file or binary file. Text files normally use UTFR. On Linux, text files normally are encoded using UTF-8 or ASCII. You can use the `file` command to detect the file type, like:

```
file /etc/passwd
file ~file4.tar.gz
```

To print out a text file's content, you can use the `cat` command. `cat` stands for concatenate, that's also the reason where the command has its name from. So, let's concatenate some files and put the results in a new file by redirecting `stdout`:

```
cat /etc/passwd /etc/grp /etc/services > /tmp/concatenated-file
```

This line concatenates the three files `passwd`, `group`, and `services` to a new file called `concatenated-files` in the `/tmp` directory. Sometimes using `cat` to print out the whole file's content is pure overkill. If we are only interested in some lines at the beginning or end of the file, we can use the `head` or `tail` commands instead. The beginning of a file is also sometimes called the file header, while the end of a file is also called the file footer. To display the first 10 lines of our new concatenated file, use:

```
head /tmp/concatenated-file
```

Alternatively, if you are only interested in the last 10 lines of our new file, use instead:

```
tail /tmp/concatenated-file
```

To change `head` and `tail` default behavior of printing the first 10 lines use the `-n` option. Head and tail have other very useful options, use the manual pages to learn more. A more important and often used feature is to use the `tail follow` option. For example, using the `follow` option with the `root` account, the `-f` flag keeps the `tail` command open and tail will listen for new file content constantly and outputs it if new text is appended to the `var/log/messages` file. If you need a live view on a file which gets written to permanently and in real-time, this command needs to be memorized. To close the tail program, use *Ctrl + C*:

```
su root -c 'tail -f /var/log/messages'
```

Now, to read a file's content the `cat` command can be used for smaller files. For bigger files, it's better to use a real text viewer program such as `less`, which has some powerful features such as searching, scrolling, and displaying line numbers. It's also very useful to learn how to navigate text files using the less command, as a lot of Linux commands are using less, also called lesser navigation, to browse text content for the page or settings, as we will see later. To open a file using less, you can use less and then the filename as an argument. You can also directly use `stdout` unless using pipes, which is very useful so we can easily navigate and scroll bigger command output, which does not fit the screen. Navigating in less is pretty simple and should be memorized because you will use it a lot in your Linux career. There is a lot more to learn. Read the manual pages for the less command to view all the available options.

A lot of movement actions can be done in the following ways:

- To scroll down a line, you can either use the arrow key or the *J* key. Here, we will only show you one of these keyboard options per action.
- To quit out of the less command, use the *Q* key.
- The uppercase *G* scrolls to the end of the file, while small g scrolls to the beginning of the file.
- The *down arrow* key scrolls down line by line.
- The *up arrow key* scrolls up line by line.
- Press the *Page Down* key to scroll down a page and press the *Page Up* key to scroll up a page.
- Press the right arrow key to scroll to the right for longer lines; to scroll back to the left, use the left arrow key.
- Press *Ctrl + G* to display file information at the bottom of the page.
- Press the *Return* key to quit the file information field.
- Type the slash key followed by search term, for example, `HTTP`, and press the *Return* key for searching for a keyword `HTTP` in the file using a forward search.
- Pressing the *n* key will jump to the next search result. Pressing the capital *N* key will jump back to the last form of search result.
- Note that the search is case insensitive if the search pattern is all lowercase; otherwise, it's case sensitive. For example, if you search for the word `HTTP` all in capital letters, it will only find patterns, which exactly have the HTTP in case-sensitive form.
- Now, jump to the end of the file by pressing capital *G*.
- A normal search using the forward slash key searches the file for a keyword from top to bottom.
- If you want to search for a keyword the other way around, from bottom to top, you can use the question mark operator, the question mark key, and then the keyword.
- Press the *n* key to jump to the next higher search result in the file. Press capital *N* to jump to the last form of search result.

- Less -N starts less in line number mode, which means that every line is prefixed by the corresponding line number.
- To go to a specific line number, for example, line 100, type the line number followed by a g, or to go to line number 20, type 20g.
- To view text files without editing it, you can also use the VIM editor.
- To start VIM in read-only mode, type view space and then the file.
- We will proceed with VIM editor in the next section.

Working with VIM text editor

In this section, we will learn how to install the vi improved, for short VIM, text editor. We will also learn all the basics of using VIM. The most simple text editor one can imagine is, this creates a new file my-lorum-file with the content lorem ipsum dollar sit, or you can create a new text file with the cat command interactively as follows

```
Another Line
this is the third line
EOF
```

Use the string EOF uppercase to stop writing to that file. Now the echo and cat commands are very useful if you need to create text files with just a few words or lines of text. If you need to edit bigger text files or want to compose your own files, for example, read-me files for your projects, it's better to use a real text editor. One of the available text editors in Linux is VIM, or vi improved, which is a very powerful text editor available for every Linux distribution. It allows mouse-free text editing, and once you get good with VIM, you can really start typing or editing text files at the speed of thought. But mastering VIM can take months or even years to get really good, because VIM is a very complex editor with a lot of different shortcuts and features Therefore, we cannot show you everything in this section, but only the fundamentals to get you started quickly with VIM.

VIM is the improved version of, and fully compatible to, vi, the text editor for UNIX developed in the '70s. On a CentOS 7 Minimal installation, VIM is not installed by default. So, let's start by installing the VIM editor – `su root -c 'yum install vim -y'`. You can open VIM with the filename to open as an argument, or without, and save a filename later. The most fundamental concept of VIM is its modes. There are three different modes. An insert mode, a command or normal mode, and an ex mode. The following screenshot shows the different modes:

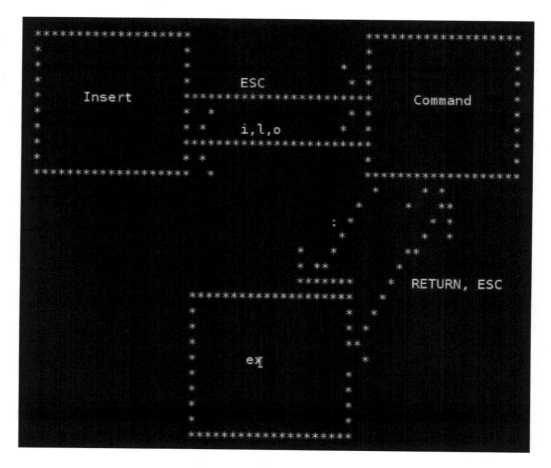

When you open VIM, you start in normal or command mode. From every mode, you can always go back to normal mode by pressing the *Esc* key. This is very useful if you don't know in which mode you are currently at. Just press the *Esc* key and you are always in normal mode. From there, you can either switch to insertion or ex mode. There are several keys available to start the insertion mode. Pressing the *i* or *o* key will bring you from command or normal mode into insertion mode, where you can start typing text. If you have finished typing text, or you want to execute another normal mode command or ex command, press the *Esc* key to go back to normal mode. From there, if you press the colon key, you go to ex mode. From there, pressing the *Return* or *Esc* key brings you back to normal mode. The insert mode is for typing or inserting text. In the insert mode, every keystroke will be printed on screen in the editor. If you want to navigate the cursor or do things such as copying and pasting, deleting of lines, text search, or undo, redo, and so on in the file, you need to change to the normal mode. In the normal mode, every keystroke is a command. Ex mode is for executing ex commands, for example, to jump to a certain line in the file, or make a substitution in the whole file, or to make a substitution of text in the whole file.

Now, we will start working with VIM practically. First things first, to exit the editor, press the following sequence in normal mode, press :q! and then press the *Return* key. If you are not in normal mode, for example, you are in insertion mode, then you first have to press the *Esc* key, then the :q!, and then press the *Return* key to exit VI. Now, let's open VIM again with the /etc/services file.

Let's first discuss basic cursor movement commands. Cursor movement commands can only be done in normal mode or command mode, which is the default mode when you start VIM. If you're in another mode, such as insertion mode, press the *Esc* key to enter the normal mode. Now, to move the cursor, you can use various keyboard shortcuts:

- To move the cursor to the right, use the *l* key
- To move the cursor to the left, use the *h* key
- To move the cursor down, use the *j* key
- To move the cursor up, use the *k* key
- You can also use the arrow keys to do exactly the preceding operations
- To move the cursor to the end of a line, press the *$* key
- To move the cursor to the beginning of a line, press the *0* key
- To move the cursor forward one word, use the *w* key

- To move the cursor backwards one word, use the *b* key
- To jump to the end of the document, use the capital *G* key, which is the same key in the less text file viewer for jumping to the end of the document as well
- To jump to the beginning of the document type gg
- This is also similar to the less command, where you used the small g once to jump to the beginning of the document
- To jump to a certain line number, type the line number; for example, line 100, followed by a capital *G*
- Searching for text patterns in the VI editor is basically the same as searching for text in the less text viewer
- Use /keyword followed by return to start a forward text search
- Press small *n* to jump to the next search result
- Press capital *N* to jump to the last former search result
- To start a backwards search, first go to the end of the document by pressing capital *G*, then use the familiar question mark keyword to search for and press the *Return* key to start a text search from bottom to top
- Press *n* to jump to the next higher search result and press *N* to jump to the next lower search result at the bottom of the text document
- Now, again jump to the beginning of the file

A very useful feature in the normal mode is to set marks at specific lines for referencing. For example, first go to the line domain. To set a marker to the specific line, type the character m followed by another character from a to z. For example, type ma. This creates a new mark referenced by the character a in the line, which starts with the domain. In the current line starting with domain, if we go to a different location in that file, for example, scrolling down pagewise and then if we now use the tick character followed by the character which represents our mark, for example 'a, we will jump back to the line where we set our reference mark a. As said before, you can set multiple marks from a to z, so let's add another mark. Just go to another line, for example, the saft line. Now, we will use b for our mark. Let's create a mark, type mb. Now if you go to a different location in the file, like in the fido line, just type 'b to scroll back to the saft line. Type 'a to go back to the domain line. Easy as that.

Now that we have learned all there is to know for basic movement commands in the normal or command mode, let's now switch over to learn some deletion commands in the normal mode. Pressing the *x* key will delete the character under the cursor, while staying in normal mode. Pressing the dd key twice deletes a line and puts the deleted text into the copy buffer. The d key can be combined with other keys too for efficient text deletion. Use dw to delete the current word under cursor. You can even combine the dw command with a number, for example to delete the next five words type 5dw. You already know that in order to jump to the end of the line, you use *$*, and to jump to the beginning of the line you use *0*. If you want to delete from the current cursor position to the end of the line use d$. On the other hand, if you want to delete from the current cursor position to the beginning of the line use d0.

Now, let's look at the undo and redo commands of the deleted text. The u key undoes the last change. For every undo step you perform, you can also perform a corresponding redo step using *Ctrl + R*. Now for copying and pasting commands, simply copy and paste the complete line type yyp. To copy multiple lines, first mark all the lines you want to copy. To do this, press *Shift + V* to start your mark, then press the down or up arrow key to select all the lines you want to copy. Now, press the *y* key to copy your text, and then press capital *P* to insert your copied text.

You can also cut text. In order to cut text lines, first mark your text using capital *V*. Now, instead of using the *y* key to yank or copy the text, press the capital *C* key to cut out the text. Note that cutting the text will put you into insertion mode. To paste the text, you need to go back to normal mode; so, press the *Esc* key now. To paste your text somewhere else, use the capital *P* key.

Now that we have discussed all the basic commands in normal or command mode, let's shift to the insert mode. There are several ways to go from normal mode to insertion mode. Normally, to enter insert mode, you can use small *i* and small *o* and capital *O* keys. Pressing small *o* inserts a new line while entering insert mode after the cursor. Pressing capital *O* inserts a new line while entering insert mode before the cursor. Pressing *i* takes you to the insert mode right after the cursor without inserting a new line.

Finally, let's discuss ex commands. Let's first make some changes to our file. Now, in order to execute ex commands, we first need to go to normal mode, pressing the *Esc* key from the insertion mode, and then pressing the colon key to start typing ex commands. For example, to write to a file, type the w. This will write and save your changes to the file. You can also use : to enter ex commands and then press wq to write and quit the VIM editor.

Now, let's open VIM again. To leave the editor, press :q and press the *Return* key. This will leave the editor if you have not made any changes. Now go back to the vi editor. Using the q ex command and pressing return will only work if you haven't made any changes to the file. Let's change the file. Now, if you want to leave the editor while you have made some changes to the file, using the ex command q will inform you that you are about to leave the editor without saving your changes. So if you want to quit the editor without saving changes, just type the :q!. Now, go back to the services file from the terminal. Another very useful ex command is to execute commands on the command line while staying in the vi editor. This can be done using the ex command exclamation mark and then the command you want to execute on the command line, for example, ls. This will switch over to the command line and present you with the result; then if you press the return key, you go back to the editor. Another very useful ex command is the sh command. Typing in sh as an ex command will switch to a command line while VI is still running in the background. Here, you can execute commands as you would normally on a command line. If you are done working on the command line, you can go back to the VIM editor by typing exit.

To search and replace a word, VIM offers us a set-like substitution mode:

1. If you want to substitute the word echo with the word hello world in the whole file, use the following command:

   `:%s/echo/HELLOWORLD/g`

2. To enable line number mode, type set number.
3. To go to a specific line, type the number line in ex mode.
4. To leave number mode, type set nonumber.
5. To open a different file in VIM, type e and then the filename.
6. To save a file under a different name, type w and then the different filename, for example my-test-file.

Summary

In this chapter, we have extensively covered the Linux filesystem, wherein we discussed file links, searching for files, file permissions, user and groups and the VIM text editor. We also looked into the functionalities of each concept.

In the next chapter, we'll cover how to work with the command line.

4
Working with the Command Line

In this chapter, we'll learn about more fundamental commands every Linux user should know, then we will learn how to install other important third-party Linux programs. We will also learn about processes and signals, introduce you to Bash shell scripting, and finally, show you how you can automate the execution of your Bash shell scripts.

We'll be covering the following topics:

- Essential Linux commands
- Additional programs
- Understanding processes
- Signals
- Working with Bash shell variables
- Bash shell scripting

Essential Linux commands

In this section, we will learn more essential Linux Bash commands that every Linux user should know. Use the `cat` command to quickly cut columns out of text files. This is like a light version of awk.

We'll be discussing the following commands:

- `cat`
- `sort`

- `awk`
- `tee`
- `tar`
- Other miscellaneous commands

First, let's create a smaller version of the `passwd` file to work with the `cat` command:

```
[root@localhost ~]# cat /tmp/passwd-truncated
root:x:0:0:root:/root:/bin/bash
bin:x:1:1:bin:/bin:/sbin/nologin
daemon:x:2:2:daemon:/sbin:/sbin/nologin
adm:x:3:4:adm:/var/adm:/sbin/nologin
lp:x:4:7:lp:/var/spool/lpd:/sbin/nologin
[root@localhost ~]# cut -d: -f1 /tmp/passwd-truncated
root
bin
daemon
adm
lp
[root@localhost ~]# cut -d: -f2,3 /tmp/passwd-truncated
x:0
x:1
x:2
x:3
x:4
[root@localhost ~]# cut -d: -f2,3 --output-delimiter " " /tmp/passwd-truncated
x 0
x 1
x 2
x 3
x 4
[root@localhost ~]# _
bin:x:1:1:bin:/bin:/sbin/nologin
daemon:x:2:2:daemon:/sbin:/sbin/nologin
adm:x:3:4:adm:/var/adm:/sbin/nologin
lp:x:4:7:lp:/var/spool/lpd:/sbin/nologin
[root@localhost ~]# cut -d: -f1 /tmp/passwd-truncated
root
bin
daemon
adm
lp
[root@localhost ~]# cut -d: -f2,3 /tmp/passwd-truncated
x:0
x:1
x:2
x:3
x:4
[root@localhost ~]# cut -d: -f2,3 --output-delimiter " " /tmp/passwd-truncated
x 0
x 1
x 2
x 3
x 4
[root@localhost ~]# egrep -v '#|^$' /etc/services | head -5 > /tmp/services-trun
cated
[root@localhost ~]#
```

−d sets the field delimiter; by default it's the tab character. −f uses a single field number or comma-separated list of field numbers that you want to extract. If using comma-separated lists also, the split input delimiter will be output, which can be changed using −− output-delimiter.

Next, let's create a smaller version of the services file without comments and empty lines. Using the cat command is very limited to the special use case that a file separator is a single character, such as a colon or the tab character. For splitting text files as multiple consecutive whitespace characters, which are often used in Linux config files, for example, in the /etc/services file, the cat command does not work. Also, when using the cat command, the field order must be fixed in every line or you will run into problems.

In the following screenshot, you can see that the services file contains no tab separator, but multiple whitespace characters marked with the star character:

```
[root@localhost ~]# egrep -v '#|^$' /etc/services | head -5 > /tmp/services-trun
cated
[root@localhost ~]# sed 's/ /*/g' /tmp/services-truncated
echo************7/tcp
echo************7/udp
discard**********9/tcp***********sink*null
discard**********9/udp***********sink*null
systat**********11/tcp**********users
[root@localhost ~]# cut -d " " -f2,3 /tmp/services-truncated


[root@localhost ~]# _
```

If you use cat on this file, it will produce nothing but garbage. To split files with multiple consecutive whitespaces, use awk instead. The tr command is like a lightweight version or subset of the set substitute mode. It translates a character set one into a character set two, reading from stdin and outputting to stdout. The syntax is self-explanatory. You can translate both single characters and ranges of characters. The character sets are similar to POSIX regular expression classes; read the manual to find out more.

Let's discuss the `sort` command. The `sort` command sorts the text file line by line. By default, it takes the whole line into account for sorting. The `-u` flag only prints out unique fields. If we take a file that has numbers instead of alphanumeric values, by default, `sort` expects alphanumeric values, so the sorting of numbers is wrong or unnatural. To fix this, use the `-n` option, which sorts using numbers. To sort values from bottom to top, use the `-r` flag. You can also influence the sort column if you need. `sort` always takes the whole line into account. To fix this, use the `-k 2.2` option to sort by the second column. There are many more sort options. Refer to the manual to find out more.

Now, in order to combine the power of `cat` or `awk`, `sort` and `unique`, let's use these tools together to print the 10 most recurring service names from the `/etc/services` file while ignoring comments and empty lines:

```
[root@localhost ~]# egrep -v "^#|^$" /etc/services | head -10
tcpmux          1/tcp                              # TCP port service multiplexer
tcpmux          1/udp                              # TCP port service multiplexer
rje             5/tcp                              # Remote Job Entry
rje             5/udp                              # Remote Job Entry
echo            7/tcp
echo            7/udp
discard         9/tcp              sink null
discard         9/udp              sink null
systat          11/tcp             users
systat          11/udp             users
[root@localhost ~]# awk -F ' ' '{print $1}' /etc/services | egrep -v '^#|^$' | s
ort | uniq -c | sort -n -k1,1 -r| head
      4 exp2
      4 exp1
      4 discard
      3 v5ua
      3 syslog-tls
      3 sua
      3 ssh
      3 nfsrdma
      3 nfs
      3 megaco-h248
[root@localhost ~]# 
```

The second command should now be pretty self-explanatory. As you can see, discard, exp1, and exp2 are the most recurring service names in the /etc/services file with four occurrences. To count all lines in the file, use the wc for the word count command. To extract the pure filename from a path, use the basename command, which is often used in scripts, as we will see later. If you know the extension of a file, you can also use the basename command to extract the filename from the extension. Similarly, to extract the path name, use the dirname command. To measure the time a command needs, execute the prefix of your command with the time command. To compare two files, use the diff command, which will print an empty output. If these files are identical, there will be no output. Otherwise, the changes between the files will be shown. The diff command can also be used for comparing two directories, file by file, using the recursive flag, which will go through all the files from A and compare them to the corresponding size files from B with the same name in folder B. The command that can be used to print out where a specific command is located in the filesystem is based on the /path variable, which we will see later.

tee is a useful command, which can be used to store an stdout command in a file, as well as print it on the command line. It is useful for keeping a record of an output while also seeing what's going on at the same time. Just give the tee command the filename you want to write to as an argument. To compress a single file, which means reduce the file size, use gzip. To uncompress, use the gunzip command.

To compress a complete subdirectory, recursively use the tar command. Note that the f option must be the last option followed by the archive name you want to create as the first argument and then the directory you want to archive and compress as the second argument. To extract an archive to any following directory, use the tar command with the following flag, -C is the output directory. hostname prints out the hostname; uptime prints out how long the server computer is powered on, and uname prints system information such as the kernel version.

In the /etc/redhat-release file, you will find the version of Red Hat Enterprise that this CentOS 7 is based on. In the /prog/meminfo file, you will find memory information, for example, how much RAM you have. In /proc/cpuinfo, you will find information about your CPUs and cores. free -m prints out useful memory information, for example, how much free RAM you've got. df prints out information about the available disk space. du -page prints out how much space the files in the current directory take. If you use it with the max-depth=1 option, you will also get a summary of the folder content. users print out all the users currently logged in to the system. The whoami command prints the name of the user who is currently using this Terminal.

Now, we'll see some very useful commands. To print the current date and time, use the date command. Use +%s to generate a unique timestamp. To print out a calendar, use the cal command. To pause, interrupt the shell execution using the sleep command. The dd program, or disk dump, is a very essential tool every Linux user needs to know. It is used to copy data from an input file or device to an output file or device. We have used dd before, in the first section, to override the filesystem's free space with zeros so we can shrink our VM images, but there are many more use cases for the dd command. dd basic syntax uses if for input file and of for output file as arguments. Also, two options are very important, the block size and the count.

You will see that the block size, which means the amount of data read at once, is 1 MB, and the count is the amount of repetitions of the block size, so that, in our example, 1 MB multiplied by 1,024 equals exactly 1 GB. dd also supports reading from stdin and writing to stdout so that the command we just used can be rewritten as dd if=/dev/zero of=/tmp/1gig_file.empty bs=1M count=1024. You can use dd not only with device files, but also to copy normal files. Also, you can use it for creating images of whole partitions, for example, for backups. To access partitions, the root account is needed.

Additional programs

In this section, we will show you some other very important Linux commands you don't want to miss. These programs are not included in the CentOS 7 minimal installation, so we first need to install it in order to install them. This section is about learning additional command-line programs. Additional because these tools are not included in the CentOS 7 minimal installation, so let's first install all of these programs using the CentOS 7 package manager, yum. In order to install new software, the root user is needed. So, first log in as root. Before we start, let's install the epel repository, which is an additional third-party repository for software that is not found in the official CentOS 7 sources, but is highly trustable and secure.

First, let's install some tools to make our user life easier. rsync is a file transfer program, pv is the pipe viewer; git is for version control; net-tools contains tools to display network information; bind-utils contain tools to query DNS information; telnet and nmap are for basic network troubleshooting; nc stands for netcat, wget is used to download files from the internet; and links is a command-line web browser.

Next, let's install some programs that give you a kind of life view on the system. This will install htop, iotop, and iftop. Finally, let's install some essential tools, which are screen, a calculator, bc, and lsof. First, let's introduce rsync. Every Linux user needs to know it as it's an awesome tool with many useful features. Basically, rsync is a file transfer program, but it does not simply copy files between a source and destination; instead, it synchronizes them, which means it only transfers a file if the source file is different from the destination qfile. This saves a lot of data overhead and time. I often use rsync with the -rav flags, which is the default to copy files verbosely and recursively with a common set of parameters.

cp copies the olip-home folder to a new location recursively. Now, if you change the source file and restart the copying process afterward, rsync first checks whether there are any differences in the source and destination files, and only transfers changes:

```
[root@localhost ~]# rsync -rav /home/olip/ /tmp/new-olip-home sending incrementa
l file list
sending incremental file list
rsync: link_stat "/tmp/new-olip-home" failed: No such file or directory (2)
rsync: link_stat "/root/sending" failed: No such file or directory (2)
rsync: link_stat "/root/incremental" failed: No such file or directory (2)
rsync: link_stat "/root/file" failed: No such file or directory (2)
created directory list
./
.bash_logout
.bash_profile
.bashrc
.mozilla/
.mozilla/extensions/
.mozilla/plugins/

sent 752 bytes  received 84 bytes  1672.00 bytes/sec
total size is 442  speedup is 0.53
rsync error: some files/attrs were not transferred (see previous errors) (code 2
3) at main.c(1052) [sender=3.0.9]
[root@localhost ~]# _
```

As shown in the preceding screenshot, we touch the `bashrc` file in the `olip-home` directory, which means update the file's timestamp, and afterward `rsync` checks and sees that the `bashrc` file has an updated timestamp, so the file gets transferred to the destination again because it's different. To copy files remotely to another server running the SSH service, and `rsync` is installed, use the following syntax: `rsync -rav`. As you can see, the colon at the end of the IP address starts the destination. Here, we will copy the `olip-home` directory to the `/tmp` directory and the other way around, to copy remote files to the local server, using `rsync .rav /home/olip/ /tmp/new-olip-home`. `rsync` has a lot of different features and is just awesome. You can refer to the manual to learn more about it. Another example of useful tools that I often use is the `-- progress` flag, which shows you the progress of the file transfer. `pv` is the pipe viewer, which is a very useful program to display traffic through `stdout`. For example, we can use it to display progress when piping big amounts of data streams, for example, using the `dd` command. `git` is a program for file version control, which can help you keep track of your file versions, as well as be used for installing programs from the Git repositories, such as the very popular GitHub service. For example, we can download the latest `pv` source code using the following command: `$ git clone https://github.com/icetee/pv.git`.

net-tools

`net-tools` is a collection of important tools for displaying network-related information, such as `netstat` to print network information, or the `route` command to view the IP routing table. The `bind-utils` we just installed contain programs to browse DNS information, for example, to see whether a certain port is open on a domain, such as port 80 on `https://www.google.com`; you will get some connection details. Type the *Esc* key to exit. `wget` is one of the most essential tools every system administrator needs to know. It can be used to download files from the internet. For example, to download a random programming command from HTTP to `stdout`, use the following command line: `wget -q0- http://whatthecommit.com/index.txt`, or type the following directly into a new file: `wget -0 /tmp/output.txt http://whatthecommit.com/index.txt`.

Nmap

Nmap is another very useful tool that can be used to troubleshoot or get information about your network. It scans the computer network and discovers and collects all kind of information about other hosts connected to it. Note that port scanning a network is a very controversial topic; since improperly using nmap can get you sued, fired, banned by your country, or even put in jail, we will only use it to retrieve very valuable information about our own private network here. For example, to scan the network for all available hosts and open ports, use the syntax: nmap network address.

You will see few IP addresses available that have various ports and services open. This can give you very important information about who is connected to your network and whether the services and computers are secure and not exposing unwanted details. nc or netcat is another very useful tool to help you debug and troubleshoot your server's network and firewall settings. For example, you can use it to see whether a certain port is open on a server. On the server, you want to verify the use, for example, the following command is used to open port 9999 and put a text file stream behind this port: nc -l -p 9999 < /etc/redhat-release. On any other server in this network, you could then try to access the server, for example, with the IP address 197, then with the IP address 192.168.1.1.200 on port 9999 and stream this file back, using the following nc command: nc 192.168.1.200 9999 > /tmp/redhat-release.

links

In this sub-section, we'll learn about links—the command-line web browser. To open the DuckDuckGo search website using the links program, use the following command line: links https://duckduckgo.com/. This will open the links web browser. Move the cursor up and down to reach the DuckDuckGo text search field. Now, you can type in your search term as you would on the normal DuckDuckGo website and then press *Enter* key to start your search. Again, use the up and down arrow keys to jump to the result of the search you want to browse to. Learning links navigation and shortcuts is outside of the scope of this book. Read the manual pages to find out more. Press the *q* key to exit links, and then confirm your choice by pressing the *Enter* key.

iotop

To get a live view of the input and output, or short I/O, bandwidth usage of your system, type iotop. iotop needs to be started with the root user. You can use iotop, for example, to learn how fast your hard disk can read and write, then press the *q* key to exit. Read the manual section on iotop to learn more about its shortcuts, for example, for sorting columns.

iftop

Let's learn about the iftop program, which gets a live view on network traffic and network bandwidth usage and monitor. Again, this tool needs to be started with the root user account. As you can see, network traffic can be displayed with this tool, press the *q* key to quit the program. Read the manual section on iftop to learn more about its shortcuts.

htop

Now, let's start htop, which is similar to the famous top program to view processes interactively. htop is the improved version of the normal top program, which adds new features such as scrolling vertically and horizontally so that you can see all the processes running on your system along with the full command lines. The htop program shows you a lot of different information about your system. Press the *q* key to quit the program. There are a lot of different shortcut options to learn; read the manual pages to learn more.

lsof

To print out a list of all open files, which means programs accessing files at the moment, use the `lsof` command. You'll get a long list; it's best to use it with `grep` to filter the content. To quickly do some math calculations on the command line, use the PC calculator. `screen` is a very useful command to detach from an SSH connection without actually disconnecting or exiting from it, which is very useful to pause your work and later go back to exactly the same point where you left, or to work from another computer. This can save a tremendous amount of time. First, in order to create a new detachable session, type `screen`. Now do your work, for example, type a text in VI. Now, imagine your day at work is over and you go home. Without the screen, you would now need to save your changes, close VI, and logout from the server. With a screen, just use the key combination *Ctrl + A + D* to detach from the current SSH session. If you have successfully detached from a session, a line will appear saying `detached from` and then the screen session ID. Now, in order to prove that we can reattach to this session, just log out from the server and then log back in to the server. Then, back on the server type screen -list to get a list of all the detached screens. To reattach to your screen, use the screen ID: `$ screen -r 23433.pts-1_localhost`. As you can see, we are exactly back where we left off. If you want to stop your screen session, type `exit`. Here, we showed you the most fundamental use cases for these programs.

Understanding processes

In this section, we will show you how processes work in Linux. Now, let's discuss everything about processes. Every program in a Linux system that is currently running is called a process. One single program can consist of multiple processes, and the process can start other processes. For example, as we already know, the Bash shell itself is a command, so, when started, it gets a process. Each command you start in this shell is a new process started by the shell process. So, for example, each time we execute the `la -al` command, the Bash shell process creates a new process in which the `ls -al` command is running. There are many, processes running all the time on every Linux system. If you have a multiprocessor CPU computer, some of those processes really are physically running in parallel all the time. Other processes, or if you have a single processor CPU, are running only semi-parallel, which means every process only runs for a few milliseconds on the CPU then pauses, which is also called being put to sleep, so the system can execute the next process for a small period of time. This system allows the execution of all processes seemingly in parallel, when in reality they are processed sequentially one after another.

All processes in a Linux system get created by another process so that every process has a parent process that created it. Only the first process does not have a parent, which in CentOS 7 is the `systemd` process. To get a list of all the running processes, run the `ps` command. Herem we use it with the `-ev` option and pipe its output into the `less` command as it does not fit the screen. You'll see that every process has a unique identifier, which is called the process identifier, or PID for short. The first process, the systemd process, has the PID of 1. The subsequent ones are in increasing order. Every process has a user ID associated to it, and also every process has a parent denoted by the parent process ID column. You'll notice that the first two processes in the list have a parent PID of 0, which means they don't have a parent.

To get a better understanding of the parent-child process relationship, you can use the `pstree` command, which we first need to install using the `psmisc` package. Afterward, just start the `pstree` command. With it you get a better understanding of which parent process created which child process, and how the relationship between the processes is. As said before, the systemd process is the first process in the system, which created all the other processes in the system. Every process also has a state; type `man ps` and go to the state section. The most important states are `running`. This means the process is currently running and will get executed by the CPU, or is in the run queue, which means it's just about to be started. You will see `sleeping` if the process execution is interrupted in favor of the next process in the waiting queue, or `stopped`, and even `defunct` or `zombie`, which means that the process terminated but the parent process does not know about it yet.

As we have learned in the previous section, you can also use the `top` or `htop` command to get a dynamic or real-time view on the processes in your system. The state column shows you the state of the process, where `r` stands for running, `s` for sleeping, and so on. If a new process gets created, the parent process will be cloned or copied exactly to the child process, so it has exactly the same data and environment as the parent process. Only the PID will be different, but the parent and child process are completely independent from each other.

Cloning

Cloning a process is also called **forking** in Linux. For example, if you execute a command, such as the `sleep` command in the shell, a new process gets created identical to the parent Bash shell process in which the `sleep` command gets executed. Normally, the parent process, in our example the Bash shell process, waits until the child process has been finished. That is why you don't get an interactive cursor as long as your subprocess is running. This is the normal behavior for every command you run in the shell. If your Bash command-line prompt is blocked, this is also called running a foreground job. To kill this foreground job, press *Ctrl + C*. You can also influence this foreground behavior by setting the ampersand symbol at the end of any command. So, let's rerun the last command with the ampersand sign. When using the ampersand sign at the end of the command, the parent process does not wait until the child process finishes, but both processes now run in parallel. This is also referred to as running a process in the background. You'll notice that running a process in the background returns the process ID of the child process, so we can reference it later. For example, for killing it, use `kill` command. In order to put the last background job into the foreground, again type `fg` and press the *Enter* key. Now, our `sleep` command is back in the foreground. To put it back into the background, press *Ctrl + Z*. This does not put our process running in the foreground directly into the background, but rather suspends the process. To put a suspended process into the background type `pg`, or in the foreground type `fg`. In order to kill any suspended or background job, you can use the `kill` command. Our processes running in the background are also called **jobs**. In order to list all the jobs you currently have in your Terminal, you can use the `jobs` command. If you have any running jobs in the background, the output will be shown from which you can reference it using the number in the brackets. In order to address such a job ID, you need to prefix it with a percentage sign. For example, to kill the job with the job ID number 1, type `kill %1`. Note that the `pg`, `fg`, and `kill` commands that we just used only work when you only have one single current background job in the Terminal. If you are working with multiple jobs in the current Terminal, you need to address them individually using the percentage sign.

Signals

Signals are used for communication between processes. If you start a new process, how can you communicate with it through your shell or any other program or process while it is running? Also, how does the parent process know when the child process is finishing? For example, how does your Bash know when the ls -al command is terminating? In Linux, this kind of notification and interprocess communication is done using signals. In Linux, if a process starts another process, the parent process is put to sleep until the child process command has finished, which will trigger a special signal and this will wake up the parent process. The parent process is put to sleep so that no active CPU time is needed for waiting. A popular signal is the seek or interrupt signal, which will be sent to the running process each time we press *Ctrl + C* in an active program. This will interrupt and stop the process immediately. Another signal we have already sent is the signal to trigger by pressing *Ctrl + Z* to suspend a process so that we can put it in the background. Instead of using key combinations to send a signal, you can also directly use the kill command to send various signals to a running process.

kill

To get a list of all the available signals which one can send to a process use kill -l. For example, the standard signal to send to a program to kill it is the SIGKILL signal, which has the signal ID 9. So, let's first create a new process and then kill it; as an example, start a new sleep process in the background. As you already have learned, putting a process into the background prints out the process ID. Most of the time, we use the kill command to kill system processes, which usually are not started by our user. So a standard way to retrieve is using the ps option, aux, and then filter by the name of the process you want to kill. Using ps with the option aux prints out the full command line, which often is helpful to differentiate the right process because often there are multiple processes with the same command name in this list. In our example, we only have one sleep process running and we can confirm the right process ID. Now, in order to kill this process, use kill -9 for sending the SIGKILL signal and then the process ID. Let's confirm this using the ps command again:

```
[root@localhost ~]# kill -l
 1) SIGHUP       2) SIGINT       3) SIGQUIT      4) SIGILL       5) SIGTRAP
 6) SIGABRT      7) SIGBUS       8) SIGFPE       9) SIGKILL     10) SIGUSR1
11) SIGSEGV     12) SIGUSR2     13) SIGPIPE     14) SIGALRM     15) SIGTERM
16) SIGSTKFLT   17) SIGCHLD     18) SIGCONT     19) SIGSTOP     20) SIGTSTP
21) SIGTTIN     22) SIGTTOU     23) SIGURG      24) SIGXCPU     25) SIGXFSZ
26) SIGVTALRM   27) SIGPROF     28) SIGWINCH    29) SIGIO       30) SIGPWR
31) SIGSYS      34) SIGRTMIN    35) SIGRTMIN+1  36) SIGRTMIN+2  37) SIGRTMIN+3
38) SIGRTMIN+4  39) SIGRTMIN+5  40) SIGRTMIN+6  41) SIGRTMIN+7  42) SIGRTMIN+8
43) SIGRTMIN+9  44) SIGRTMIN+10 45) SIGRTMIN+11 46) SIGRTMIN+12 47) SIGRTMIN+13
48) SIGRTMIN+14 49) SIGRTMIN+15 50) SIGRTMAX-14 51) SIGRTMAX-13 52) SIGRTMAX-12
53) SIGRTMAX-11 54) SIGRTMAX-10 55) SIGRTMAX-9  56) SIGRTMAX-8  57) SIGRTMAX-7
58) SIGRTMAX-6  59) SIGRTMAX-5  60) SIGRTMAX-4  61) SIGRTMAX-3  62) SIGRTMAX-2
63) SIGRTMAX-1  64) SIGRTMAX
[root@localhost ~]#
```

As you can see, the `sleep` command has been successfully killed. In the previous section, we use the `kill` command with the percentage job ID, but what is the difference in using the `kill` command with the PID instead of the job ID? Background and suspended processes are usually manipulated via the job number or job ID. This number is different from the process ID and is used because it is shorter. Killing processes using the PID is most often used to kill malfunctioning system processes using the root account. In addition, a job can consist of multiple processes running in a series or at the same time in parallel. Using the job ID is easier than tracking individual processes.

hang-up

Finally, let's discuss the `SIGUP` signal, or the hang-up signal. In CentOS 7, if you run a program in the background, like the `sleep` command, and log out of the system, then log in again, you'll see the command or process still running. So, in CentOS 7, we can easily run background processes and log out of the SSH session, which is useful to run programs that need to run all the time or to do some heavy calculations that take hours, days, or even months. In other Linux distributions, if you log out of the system, the kernel will send the hang-up signal, or in short `SIGUP`, to all running background processes and terminate them. In such systems, to disable the hang-up signal that is sent to your processes, use `nohup`; prefix your command with the `nohup` command, such as `nohup sleep 1000 &`. This way you can safely log out of the system and your job will not stop running. But, as mentioned before, on a CentOS 7 system, you don't have to do this.

Working with Bash shell variables

In this section, we will introduce you to Linux Bash shell variables. Bash shell variables are a great way to give symbolic names to any dynamic values, so we can reference values by a name. This helps to create very flexible and convenient systems where you often only have to change a single value, and all processes on your computer accessing this value can change their behavior automatically. Using shell variables provides a simple way to share configuration settings between multiple applications and processes in Linux, as we will see in the next section. To define a new environment variable, use the following syntax MY_VALUE=1, name of the variable equals, then the value. All Bash shell variables must not contain spaces or special characters, and, by convention, often shell variables are all uppercase. To access the stored value of the shell variable, which is nothing more than a shell expansion of the stored value, prefix the variable with the dollar sign. You can also look at shell variables as containers for dynamic values. You can also change the value of a shell variable anytime if you want. You can also copy a shell variable's content to another variable using the following syntax: MY_NEW_VALUE=$MY_VALUE. To unset a shell variable's content, use the unset command. For assigning shell variables, the same quoting and escaping rules apply as for any other Bash topics we have learned in the shell quoting and globbing sections in the previous chapters. For example, first assign the string b to the shell variable a. Now, for embedding spaces in the string, quotes must be used. Other shell expansions such as other shell variables can also be expanded in the assignment of a string. For embedding double quotes in a string, use single quotes to surround. There are a number of predefined and global shell environment variables to configure system-wide settings, such as home, path, shell, and so forth.

While there are no official standard for most environment variables in Linux, a lot of programs are using common variable names. For example, if you set a value for the PROXY environment variable, all programs and services that make use of this variable can now access this new centralized information without the need for you to tell each program or service individually that something has changed. Another very important system environment variable is the PATH variable. It is used by the Bash shell itself. It contains all the paths separated by a colon where the Bash shell tries to look up places for executable files, so you don't have to provide the full path for a command, which is included in this path. For example, if we create a new script file in a new local script folder called my-script.sh, we need to provide its full name location in order to execute it; there is no other way we can execute a script. But we cannot run it, for example, from the /tmp directory because Bash cannot find it in its path. Now, if we add the script's location to the path environment variable, we are able to run our script from everywhere without having to provide the full path, and even autocomplete is working. But what is the difference between a Bash shell variable and an environment variable?

Normal shell variables are not part of the so-called process environment or, in other words, they are not visible in any sub or child process. This is because when executing a process, only the environment gets cloned, and not the local shell variables. You can test this by creating the following shell variable using MYVAR=helloworld and then use it in the script that we will run as a subprocess:

```
[root@localhost ~]# MYVAR=helloworld
[root@localhost ~]# printf '#!/bin/bash\necho $MYVAR\n' > ~/scripts/local_var.sh
[root@localhost ~]# cat ~/scripts/local_var.sh
#!/bin/bash
echo $MYVAR
[root@localhost ~]# chmod +x ~/scripts/local_var.sh
[root@localhost ~]# ~/scripts/local_var.sh

[root@localhost ~]#
```

As you can see, we create a new shell variable called MYVAR, and then create a script that references or tries to access this environment variable. What happens now if we execute this script? As you can see, the child process, or subprocess, is not able to access the MYVAR Bash shell variable from the parent, but you can change this behavior by defining our MYVAR shell variable as an environment variable. Any child process gets a copy of the parent's environment during process creation, including all environment variables, but not the local shell variables. If you prefix the shell variable with the word export, the child process can access this environment variable because the environment is being copied from the parent process to the child process when a new process is created. But even environment variables like shell variables don't survive logging out of the system, which means that if you close your SSH session, all your defined variables are gone.

If you want to create a system-wide environment variable that is present for every user and survives logging out of the system, put your variable into the `/etc/environment` file using your root user account. You can also make a shell variable available for a child process using the following syntax by prefixing the shell variable name before running the command, such as `MYVAR=NEW_Helloworld ~/scripts/local_var.sh`. This way you don't have to define a shell variable as an environment variable. Another very important rule is that a child process will never be able to change the parent's environment variables, because the child and parent are independent of each other, and the child only has a local copy of the parent's environment. To test this out, try the following:

```
[root@localhost ~]# unset CHILDVAR
[root@localhost ~]# echo $CHILDVAR

[root@localhost ~]# printf '#!/bin/bash\nexport CHILDVAR=Hello_from_child\n' > ~/scripts/child.sh
[root@localhost ~]# cat ~/scripts/child.sh
#!/bin/bash
export CHILDVAR=Hello_from_child
[root@localhost ~]# chmod +x ~/scripts/child.sh
[root@localhost ~]# ~/scripts/child.sh
[root@localhost ~]# echo $CHILDVAR

[root@localhost ~]#
```

First, let's clear all the possible former values a local child Bash shell variable has. Next, create a script that creates a new environment variable called CHILDVAR with the value Hello_from_child. Now, what happens if we execute the script? If we execute the script, the CHILDVAR environment variable will be set in the child process, and this CHILDVAR environment variable is not visible for the parent process. In summary, any shell variable or environment variable that you define in a script can never be seen in the parent process. If you want to make shell variables available from a child process to a parent process, first you need to create a so-called source file in your child process where you define your environment variables in `vi ~/scripts/child.sh`.

Next, execute the script in your child process:

```
[root@localhost ~]# ~/scripts/child.sh
[root@localhost ~]# cat my-source-file.source
export CHILDVAR=Hello_from_child

[root@localhost ~]# echo $childvar

[root@localhost ~]# source my-source-file.source
[root@localhost ~]# echo $CHILDVAR
Hello_from_child
[root@localhost ~]#
```

This creates the source file for the parent process. Now, in the parent process, first we check whether the CHILDVAR environment variable is available. If it's not, let's source it using the source command. Finally, let's recheck whether the CHILDVAR environment variable is now accessible. If it is, then this is a valid way to create environment variables in a child process and make them available.

Introduction to Bash shell scripting

In this section, we will introduce you to the core concept of Bash shell scripting. Another very important feature of Bash shell scripts are functions. We use functions excessively in Bash shell scripts to make reoccurring tasks or commands reusable. Functions encapsulate a task to make it more modular. Functions usually take in data, process it, and return a result. Once a function is written, it can be used over and over again, but we can also work with functions on the command line.

Let's discuss the general syntax of a function by creating one:

```
$ say_hello90 {
>echo "My name is $1";
>}
```

The first word is the function name followed by opening and closing brackets, which are used to define a function, followed by a curly opening bracket; all the commands belonging to a function are defined within the open and closing brackets, which is also called the function body. Functions can have arguments as normal commands, which will be accessible to the function body from outside. To access a certain argument in the function, use the dollar number notation. So $1 is the first argument, $2 would be the second, and so on. Let's take a look at our say_hello function. If we call this function with one argument, the function will be executed with one argument, and this argument will be taken in the function body, where we can access the first argument with the $1 variable, which is nothing more than a normal shell expansion.

Functions can also call other functions in their body. Now, let's learn to put your shell commands in a shell script file. Script files are just plain text files which contain different Linux commands, control structures, loops, and so on. Usually, they are written to solve everyday computer problems and fit your own individual needs instead of having to execute single commands one by one manually. There are two ways to execute a text file as a shell script. The first way is to use it as an argument for the Bash command. Another way to execute it without using it as an argument for the Bash command is to first make the script executable and then put the so-called shebang line at the first line, which tells the command line that this file is a Bash script and should be started with the Bash interpreter. In our example, #!/bin/bash is the shebang line and tells Bash that this is a Bash shell script. Now, to start it with the shebang approach, make it executable and then you can just run it on the command line, as following:

```
$ vi /tmp/new-script.sh
$ chmod +x /tmp/new-script.sh
/tmp/new-script.sh
```

Similar to using functions, we can also access command-line arguments in shell scripts, such as $ vi /tmp/new-script.sh. The first argument can be accessed using $1, the second argument $2, and so on. In shell scripts, you can also access the name of the shell script using the $0. The total number of arguments can be accessed using the $#. So, for example, to write a check that your script needs at least two arguments do the following:

```
#!/bin/bash
echo "Hello World"
echo "..........."
if [[ $# -lt 2 ]]
then
echo "Usage $0 param1 param2"
echo $1
echo $2
echo $0
```

```
echo $#
```

So, what this script does is check whether the number of command-line arguments are at least two and, if this is not the case, then a usage format will be printed out stating that you need two parameters, press *Enter*, and then an exit value of 1 will be returned, which means that this script has thrown an error, because, as we already know, a script will return 0 on successful execution. Let's test this script out:

```
[olip@localhost ~]$ vi /tmp/new-script.sh
[olip@localhost ~]$ /tmp/new-script.sh  argument1
Hello World
- - - - - - - - - -
Usage /tmp/new-script.sh param1 param2
[olip@localhost ~]$ /tmp/new-script.sh  argument1 argument2
Hello World
- - - - - - - - - -
argument1
argument2
/tmp/new-script.sh
2
```

If we start the script with only one argument, it will print out the usage format. However, if we start it with two arguments, it will correctly work. When it comes to shell scripting, there is much more to learn and we could only show you the very basics to get you started. You can refer to the Bash manual or just start reading the various shell scripts that are shipped with your CentOS 7 OS for free. Type the following command to get a list of all the .sh files: su -c 'find / -name "*.sh"', which is the default extension for shell script files in your system. Just start by opening one of the available shell script files in your system and try to understand it, for example, /usr/libexec/grepconf.sh.

Implementing Bash shell scripting

Besides the logical and and or expressions that we used in the previous section, if we need to make a decision based on a command's exit status, variable value, command output, and so on, we need to understand the if statement or conditional branch. In plain words, the if statement means that, based on some condition, our script or command line should perform one action, otherwise it should perform something else.

Let's work with the exit code from the previous section again to demonstrate:

```
[root@localhost ~]# ls /home/olip
my-source-file-source  nohup.out  pv  stuff  stuff2
[root@localhost ~]# EXIT=$?
[root@localhost ~]# if [[ $EXIT -eq 0 ]]
> then
> echo "running ls command was successful"
> echo "Yippie"
> fi
running ls command was successful
Yippie
[root@localhost ~]# EXIT=1
[root@localhost ~]# if ! [[ $EXIT -eq 0 ]]
> then
> echo "EXIT value is not zero"
> fi
EXIT value is not zero
[root@localhost ~]# NUMBER=5
[root@localhost ~]# if [[ $NUMBER -eq 5 ]]
> then
> echo "Number is true"
> fi
Number is true
[root@localhost ~]# PASSWORD="my_secret_pass"
[root@localhost ~]# if[[ $PASSWORD -eq "Hello_my_world_555" || $PASSWORD -eq "my
```

In this example, we issued the `ls` command to see the content of the `oiip` home directory. We stored the exit status of the `ls` command in the `EXIT` Bash variable. In the next line, we now state the if condition. This can be read as: `if` the Bash variable `EXIT` equals 0, then print out two lines of text, and this `if` condition with the reverse if word, fi. As you see, the two lines have been printed out, which means the if condition was true, so the exit value was 0. It's important to note that you have to be very careful that you set the spaces and new lines exactly as I did in the preceding example, but you can also put the complete if statement in one line, which you can see if you press the up arrow key to show the last command in the history. As you can see, the shell internally uses a semicolon space instead of new lines to separate most of the expressions, which is a bit hard to read, especially if you're writing more complex Bash shell script one-liners. To negate any if expression which means that the `if` statement evaluates to true if the condition is not met, use the following:

```
$ EXIT=1
$ if ! [[ $EXIT -eq 0 ]]
>then
>echo "EXIT value is not zero"
>fi
EXIT value is not zero
```

In this example, the if condition can be read as: if the exit value equals not 0, then print out the text. In our example, this is true because the exit value is 1. If conditions can include a lot of different tests, which are too much to demonstrate here. Here, follow the most important ones. To test for equality, use the −eq test as we have just seen. You can use it for numbers. For string comparisons, use the == operator instead. You can also use the logical and and or expressions as introduced in the last section, for example, to also test for alternatives. This example can be read as: if the password equals to Hello_my_world_555 or if the password equals to my_secret_pass. In this example, the password is correct. You can also use regular expressions using the equals tilde operator. This statement can be read as: the if condition is true if the string matches at the beginning of the line, where the first two characters are variables, but then there must be an rem, which is true. For numeric values, you can also test for less than or greater than numbers using −lt and −gt instead of −eq, for example, to test for less than or to test for greater than.

Another group of very important if conditions are file tests. There exist vast number of very powerful file tests to see if a file or directory meets a special property. There are a vast number of very powerful file tests to see whether a file or directory, for example to test whether the file exists, use the −a file test, or to check whether a directory exists use the −d file test. This is shown in the following screenshot:

```
[root@localhost ~]# FILE=/etc/environment
[root@localhost ~]# if [[ -a $FILE ]]
> then
> echo "the tested file does exists"
> fi
the tested file does exists
[root@localhost ~]# DIR=/home/olip
[root@localhost ~]# if [[ -d $DIR ]]
> then
> echo "the tested dir does exists"
> echo "this is really awesome so i also print out its content"
> ls $DIR
> fi
the tested dir does exists
this is really awesome so i also print out its content
my-source-file-source   nohup.out   pv  stuff  stuff2
[root@localhost ~]#
```

To learn more about all the existing file tests, as well as all available comparison operators, open the Bash manual and search for conditional expressions. The general syntax for the most simple if statements we have just learned is that, if the condition is true, all the commands between the beginning if and the ending `fi` are executed. Now, you can also incorporate an `else` branch, which will be executed if the condition is not true. The following screenshot shows the execution:

```
[root@localhost ~]# ls /var/log/audit
audit.log
[root@localhost ~]# EXIT=$?
[root@localhost ~]# if [[ $EXIT -eq 0 ]]
> then
> echo "running ls command was successful"
> echo "Yippie"
> else
> echo "cannot access the files in /var/log/audit"
> echo "I am very sorry for that :("
> fi
running ls command was successful
Yippie
[root@localhost ~]#
```

The else branch is introduced by the `else` keyword. In our example, the if condition is not true, so the else branch will be executed. If you have several independent conditions to check, you can also use the `elif` statement, which is better than writing multiple `if` statements one after another. So, instead of writing three single `if` statements to check for conditions equal to, less than, and greater than, you can use the more compact `elif` notations instead:

```
[root@localhost ~]# if [[ $VALUE -lt 5 ]]
> then
> echo "value is less than 5"
> elif [[ $VALUE -eq 5 ]]
> then
> echo "value is equal to 5"
> elif [[ $VALUE -gt 5 ]]
> then
> echo "value is bigger than 5"
> fi
value is less than 5
[root@localhost ~]#
```

Next, we'll discuss loops. One of the most important loops in the Bash shell is the `for in` loop. It can be used to iterate over a series of words. The word delimiter can be a space or a new line. Now, if we use such a list of space or new line separated words with the `for` loop, it will iterate over every item in that list and we can use the current value in the body of the for loop, where we can also execute commands. This block will then be repeated as often as we have elements in this list. The name of the loop variable in our example, we have called it `count`, is free to choose:

```
[root@localhost ~]# for count in 1 2 3 4
> do
> echo $count
> done
1
2
3
4
[root@localhost ~]#
```

This example can be read as: for, go through the list of 1, 2, 3 and 4, and in each iteration of it, save the current value in the count variable and then, in the body of the loop, print out its content. But what can we do with the `for in` loop? For example, the following Bash built-in expands to a list of consecutive numbers: `$ echo {1..20}`. You can also do the same with the `seq` command, but this produces a new line-separated list instead. So, if we need to run a loop, we can just do the following. New line-separated lists do all the work, but don't forget to put the command in dollar bracket notation. As we already know, the shell globbing character outputs a list of all the files separated by a space, so we can also do so. An important use case for using files in the for in loop is to rename multiple files, for example, in a directory with a different filename extension. Note that, in this example, we use the `basename` command and surround it with the dollar bracket notation to return the pure filename:

```
[root@localhost ~]# mkdir ~/stuff
[root@localhost ~]# touch ~/stuff/1.txt ~/stuff/2.txt ~/stuff/3.txt ~/stuff/4.tx
t ~/stuff/*.txt
[root@localhost ~]# ls ~/stuff
1.txt  2.txt  3.txt  4.txt  *.txt
[root@localhost ~]# for file in ~/stuff/*.txt
> do
> mv $file ~/stuff/$(basename $file .txt).doc
> done
[root@localhost ~]# ls ~/stuff
1.doc  2.doc  3.doc  4.doc  *.txt
[root@localhost ~]#
```

As you can see, we created a new directory with five files having the extension .txt. Then, we loop over our five files using a for each loop, and, for every file, we move the file to a doc extension. There are other very important loops as well as the while loop. You can refer to the Bash manual and search for while.

Automating script execution

In this section, we will show you how to automate Bash shell script execution. The cron system, which is available on every Linux system, allows for the automation of commands or scripts by enabling the administrator to determine a predefined schedule based on any hour, day, or even month. It is a standard component of the CentOS 7 operating system, and in this section we will introduce you to the concept of managing recurring tasks in order to take advantage of this invaluable tool.

First, let's create a new script, which will download an elegant and useful Linux command-line example from the incredible **Commandlinefu** web page and put it in the motd, or message of the day, file in the Linux system so that it is visible whenever a user logs into the system. The motd file is a simple text file from which the content will be displayed on successful login. We then run the script as a cron job so that the message of the day will be updated every day, which is very useful to learn a new and elegant command-line solution each day.

In order to do that, first log in as root, as the cron system is located in the system directories. Next, make a copy of the original motd file. Afterward, let's create our script file to update the motd file in the system:

```
[root@localhost ~]# su -
Last login: Wed Jun 27 05:27:55 EDT 2018 on tty1
[root@localhost ~]# cp /etc/motd /etc/motd.BAK
cp: overwrite '/etc/motd.BAK'? y
[root@localhost ~]# mkdir scripts
mkdir: cannot create directory 'scripts': File exists
[root@localhost ~]# vi ~/scripts/motd-commandlinefu-update.sh_
```

```
#!/bin/bash
Wget -O /etc/motd http://www.commandlinefu.com/commands/random/plaintext
```

This script is normal batch script and downloads a random Commandlinefu example from the web page, `http://www.commandlinefu.com/commands/random/plaintext`, using the `wget` program and saves the downloaded file as `/etc/motd`. So, we can directly see the content when we log in to the system. Now, let's test drive our new script:

```
[root@localhost ~]# chmod +x ~/scripts/motd-commandlinefu-update.sh
[root@localhost ~]# ~/scripts/motd-commandlinefu-update.sh
--2017-05-26 02:23:00--  http://www.commandlinefu.com/commands/random/plaintext
Resolving www.commandlinefu.com (www.commandlinefu.com)... 104.27.175.104, 104.27.174.104, 2400:cb00:2048:1::681b:ae68, ...
Connecting to www.commandlinefu.com (www.commandlinefu.com)|104.27.175.104|:80... connected.
HTTP request sent, awaiting response... 302 Found
Location: http://www.commandlinefu.com/commands/collection/3640/plaintext [following]
--2017-05-26 02:23:00--  http://www.commandlinefu.com/commands/collection/3640/plaintext
Reusing existing connection to www.commandlinefu.com:80.
HTTP request sent, awaiting response... 200 OK
Length: unspecified [text/plain]
Saving to: '/etc/motd'

    [ <=>                                                                    ] 238

2017-05-26 02:23:00 (11.6 MB/s) - '/etc/motd' saved [238]

[root@localhost ~]# cat /etc/motd
# commandlinefu.com - questions/comments: tech@commandlinefu.com

# Display summary of git commit ids and messages for a given branch
git log --pretty='format:%Cgreen%H %Cred%ai %Creset- %s'

# AD: Diff 2 entire servers at ScriptRock.com
[root@localhost ~]# ~/scripts/motd-commandlinefu-update.sh
--2017-05-26 02:35:45--  http://www.commandlinefu.com/commands/random/plaintext
Resolving www.commandlinefu.com (www.commandlinefu.com)... 104.27.175.104, 104.27.174.104, 2400:cb00:2048:1::681b:af68, ...
Connecting to www.commandlinefu.com (www.commandlinefu.com)|104.27.175.104|:80... connected.
HTTP request sent, awaiting response... 302 Found
Location: http://www.commandlinefu.com/commands/collection/13032/plaintext [following]
--2017-05-26 02:35:47--  http://www.commandlinefu.com/commands/collection/13032/plaintext
Reusing existing connection to www.commandlinefu.com:80.
HTTP request sent, awaiting response... 200 OK
Length: unspecified [text/plain]
Saving to: '/etc/motd'
```

As you can see, the script has been successfully downloading a Commandlinefu from the `http://www.commandlinefu.com/` web page. To test whether the Commandlinefu web page URL we use truly returns a random command-line example, let's restart our script:

```
[root@localhost ~]# cat /etc/motd
# commandlinefu.com - questions/comments: tech@commandlinefu.com

# Display summary of git commit ids and messages for a given branch
git log --pretty='format:%Cgreen%H %Cred%ai %Creset- %s'

# AD: Diff 2 entire servers at ScriptRock.com
[root@localhost ~]# ~/scripts/motd-commandlinefu-update.sh
--2017-05-26 02:35:45--  http://www.commandlinefu.com/commands/random/plaintext
Resolving www.commandlinefu.com (www.commandlinefu.com)... 104.27.175.104, 104.27.174.104, 2400:cb00:2048:1::681b:af68, ...
Connecting to www.commandlinefu.com (www.commandlinefu.com)|104.27.175.104|:80... connected.
HTTP request sent, awaiting response... 302 Found
Location: http://www.commandlinefu.com/commands/collection/13032/plaintext [following]
--2017-05-26 02:35:47--  http://www.commandlinefu.com/commands/collection/13032/plaintext
Reusing existing connection to www.commandlinefu.com:80.
HTTP request sent, awaiting response... 200 OK
Length: unspecified [text/plain]
Saving to: '/etc/motd'

    [ <=>                                                                      ] 289

2017-05-26 02:35:47 (7.70 MB/s) - '/etc/motd' saved [289]

[root@localhost ~]# cat /etc/motd
# commandlinefu.com - questions/comments: tech@commandlinefu.com
```

As you can see, the command-line example is different this time. Now, based on your own preferred schedule of script execution, you need to decide how often you want to execute the script. There are some special cron directories in the filesystem for execution of system-wide cron jobs, and you can access them using `# ls /etc/cron* -d`. The folders are called `cron.daily`, `cron.hourly`, `cron.weekly`, and `cron.monthly` and are in the `/etc` directory, and their names refer to the time point that they are run. So, if we want our new Commandlinefu script to be started on a daily basis, just drop the script file into the `cron.daily` directory or create a symbolic link to it using `cd /etc/cron* -d`. If you want to run it using a different schedule, just drop it into the `cron.hourly`, `cron.monthly`, or `cron.weekly` directories. Just remove the script or the symbolic link from the folder if you don't want to execute it anymore. If you don't want to run system-wide cron jobs, you can also use the `crontab` command as a normal user. You can read the `crontab` manual to learn more about this command. Finally, let's test whether the `motd` file is working. Exit out of the SSH session and then log in again:

```
        crontab - maintains crontab files for individual users

SYNOPSIS
        crontab [-u user] file
        crontab [-u user] [-l | -r | -e] [-i] [-s]
        crontab -n [ hostname ]
        crontab -c

DESCRIPTION
        Crontab  is the program used to install, remove or list the tables used
        to serve the cron(8) daemon.  Each user can have their own crontab, and
        though these  are  files  in  /var/spool/, they are not intended to be
        edited directly.  For SELinux in MLS mode, you can define more crontabs
        for each range.  For more information, see selinux(8).

        In  this version of Cron it is possible to use a network-mounted shared
        /var/spool/cron across a cluster of hosts and specify that only one  of
        the  hosts  should  run the crontab jobs in the particular directory at
        any one time.  You may also use crontab(1) from any of these  hosts  to
        edit  the  same shared set of crontab files, and to set and query which
        host should run the crontab jobs.

[root@localhost scripts]# exit
logout
[root@localhost ~]# __
```

As you can see, it's working beautifully. Based on the cron job we created, tomorrow there should be a different command-line example presented here.

In this chapter, we have introduced you to the Linux cron system for script automation.

Summary

In this chapter, we've discussed topics ranging from essential Linux commands, signals, processes and Bash shell scripting.

In the next chapter, we'll cover advanced command-line concepts.

5
More Advanced Command Lines and Concepts

In this chapter, we are going to take a look at the following:

- Basic networking concepts
- Installing new software and updating the system
- Introduction to services
- Basic system troubleshooting and firewalling
- Introduction to ACL
- `setuid`, `setgid`, **and** `sticky bit`

Basic networking concepts

In this section, you will learn the foundations of networking in Linux. Everything about networking is within the classic domain of Unix and Linux, and, in fact, the old Unix folks do say that Unix has been created for network communication. Linux is considered one of the best systems to use, learn, test, play, diagnose, and troubleshoot computer networks because a lot of great tools are available in Linux for free and come right out of the box, or just need a single command to install. There's a lot to learn about the subject of computer networks, and here we can only teach you the fundamentals of it using the CentOS 7 Linux operating system.

Now, let's learn about computer networks from 10,000 up. The two most fundamental concepts in networking are the network, or subnetwork, and the IP address. The three most important facts every Linux user needs to know are the network, or sometimes called the subnetwork, the IP address, and the rules of the network:

- Rule 1: The network

  Every network, or sometimes called subnetwork, has a so-called network address consisting of only numbers, which looks like this:

- Rule 2: The IP address

  Every computer needs an IP address for communication, which is part of a subnetwork's address. In our example, the first three numbers divided by dots are the same between the IP addresses and the network address:

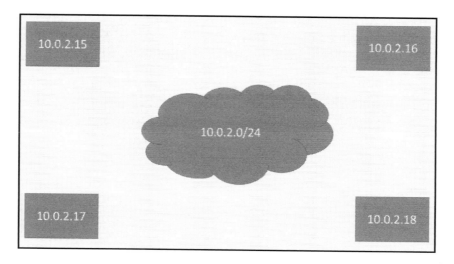

- Rule 3: The same network

The easiest way for network communication between two or multiple computers is to connect them physically (for example, by using network cables and a single switch), and then put them in the same network, which means choosing all of the computers' IP addresses from the same range as our subnetwork's network address. In our example, choose 10.0.2 as the first three digits for all our IP addresses. As you can see, only the last digit is variable. Every computer that wants to talk to another computer in the same network then only needs the correct IP address of the recipient. This is also the basic setup of almost all private networks you may have at home:

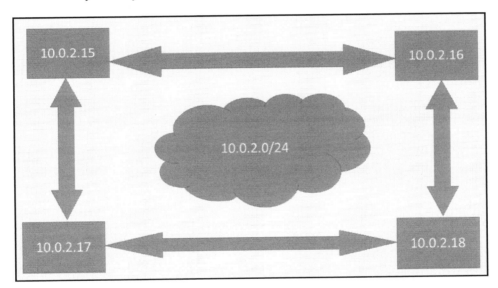

As we have just learned, for normal network communication, all participants need to be in the same network. If this was all there was to networking, we would have to stop here and modern communication and the World Wide Web would not exist. The reality is that there are millions of networks connected together around the globe, such as our own private one, which are all connected through routers. If you want to communicate with another machine in your network or any other network, your computer needs to have a so-called IP routing table that defines static routes or the next hop towards a particular destination. This IP routing table is part of every Linux operating system. For example, if we have a private network consisting of three subnetworks with the following IP network addresses, if you want to get into contact with another computer in your subnetwork, your routing table could work the following way. If there is an entry in the table that defines what to do if someone wants to access the IP address of the 10.0.2.0 subnetwork, for example, with the IP 10.0.2.15, there is a route entry in the table that defines that you should hop to the 10.0.2.0 network:

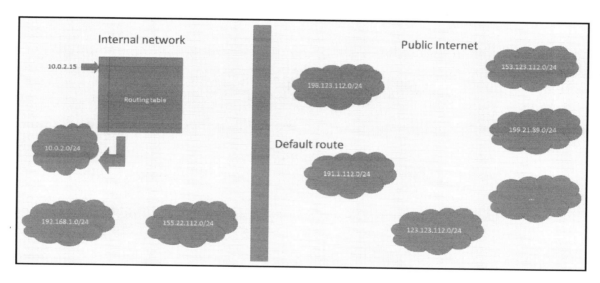

The same happens if you want to access the machine with the IP address `192.168.122.` Because there is an entry in the table, the routing table will hop to the `192.168.1.0` network that this computer is part of:

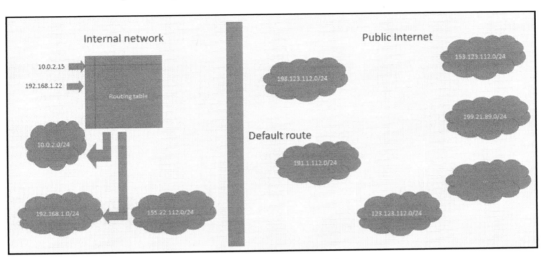

For all the other IP addresses where there is no explicit rule, the so-called default route will be used. In most private networks, the default rule is the IP address of a real hardware router, which basically is the same as an IP routing table, but which can do more, as it is connected to other routers around the globe where it will find its way to the correct destination address:

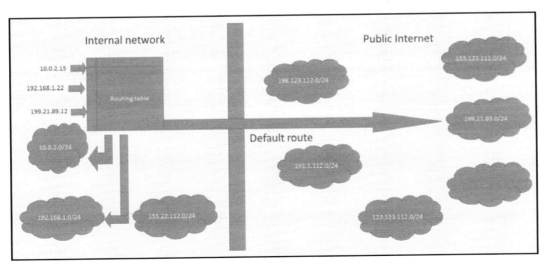

This is also called dynamic routing, as the router or path between the source and the destination can vary depending on which routers it will use. Normally, each private network that most internet service providers offer has only one public IP address that connects to the public internet:

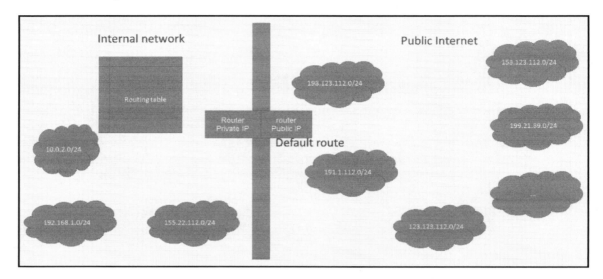

All machines from our private network need to go via this router, with its single public IP address, if they want to communicate with other computers in the public internet.

On the other hand, if an outside public machine from the internet wants to access the private computers from our subnetwork, the router needs to handle the correct delivery of messages to the correct recipient, which has an internal IP address only visible within our private network.

But how can you define an IP address for a computer? The IP address needs to be set on an OS level in the correct configuration location associated with a certain network interface:

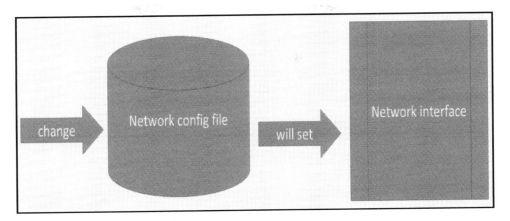

But, as mentioned before, the IP addresses need to be unique in the same subnetwork; otherwise, the correct recipient for a network message cannot be found.

So, how can you take care of that? The first approach is to manually manage a list of computers and all free and reserved IP addresses available in this network. Here, we need to assign static IP addresses, which means every computer gets an IP address hardcoded into the system, which will not change and remain stable:

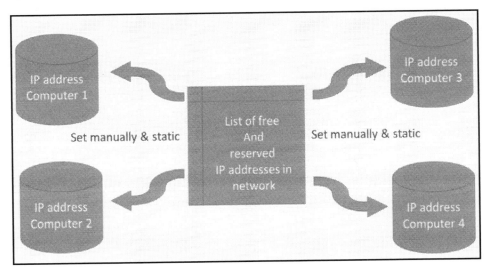

Often, important services in networks, such as a mail or web server, have a static IP because they must be reachable under the same address all the time from multiple other computers or services. But, as you can imagine, this system is very inflexible and needs manual intervention all the time. Just think about a public wireless hotspot and all the people who are connecting to this network all the time with multiple devices, such as smartphones, laptops, and tablets. A much better solution is to use a so-called DHCP server. This is a service running in your network that listens to new devices and keeps a database of all devices currently connected to the network. It automatically assigns or revokes, and manages, in a very reliable manner, IP addresses to all the machines connected:

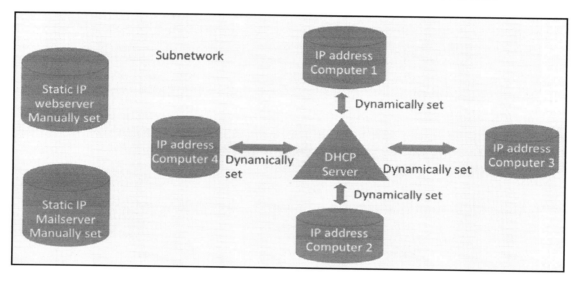

The IP addresses assigned to the computers are dynamic, which means tomorrow, your computer can have an IP address other than the one used today. The great thing about this system is that it can also send additional information about your network to the computers connected, for example, the IP address of a private DNS or mail server in your network, as can be seen in the following diagram:

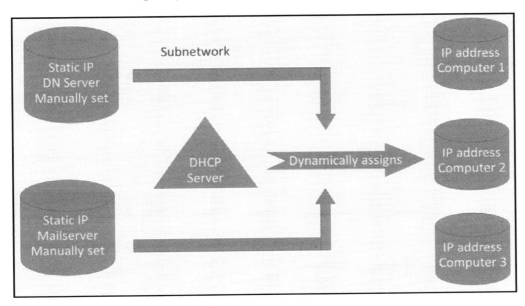

A DNS server is another very important networking feature that we need to know about. As we have just learned, computers communicate with each other using IP addresses only, which are just numbers. As we humans are not so good at memorizing or recalling long sequences of numbers, but are much better working with names for objects or things, a system has been developed to assign names or aliases to these IP addresses so that we can address computers by names instead.

A DNS server has a database that stores these relationships. As computers can only work with numbers and not names on the network, every time we want to connect the computer using a name, a corresponding DNS server gets asked internally to translate the name to its corresponding IP address so that we can make the right connection with the IP address instead. Now, for resolving names of the normal internet, such as google.com, we will use some public DNS servers normally provided by your ISP or from another source:

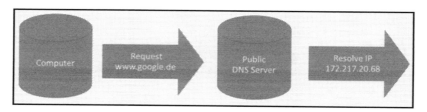

But how can we give names to our internal private computers' IP addresses in our subnetwork when the public DNS servers don't have this information? One solution would be to install and set up our own private DNS server and add new names to IP address relationships.

As this needs a lot of work to install and configure. An easier, and quicker, solution is to put the name to an IP address relationship locally in a special file called the /etc/hosts file:

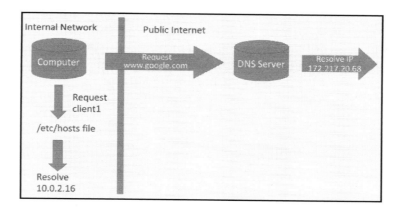

The biggest disadvantage of using the hosts file is that you have to put this file on every single computer in your network that wants to resolve network names, and also you have to keep this file up to date at all times so that each time a new computer is added to the network, every computer in the network needs to update their hosts file.

Until now, we have only spoken of names to IP address relationships when it comes to DNS servers and the hosts file. But here we need to discuss the anatomy of such a name in greater detail. For example, you could give all the computers in your network hostnames of the persons working with them:

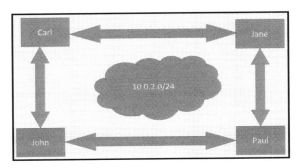

You can also use any name schema you like, but, as you can imagine, these hostnames are not unique enough to fully qualify a computer in a network so that we can address it directly. Bear in mind that our private network can consist of several different subnetworks, for example, one for the IT department, and one for the human resources department:

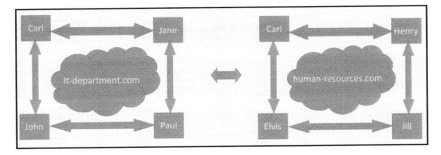

Here, two people can easily exist with the same name in different subnetworks, so this would not work because the computer hostname, Carl, exists in both networks and we just cannot use the hostname alone to differentiate between unique computer names. Therefore, we can also give names to subnetworks or network addresses. This kind of name is also called the DNS name, or domain name. The hostname or name of the computer plus the DNS name, combined together and separated by a dot, is called the **fully-qualified domain name (FQDN)**, and really is needed each time we need to access computers in different networks outside our own local subnetwork:

```
●  carl.my-company.com

   Hostname    DNS Name

FQDN (Hostname + DNS Name)
```

So here, using the fully-qualified name to address Carl at **it-department.com** will not clash with the Carl in the **human-resources.com** subnetwork.

Let's recap! The hostname is a computer name (for example, Carl), the DNS name is the name of a network or subnetwork, such as my-company.com or google.com, and the fully-qualified domain name is the hostname plus the DNS name separated by a dot (for example, Carl.my-company.com or mail.google.com).

In Chapter 1, *Introduction to Linux*, of this book, we set up three VMs called **Master, client1**, and **client2**. We configured the network of our three machines to have one network interface per VM, always with the same isolated IP 10.0.2.15, which means no internal connections between the three VMs can be made because they all have the same IP:

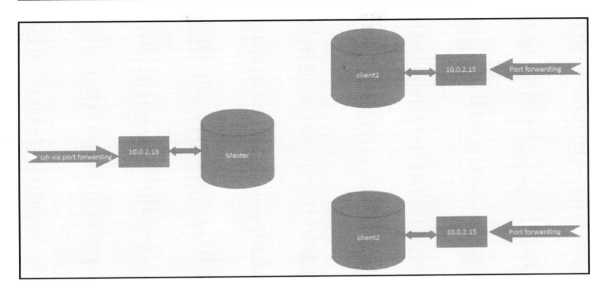

We use VirtualBox port forwarding to access our machines from outside through SSH using the host ports 2222, 2223, and 2224, which all map to port 22, the internal SSH port of the machines. Now, we want to make the machines able to communicate with each other using an internal private network. As each network interface can only have one IP address, we will accomplish this by adding a second virtual network adapter with a new IP address from another subnetwork to each machine, so that every VM has one network adapter for public access via SSH, and one for internal subnetwork communication:

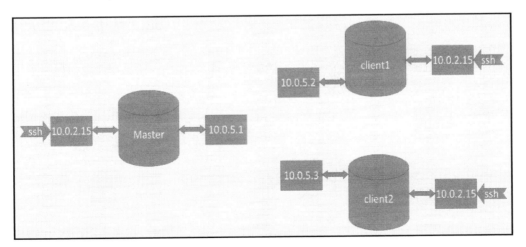

As you can see, we use a second subnetwork called `10.0.5` instead of our `10.0.2` for our internal network:

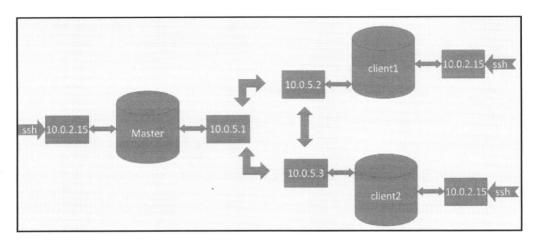

If you type in the `ip addr list`, you will get a list of all the network interfaces currently attached to your computer:

```
[root@localhost ~]# ip addr list_
2: enp0s3: <BROADCAST,MULTICAST,UP,LOWER_UP> mtu 1500 qdisc pfifo_fast state UP
qlen 1000
    link/ether 08:00:27:ae:27:f9 brd ff:ff:ff:ff:ff:ff
3: enp0s8: <BROADCAST,MULTICAST,UP,LOWER_UP> mtu 1500 qdisc pfifo_fast state UP
qlen 1000
    link/ether 08:00:27:27:de:c9 brd ff:ff:ff:ff:ff:ff
    inet 10.0.3.15/24 brd 10.0.3.255 scope global dynamic enp0s8
        valid_lft 84676sec preferred_lft 84676sec
    inet6 fe80::a00:27ff:fe27:dec9/64 scope link
        valid_lft forever preferred_lft forever
4: enp0s9: <BROADCAST,MULTICAST,UP,LOWER_UP> mtu 1500 qdisc pfifo_fast state UP
qlen 1000
    link/ether 08:00:27:6c:9b:91 brd ff:ff:ff:ff:ff:ff
    inet 10.0.4.15/24 brd 10.0.4.255 scope global dynamic enp0s9
        valid_lft 85458sec preferred_lft 85458sec
    inet6 fe80::a00:27ff:fe6c:9b91/64 scope link
        valid_lft forever preferred_lft forever
5: enp0s10: <BROADCAST,MULTICAST,UP,LOWER_UP> mtu 1500 qdisc pfifo_fast state UP
 qlen 1000
    link/ether 08:00:27:8f:96:d1 brd ff:ff:ff:ff:ff:ff
    inet 10.0.5.15/24 brd 10.0.5.255 scope global dynamic enp0s10
        valid_lft 84676sec preferred_lft 84676sec
    inet6 fe80::a00:27ff:fe8f:96d1/64 scope link
        valid_lft forever preferred_lft forever
[root@localhost ~]#
```

The first device is the loopback device, which is a non-physical device so that we can make a network connection to our own computer. It always has the IP address `127.0.0.1`. The second network interface is enp0s3, which is a virtual network interface provided by the VirtualBox configuration. This reflects to adapt the one in the following setup:

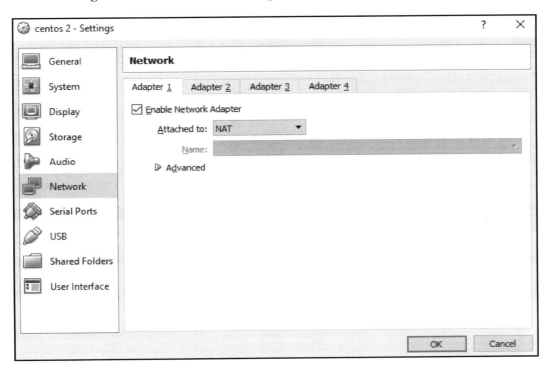

This virtual network interface has the IP address `10.0.2.15` and is mainly used so we can SSH to the machine.

Now, let's add another network interface to our virtual machine:

1. In order to do that, first shut down the machine:

```
[olip@localhost ~]$ ip addr list
1: lo: <LOOPBACK,UP,LOWER_UP> mtu 65536 qdisc noqueue state UNKNOWN qlen 1
    link/loopback 00:00:00:00:00:00 brd 00:00:00:00:00:00
    inet 127.0.0.1/8 scope host lo
       valid_lft forever preferred_lft forever
    inet6 ::1/128 scope host
       valid_lft forever preferred_lft forever
2: enp0s3: <BROADCAST,MULTICAST,UP,LOWER_UP> mtu 1500 qdisc pfifo_fast state UP qlen 1000
    link/ether 08:00:27:82:d9:50 brd ff:ff:ff:ff:ff:ff
    inet 10.0.2.15/24 brd 10.0.2.255 scope global dynamic enp0s3
       valid_lft 85581sec preferred_lft 85581sec
    inet6 fe80::f78b:4a5f:1efa:d09b/64 scope link
       valid_lft forever preferred_lft forever
[olip@localhost ~]$ shutdown -h now
==== AUTHENTICATING FOR org.freedesktop.login1.power-off ====
Authentication is required for powering off the system.
Authenticating as: root
Password:
==== AUTHENTICATION COMPLETE ====
Connection to 127.0.0.1 closed by remote host.
Connection to 127.0.0.1 closed.
[instructor@videotraining cli-presenter]$
```

2. Now, to add a new network interface for internal communication between your virtual machines, add a second network interface to each machine in the following way. First, open your VM **Settings**, go to **Network**, open the tab **Adapter 2**, enable it, and attach it to the internal network. As you can see, the name of the internal network is called internet. We will put all our other VMs in the same network:

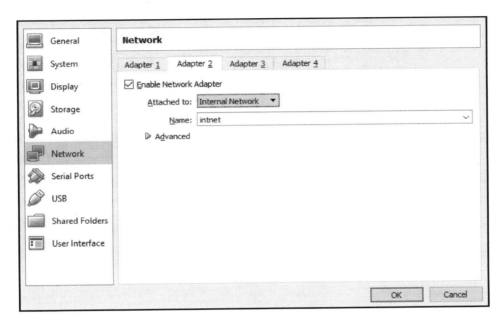

3. Now, press **OK** to proceed.
4. Do the same for every VM you want to have as part of your internal network for communication between the machines.

5. Now let's start one of your VMs to test the network settings.

6. Now, if you again run the IP address list, you will see that our newly added network interface appears at interface number 3 with the name `enp0s8`. Also, you will see that currently, no IP address has been associated to this device automatically:

```
CentOS Linux 7 (AltArch)
Kernel 3.10.0-693.2.2.el7.centos.plus.i686 on an i686

localhost login: root
Password:
Last login: Wed Jun 27 01:25:33 on tty1
[root@localhost ~]# ip addr list
1: lo: <LOOPBACK,UP,LOWER_UP> mtu 65536 qdisc noqueue state UNKNOWN qlen 1
    link/loopback 00:00:00:00:00:00 brd 00:00:00:00:00:00
    inet 127.0.0.1/8 scope host lo
       valid_lft forever preferred_lft forever
    inet6 ::1/128 scope host
       valid_lft forever preferred_lft forever
2: enp0s3: <BROADCAST,MULTICAST,UP,LOWER_UP> mtu 1500 qdisc pfifo_fast state UP
qlen 1000
    link/ether 08:00:27:ca:86:38 brd ff:ff:ff:ff:ff:ff
3: enp0s8: <BROADCAST,MULTICAST,UP,LOWER_UP> mtu 1500 qdisc pfifo_fast state UP
qlen 1000
    link/ether 08:00:27:04:03:39 brd ff:ff:ff:ff:ff:ff
    inet6 fe80::b4ce:33cc:698d:103b/64 scope link
       valid_lft forever preferred_lft forever
```

7. Let's get some information about our current network. Let's show the IP routing table for our network devices:

```
[root@localhost ~]# ip addr list
1: lo: <LOOPBACK,UP,LOWER_UP> mtu 65536 qdisc noqueue state UNKNOWN
    link/loopback 00:00:00:00:00:00 brd 00:00:00:00:00:00
    inet 127.0.0.1/8 scope host lo
       valid_lft forever preferred_lft forever
    inet6 ::1/128 scope host
       valid_lft forever preferred_lft forever
2: enp0s3: <BROADCAST,MULTICAST,UP,LOWER_UP> mtu 1500 qdisc pfifo_fast state UP
qlen 1000
    link/ether 08:00:27:ae:27:f9 brd ff:ff:ff:ff:ff:ff
[root@localhost]# ip route show
default via 10.0.2.2 dev enp0s3 proto static metric 100
10.0.2.0/24 dev enp0s3 proto kernel scope link src 10.0.2.15 metric 100
[root@localhost]#
[root@localhost ~]#
```

As you can see, the `enp0s3` network adapter with the IP address `10.0.2.15`, which is the interface we used to connect via SSH from the host machine using port forwarding, currently has two routes in the IP routing table. The first route is the route for the subnetwork we are currently a member of, `10.0.2.0`. This means that this route will be taken if we try to contact another computer in our subnetwork. For example, `10.0.2.16`. All the other IP addresses we want to reach are using the default route, which points to the IP address `10.0.2.2`. This is the IP address of our router. So, for example, if you want to go to www.google.com, first the domain name will be translated to an IP address using a DNS server, and then it will be matched against our routes there. We can use the `nslookup` command to resolve any domain name into an IP address using the system's default DNS server. As you can see, the `google.com` domain name has the following IP address:

```
    inet 10.0.4.15/24 brd 10.0.4.255 scope global noprefixroute dynamic enp0s9
        valid_lft 86277sec preferred_lft 86277sec
    inet6 fe80::9c5f:e9b9:7645:ef1b/64 scope link noprefixroute
        valid_lft forever preferred_lft forever
5: enp0s10: <BROADCAST,MULTICAST,UP,LOWER_UP> mtu 1500 qdisc pfifo_fast state UP
group default qlen 1000
    link/ether 08:00:27:8f:96:d1 brd ff:ff:ff:ff:ff:ff
    inet 10.0.5.15/24 brd 10.0.5.255 scope global noprefixroute dynamic enp0s10
        valid_lft 86277sec preferred_lft 86277sec
    inet6 fe80::e882:1439:983c:3dde/64 scope link noprefixroute
        valid_lft forever preferred_lft forever
[root@localhost ~]# ip route show
default via 10.0.4.2 dev enp0s9 proto dhcp metric 101
default via 10.0.5.2 dev enp0s10 proto dhcp metric 102
10.0.4.0/24 dev enp0s9 proto kernel scope link src 10.0.4.15 metric 101
10.0.5.0/24 dev enp0s10 proto kernel scope link src 10.0.5.15 metric 102
[root@localhost ~]# nslookup google.com
Server:         192.168.0.6
Address:        192.168.0.6#53

Non-authoritative answer:
Name:   google.com
Address: 216.58.203.206

[root@localhost ~]#
```

Since the IP addresses starting with 172 are not part of our subnetwork, the default route will be used. Behind the 10.0.2.2 IP address sits a real hardware router; it will take care of the proper routing between the virtual machine and the google.com website.

Before we create a new network connection between our three virtual machines using the enp0s8 network interface, let's set three unique FQDNs. We will do this using the root account.

To print out the FQDN, use the hostnamectl status command:

```
[root@localhost ~]# hostnamectl status
        Static hostname: localhost.localdomain
              Icon name: computer-vm
                Chassis: vm
             Machine ID: 0210766d29dc44af8c4f76190fa655f7
                Boot ID: c547488b0bbd4c8c8aad963bf446ce24
         Virtualization: kvm
       Operating System: CentOS Linux 7 (Core)
            CPE OS Name: cpe:/o:centos:centos:7
                 Kernel: Linux 3.10.0-327.el7.x86_64
           Architecture: x86-64
[root@localhost ~]#
```

As you can see, currently we have the FQDN of localhost.localdomain. Now, to change the FQDN, use the set-hostname option of the hostnamectl command. In our example, we used the hostname or computer name master and the DNS name, centos7vt.com. The fully-qualified domain name is master.centos7vt.com.

Let's recheck using the status option. On our two other VMs, we will later set the hostnames, client1 and client2, and the same DNS name, centos7vt.com. You can also set the FQDN by editing the /etc/hostname file.

To change your system's default DNS server IP address, open the file called `/etc/resolv.conf`. Under the keyword name server, you can change or add new name servers. For example, to add a new name server, introduce a new name server line and change the IP address. In this example, we will use Google's official DNS server address, or you can just use 1:

```
# Generated by NetworkManager
search fritz.box centos7vt.com
nameserver 192.168.178.1
nameserver 8.8.8.8
```

```
:"/etc/resolv.conf" 4L, 105C written
```

Next, let's set up a new static network configuration for our new network adapter, `enp0s8`. On CentOS 7, all the network configuration files can be found at `/etc/sysconfig/network-scripts`:

```
[root@localhost ~]# cd /etc/sysconfig/network-scripts
[root@localhost network-scripts]# ls
ifcfg-enp0s3   ifdown-ppp        ifup-ib      ifup-Team
ifcfg-lo       ifdown-routes     ifup-ippp    ifup-TeamPort
ifdown         ifdown-sit        ifup-ipv6    ifup-tunnel
ifdown-bnep    ifdown-Team       ifup-isdn    ifup-wireless
ifdown-eth     ifdown-TeamPort   ifup-plip    init.ipv6-global
ifdown-ib      ifdown-tunnel     ifup-plusb   network-functions
ifdown-ippp    ifup              ifup-post    network-functions-ipv6
ifdown-ipv6    ifup-aliases      ifup-ppp
ifdown-isdn    ifup-bnep         ifup-routes
ifdown-post    ifup-eth          ifup-sit
[root@localhost network-scripts]# _
```

As you can see, for the `enp0s3` network interface, a corresponding network interface configuration file called `ifcfg-enp0s3`. Let's view its content by typing `cat ifcfg-eno0s3` exists:

```
ifdown-bnep    ifdown-Team       ifup-isdn    ifup-wireless
ifdown-eth     ifdown-TeamPort   ifup-plip    init.ipv6-global
ifdown-ib      ifdown-tunnel     ifup-plusb   network-functions
ifdown-ippp    ifup              ifup-post    network-functions-ipv6
ifdown-ipv6    ifup-aliases      ifup-ppp
ifdown-isdn    ifup-bnep         ifup-routes
ifdown-post    ifup-eth          ifup-sit
[root@localhost network-scripts]# cat ifcfg-enp0s3
TYPE=Ethernet
BOOTPROTO=dhcp
DEFROUTE=yes
PEERDNS=yes
PEERROUTES=yes
IPV4_FAILURE_FATAL=no
IPV6INIT=yes
IPV6_AUTOCONF=yes
IPV6_DEFROUTE=yes
IPV6_PEERDNS=yes
IPV6_PEERROUTES=yes
IPV6_FAILURE_FATAL=no
NAME=enp0s3
UUID=fa293265-7a0e-49ca-812a-4b7c8a331f52
DEVICE=enp0s3
ONBOOT=no
[root@localhost network-scripts]# _
```

The most important things to know about this Ethernet network device are that it's getting its IP address from a DHCP server, the device is activated on boot up, and has the device ID `enp0s3`. The other items you see in this configuration file can also become very important when configuring different network devices in different environments. Since there is no visual manual page for the `if` configuration file format, please refer to the excellent documentation at `/usr/share/doc/initscripts-* sysconfig.txt`:

```
==============================

Generic options:

/etc/sysconfig/*

    CGROUP_DAEMON=
        List of control groups that the daemon will be run in. For example,
        CGROUP_DAEMON="cpu:daemons cpuacct:/" will run it in the daemons
        group for the CPU controller, and the '/' group for the CPU accounting
        controller.

/etc/sysconfig/authconfig

    used by authconfig to store information about the system's user
    information and authentication setup; changes made to this file
    have no effect until the next time authconfig is run

    USEHESIOD=no
        Whether or not the hesiod naming service is in use.  If not set,
        authconfig examines the passwd setting in /etc/nsswitch.conf.
    USELDAP=no
        Whether or not LDAP is used as a naming service.  If not set,
/usr/share/doc/initscripts-9.49.41/sysconfig.txt
```

If you open the file and search for ifcfg, you will come to the section where all the different items of the ifcfg file format are being explained. For example, the BOOTPROTO item can have the values none, bootp, and dhcp. Since both bootp and dhcp refer to a DHCP client for our new network device, enp0s8, that we want to configure as a static device, we will use the BOOTPROTO none, but what items do we need for setting up our simple static network connection? Since we are setting up an internal network only, we don't need any routing set up and only need very little information in our **interface config (ifcfg)** file.

So we will need the following items: the name, the device, the IP address, because we will hardcode a static IP address, and the BOOTPROTO, which we will set to none. So let's review our plan network configuration from the introduction.

As you will remember, the master node we are currently logged in should have a second network interface with the static IP address 10.0.5.1. **Client1** should have a second network adapter with the static IP address 10.0.5.2, and **client2** should have 10.0.5.3, all for internal network communication between the nodes:

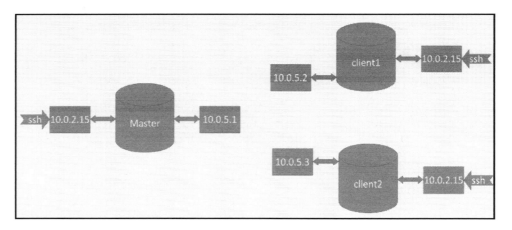

So let's configure our new device:

1. As you can see, we are currently in the network scripts folder, where all our network interface's configuration files can be found. So let's first create a new configuration file for our new network interface:

```
[root@localhost network-scripts]# pwd
/etc/sysconfig/network-scripts
[root@localhost network-scripts]# ls
ifcfg-enp0s3   ifdown-ppp      ifup-ib        ifup-Team
ifcfg-lo       ifdown-routes   ifup-ippp      ifup-TeamPort
ifdown         ifdown-sit      ifup-ipv6      ifup-tunnel
ifdown-bnep    ifdown-Team     ifup-isdn      ifup-wireless
ifdown-eth     ifdown-TeamPort ifup-plip      init.ipv6-global
ifdown-ib      ifdown-tunnel   ifup-plusb     network-functions
ifdown-ippp    ifup            ifup-post      network-functions-ipv6
ifdown-ipv6    ifup-aliases    ifup-ppp
ifdown-isdn    ifup-bnep       ifup-routes
ifdown-post    ifup-eth        ifup-sit
[root@localhost network-scripts]# _
        inet6 ::1/128 scope host
            valid_lft forever preferred_lft forever
2: enp0s3: <BROADCAST,MULTICAST,UP,LOWER_UP> mtu 1500 qdisc pfifo_fast state UP
group default qlen 1000
        link/ether 08:00:27:ae:27:f9 brd ff:ff:ff:ff:ff:ff
3: enp0s8: <BROADCAST,MULTICAST,UP,LOWER_UP> mtu 1500 qdisc pfifo_fast state UP
group default qlen 1000
        link/ether 08:00:27:27:de:c9 brd ff:ff:ff:ff:ff:ff
        inet6 fe80::b0b0:8462:5c93:3015/64 scope link noprefixroute
            valid_lft forever preferred_lft forever
4: enp0s9: <BROADCAST,MULTICAST,UP,LOWER_UP> mtu 1500 qdisc pfifo_fast state UP
group default qlen 1000
        link/ether 08:00:27:6c:9b:91 brd ff:ff:ff:ff:ff:ff
        inet 10.0.4.15/24 brd 10.0.4.255 scope global noprefixroute dynamic enp0s9
            valid_lft 84921sec preferred_lft 84921sec
        inet6 fe80::9c5f:e9b9:7645:ef1b/64 scope link noprefixroute
            valid_lft forever preferred_lft forever
5: enp0s10: <BROADCAST,MULTICAST,UP,LOWER_UP> mtu 1500 qdisc pfifo_fast state UP
group default qlen 1000
        link/ether 08:00:27:8f:96:d1 brd ff:ff:ff:ff:ff:ff
        inet 10.0.5.15/24 brd 10.0.5.255 scope global noprefixroute dynamic enp0s10
            valid_lft 84921sec preferred_lft 84921sec
        inet6 fe80::e882:1439:983c:3dde/64 scope link noprefixroute
            valid_lft forever preferred_lft forever
[root@localhost network-scripts]#
```

2. We will make our life easy by copying the existing configuration file for the `enp0s3` network device to the new `enp0s8` configuration file. Now let's open this new configuration file:

```
        valid_lft forever preferred_lft forever
2: enp0s3: <BROADCAST,MULTICAST,UP,LOWER_UP> mtu 1500 qdisc pfifo_fast state UP
group default qlen 1000
       link/ether 08:00:27:ae:27:f9 brd ff:ff:ff:ff:ff:ff
3: enp0s8: <BROADCAST,MULTICAST,UP,LOWER_UP> mtu 1500 qdisc pfifo_fast state UP
group default qlen 1000
       link/ether 08:00:27:27:de:c9 brd ff:ff:ff:ff:ff:ff
       inet6 fe80::b0b0:8462:5c93:3015/64 scope link noprefixroute
          valid_lft forever preferred_lft forever
4: enp0s9: <BROADCAST,MULTICAST,UP,LOWER_UP> mtu 1500 qdisc pfifo_fast state UP
group default qlen 1000
       link/ether 08:00:27:6c:9b:91 brd ff:ff:ff:ff:ff:ff
       inet 10.0.4.15/24 brd 10.0.4.255 scope global noprefixroute dynamic enp0s9
          valid_lft 84921sec preferred_lft 84921sec
       inet6 fe80::9c5f:e9b9:7645:ef1b/64 scope link noprefixroute
          valid_lft forever preferred_lft forever
5: enp0s10: <BROADCAST,MULTICAST,UP,LOWER_UP> mtu 1500 qdisc pfifo_fast state UP
 group default qlen 1000
       link/ether 08:00:27:8f:96:d1 brd ff:ff:ff:ff:ff:ff
       inet 10.0.5.15/24 brd 10.0.5.255 scope global noprefixroute dynamic enp0s10
          valid_lft 84921sec preferred_lft 84921sec
       inet6 fe80::e802:1439:983c:3dde/64 scope link noprefixroute
          valid_lft forever preferred_lft forever
[root@localhost network-scripts]# cp ifcfg-enp0s3 ifcfg-enp0s8
[root@localhost network-scripts]# vi ifcfg-enp0s8
```

3. Let's change the boot protocol to none for the static IP configuration. Most of the items are not needed, so just delete the lines. Change the name of the device to s8; UUID is not needed here. Also, change the device ID, leave the ONBOOT as yes, so the interface will come up on server restart, and finally, add a new line that defines the hardcoded IP address of our static internet network configuration. Use the IP address 10.0.5.1 for our master server:

```
TYPE=Ethernet
BOOTPROTO=dhcp
DEFROUTE=yes
PEERDNS=yes
PEERROUTES=yes
IPV4_FAILURE_FATAL=no
IPV6INIT=yes
IPV6_AUTOCONF=yes
IPV6_DEFROUTE=yes
IPV6_PEERDNS=yes
IPV6_PEERROUTES=yes
IPV6_FAILURE_FATAL=no
NAME=enp0s3
UUID=fa293265-7a0e-49ca-812a-4b7c8a331f52
DEVICE=enp0s3
ONBOOT=no




"ifcfg-enp0s8" 16L, 277C
```

4. Now save the file and exit.
5. We then need to hard reset our enp0s8 network interface so that the changes we made to the configuration file can be applied to the device and the static IP address can get active. In order to do so, first shut down the enp0s8 device using the ifdown command.
6. Then bring it back online using the ifup command.
7. Finally, let's review the ip addr list command.

If you compare the output of enp0s8 before we restarted the device and afterwards, you will see that the changes we made to the configuration file were valid, and now we have a static IP of 10.0.5.1 for our enp0s8 network device.

Now, after we set up the static network configuration for the enp0s8 network adapter, let's recheck our IP routing table with the `ip route show` command. If you compare the routing table before and after we have set up the new network interface, `enp0s8`, you will see that a new route has been created for routing network communications in our new `10.0.0.0` subnetwork.

The last thing still left on the master node, as we don't have a private DNS server, is to set up our network's computer names to IP relationships in the `/etc/hosts` file. Always start adding new entries at the end of the file by using the fully-qualified domain names first, and then you can add further short hostnames. You can always add multiple names for the same IP address:

```
127.0.0.1   localhost localhost.localdomain localhost4 localhost4.localdomain4
::1         localhost localhost.localdomain localhost6 localhost6.localdomain6
10.0.5.1    master.centos7vt.com
10.0.5.2    client1.centos7vt.com
10.0.5.3    client2.centos7vt.com
10.0.5.1    master
10.0.5.1    chief
10.0.5.1    meister
10.0.5.1    m
10.0.5.2    client1
10.0.5.2    c1
10.0.5.3    client2
10.0.5.3    c1_




-- INSERT --                                                    13,13            All
```

The first entry will be our own machine we just set up. The other entries are for our clients we are about to set up shortly. Save and exit the file. Now start the two client VMs. After booting up the VMs is complete, open two new tabs in your Terminal emulator of your choosing. The first tab on the left holds the connection to the master node. On the next tab to the right, please log in to the client2 VM using the SSH port forwarding on port 2223. In the third tab, log into the client2 VM on port 2224. Now go to the middle tab where our client1 VM is open.

Here let's repeat the steps to configure our `enp0s8` network interface so we can make the connection between our servers:

1. First, log in as root.
2. Next, set a fully-qualified domain name to `client1.centos7vt.com`.
3. Next, create a configuration file for our new **enp0s8** static network connection. Here, enter the same information as on the master; only change the IP address to the `10.0.5.2`. Save and exit the file.
4. Next, restart the network interface:

```
[root@localhost olip]# ifdown enp0s8
Device 'enp0s8' successfully disconnected.
[root@localhost olip]# ifup enp0s8
Connection successfully activated (D-Bus active path: /org/freedesktop/NetworkMa
nager/ActiveConnection/15)
```

As you can see, we have successfully assigned the `10.0.5.2` IP address to our enp0s8 network interface. Finally, add entries to the `/etc/hosts` file so that we can resolve other domain names in our subnetwork. Add the same information as on the master:

```
127.0.0.1   localhost localhost.localdomain localhost4 localhost4.localdomain4
::1         localhost localhost.localdomain localhost6 localhost6.localdomain6
10.0.5.1    master.centos7vt.com
10.0.5.2    client1.centos7vt.com
10.0.5.3    client2.centos7vt.com
10.0.5.1    master
10.0.5.1    chief
10.0.5.1    meister
10.0.5.1    m
10.0.5.2    client1
10.0.5.2    cl
10.0.5.3    client2
10.0.5.3    cl

-- INSERT --                                               13,13          All
```

Save and exit the file. Next, do the same steps for the `client2` VM in the third tab. First log, in as root, use `client2` for the hostname, use the `10.0.5.3` for the IP address, restart your network interface, and finally, add entries to the `/etc/hosts` file.

Now that we have set up our private network for communication, the easiest way to test whether it is working properly is to use the `ping` command. This command can be used to see whether another host is alive and reachable. If it is not reachable, the following error message will be printed:

```
[root@localhost network-scripts]# ping -c 3 10.0.5.10
PING 10.0.5.10 (10.0.5.10) 56(84) bytes of data.
From 10.0.5.15 icmp_seq=1 Destination Host Unreachable
From 10.0.5.15 icmp_seq=2 Destination Host Unreachable
From 10.0.5.15 icmp_seq=3 Destination Host Unreachable

--- 10.0.5.10 ping statistics ---
3 packets transmitted, 0 received, +3 errors, 100% packet loss, time 2000ms
pipe 3
[root@localhost network-scripts]#
```

Now let's start our connection tests from the `master` in the first tab. First, let's test if we can reach `client1` with the IP address `10.0.5.2`:

```
[root@localhost network-scripts]# ping -c 3  10.0.5.2
PING 10.0.5.2 (10.0.5.2) 56(84) bytes of data.
64 bytes from 10.0.5.2: icmp_seq=1 ttl=64 time=0.436 ms
64 bytes from 10.0.5.2: icmp_seq=2 ttl=64 time=0.291 ms
64 bytes from 10.0.5.2: icmp_seq=3 ttl=64 time=0.261 ms

--- 10.0.5.2 ping statistics ---
3 packets transmitted, 3 received, 0% packet loss, time 2003ms
rtt min/avg/max/mdev = 0.261/0.329/0.436/0.077 ms
[root@localhost network-scripts]#
```

As you can see, it works. Also, test if we can reach `client2` with the IP address `10.0.5.3`:

```
[root@localhost network-scripts]# ping -c 3  10.0.5.2
PING 10.0.5.2 (10.0.5.2) 56(84) bytes of data.
64 bytes from 10.0.5.2: icmp_seq=1 ttl=64 time=0.436 ms
64 bytes from 10.0.5.2: icmp_seq=2 ttl=64 time=0.291 ms
64 bytes from 10.0.5.2: icmp_seq=3 ttl=64 time=0.261 ms

--- 10.0.5.2 ping statistics ---
3 packets transmitted, 3 received, 0% packet loss, time 2003ms
rtt min/avg/max/mdev = 0.261/0.329/0.436/0.077 ms
[root@localhost network-scripts]# ping -c 3  10.0.5.3
PING 10.0.5.3 (10.0.5.3) 56(84) bytes of data.
64 bytes from 10.0.5.3: icmp_seq=1 ttl=64 time=0.414 ms
64 bytes from 10.0.5.3: icmp_seq=2 ttl=64 time=0.270 ms
64 bytes from 10.0.5.3: icmp_seq=3 ttl=64 time=0.280 ms

--- 10.0.5.3 ping statistics ---
3 packets transmitted, 3 received, 0% packet loss, time 2003ms
rtt min/avg/max/mdev = 0.270/0.321/0.414/0.067 ms
[root@localhost network-scripts]#
```

As you can see, this also works.

As a next step, test if our `/etc/hosts` configuration is also working. In order to do so, let's ping the various hostnames we set up in this file. The fully-qualified domain name of client1 is working. Also, the hostname client1 is working. C2 is also working as a short name for client2. The fully-qualified domain name of client2 is also working. The short name client2 is working and the very short name c2 is also working for client2:

```
--- client1 ping statistics ---
3 packets transmitted, 3 received, 0% packet loss, time 2003ms
rtt min/avg/max/mdev = 0.962/2.028/4.065/1.440 ms
[olip@localhost ~]$ ping -c 3  c2
PING c2 (10.0.5.3) 56(84) bytes of data.
64 bytes from client2.centos7vt.com (10.0.5.3): icmp_seq=1 ttl=64 time=1.33 ms
64 bytes from client2.centos7vt.com (10.0.5.3): icmp_seq=2 ttl=64 time=0.729 ms
64 bytes from client2.centos7vt.com (10.0.5.3): icmp_seq=3 ttl=64 time=1.16 ms
```

Now let's move to client1. Here, let's test if we can reach the master server:

```
[root@localhost olip]# ping -c 3  master
PING master (10.0.5.1) 56(84) bytes of data.
64 bytes from master.centos7vt.com (10.0.5.1): icmp_seq=1 ttl=64 time=2.15 ms
64 bytes from master.centos7vt.com (10.0.5.1): icmp_seq=2 ttl=64 time=0.976 ms
64 bytes from master.centos7vt.com (10.0.5.1): icmp_seq=3 ttl=64 time=1.23 ms

--- master ping statistics ---
3 packets transmitted, 3 received, 0% packet loss, time 2013ms
rtt min/avg/max/mdev = 0.976/1.455/2.151/0.504 ms
[root@localhost olip]# 
```

Yes, it's working. Also, you can test the master server under a different name. Let's also test the client2 connection. Test the master under a different name, and also test client1. In summary, we can say that the network configuration between our three VM machines is now working properly.

Installing new software and updating the system

In this section, we will show you how you can install new software on your computer and how to update your CentOS 7 system.

First, let's show all the currently installed RPM packages on the system. Type yum list installed:

```
[root@localhost ~]# yum list installed
Loaded plugins: fastestmirror
Loading mirror speeds from cached hostfile
 * base: centos.excellmedia.net
 * epel: del-mirrors.extreme-ix.org
 * extras: centos.excellmedia.net
 * updates: centos.excellmedia.net
```

In the installation chapter in `Chapter 1`, *Introduction to Linux*, we already demonstrated how you can do a full system update using the `yum` command, which will update all of the RPM packages that are already included in the minimal installation, and also all the packages we have installed afterwards.

To get a list of all the updates currently available for all the software packages already installed on your system, type the following command to see what's new: `yum check update`:

```
valgrind.x86_64                      1:3.13.0-10.el7              installed
vim-common.x86_64                    2:7.4.160-4.el7             @base
vim-enhanced.x86_64                  2:7.4.160-4.el7             @base
vim-filesystem.x86_64                2:7.4.160-4.el7             @base
vim-minimal.x86_64                   2:7.4.160-4.el7             @base
virt-what.x86_64                     1.18-4.el7                  installed
wget.x86_64                          1.14-15.el7_4.1            @base
which.x86_64                         2.20-7.el7                  @anaconda
wpa_supplicant.x86_64                1:2.6-9.el7                 installed
xcb-util.x86_64                      0.4.0-2.el7                 @anaconda
xfsprogs.x86_64                      4.5.0-15.el7                installed
xml-common.noarch                    0.6.3-39.el7                @anaconda
xmlrpc-c.x86_64                      1.32.5-1905.svn2451.el7    @anaconda
xmlrpc-c-client.x86_64               1.32.5-1905.svn2451.el7    @anaconda
xulrunner.x86_64                     31.6.0-2.el7.centos         @anaconda
xz.x86_64                            5.2.2-1.el7                 installed
xz-libs.i686                         5.2.2-1.el7                 installed
xz-libs.x86_64                       5.2.2-1.el7                 installed
yum.noarch                           3.4.3-158.el7.centos        installed
yum-metadata-parser.x86_64           1.1.4-10.el7                @anaconda
yum-plugin-fastestmirror.noarch      1.1.31-45.el7               installed
zip.x86_64                           3.0-11.el7                  installed
zlib.i686                            1.2.7-17.el7                installed
zlib.x86_64                          1.2.7-17.el7                installed
[root@localhost ~]#
```

Here, all the RPM software packages are listed with the new version of the updates you can install. All updates must be done using the root user. So first log in as root. To update only a single ROM software package, such as the `vim-minimal` package, which was presented in the list of available software updates, use `yum update` and then incorporate the name of the package; for example, `vim-minimal`. Type yes when asked to update the software package, and type `yes` again to confirm the importing of the GBG key:

```
Resolving Dependencies
There are unfinished transactions remaining. You might consider running yum-comp
lete-transaction, or "yum-complete-transaction --cleanup-only" and "yum history
redo last", first to finish them. If those don't work you'll have to try removin
g/installing packages by hand (maybe package-cleanup can help).
The program yum-complete-transaction is found in the yum-utils package.
--> Running transaction check
---> Package vim-enhanced.x86_64 2:7.4.160-4.el7 will be installed
--> Finished Dependency Resolution

Dependencies Resolved

================================================================================
 Package            Arch          Version               Repository       Size
================================================================================
Installing:
 vim-enhanced       x86_64        2:7.4.160-4.el7       base            1.0 M

Transaction Summary
================================================================================
Install  1 Package

Total download size: 1.0 M
Installed size: 2.2 M
Is this ok [y/d/N]: _
```

As we can see, the `vim-minimal` package has been successfully updated to the latest version. As we have already learned in `Chapter 1`, *Introduction to Linux,* in this book, just type `yum update` to do a full system update of all the packages currently installed on your system. Now let's press the *N* key to cancel the download and installation of the updates of all the packages. Most yum commands need some kind of confirmation by the user; for example, to confirm the update of software packages. If you are absolutely sure that you will answer yes to any question, you can further automate the `yum` command of your choosing by providing the `-y` flag. This works on almost any command. This will perform the yum action of your choosing without further confirmation by the user.

 Please note that there is a big ongoing debate as to whether you need to restart your system after packages have been updated. The consensus is that normally this is not needed, but, if the kernel or glibc software packages have been updated, you should do it. Of course, you should really do it for security reasons.

We can also see that the reboot is necessary when we compare the currently installed kernel with the currently running kernel in the system:

```
[olip@localhost root]$ yum list installed | grep kernel
abrt-addon-kerneloops.x86_64        2.1.11-50.el7.centos        installed
kernel.x86_64                       3.10.0-327.el7              @anaconda
kernel.x86_64                       3.10.0-862.3.3.el7          installed
kernel-devel.x86_64                 3.10.0-327.el7              @anaconda
kernel-devel.x86_64                 3.10.0-862.3.3.el7          installed
kernel-headers.x86_64               3.10.0-862.3.3.el7          installed
kernel-tools.x86_64                 3.10.0-862.3.3.el7          installed
kernel-tools-libs.x86_64            3.10.0-862.3.3.el7          installed
[olip@localhost root]$ _
```

The currently running kernel ends with `514.el7`. The currently installed latest kernel ends with `514.21`, so we are currently not running the latest kernel. So let's reboot the system. After rebooting has finished and you are logged in as the root user back to the system, type the `uname -r` command again, and now we can see that we are now running the latest kernel, so rebooting was necessary in this instance:

```
[olip@localhost root]$ uname -r
3.10.0-327.el7.x86_64
[olip@localhost root]$
```

Now, to search in your package repositories using a keyword (for example, `Apache2 Web Server`), use the `yum search` command and then the keyword. This will print out a list of all the software packages matching the keyword; in our example, apache, in the package name or in the package description:

```
xerces-c-devel.i686  : Header files, libraries and development documentation for
                     : xerces-c
xerces-c-devel.x86_64 : Header files, libraries and development documentation
                     : for xerces-c
xerces-c-doc.noarch  : Documentation for Xerces-C++ validating XML parser
xerces-j2-demo.noarch : Demonstrations and samples for xerces-j2
xerces-j2-javadoc.noarch : Javadocs for xerces-j2
xml-commons-apis.noarch : APIs for DOM, SAX, and JAXP
xml-commons-apis-javadoc.noarch : Javadoc for xml-commons-apis
xml-commons-apis-manual.noarch : Manual for xml-commons-apis
xml-commons-apis12-javadoc.noarch : Javadoc for xml-commons-apis12
xml-commons-apis12-manual.noarch : Documents for xml-commons-apis12
xml-commons-resolver.noarch : Resolver subproject of xml-commons
xml-commons-resolver-javadoc.noarch : Javadoc for xml-commons-resolver
xml-security-c-devel.x86_64 : Development files for xml-security-c
xml-stylebook-demo.noarch : Examples for xml-stylebook
xml-stylebook-javadoc.noarch : API documentation for xml-stylebook
xmlgraphics-commons-javadoc.noarch : Javadoc for xmlgraphics-commons
xmlrpc-client.noarch : XML-RPC client implementation
xmlrpc-common.noarch : Common classes for XML-RPC client and server
                     : implementations
xmlrpc-javadoc.noarch : Javadoc for xmlrpc
xmlrpc-server.noarch : XML-RPC server implementation
yawn-server.noarch : Standalone web server for yawn
[olip@localhost root]$ 
```

 If you want to get more information about one of the package names (for example, the HTTP package name), you can use the `yum info` subcommand.

Another really useful feature is if you know the name of a file or command included in an RPM package, but actually don't know the name of the RPM package where this command or file is from, you can use the `yum whatprovides` command, prefixing the command or file you are searching for with an `*/`:

```
[nlip@localhost root]$ yum whatprovides */ifconfig
[root@localhost ~]# yum whatprovides */ifconfig
Loaded plugins: fastestmirror
Loading mirror speeds from cached hostfile                         | 7.9 kB    00:00
epel/x86_64/metalink
 * base: centos.excellmedia.net
 * epel: del mirrors.extreme ix.org
 * extras: centos.excellmedia.net
 * updates: centos.excellmedia.net
base                                                               | 3.6 kB    00:00
extras                                                             | 3.4 kB    00:00
updates                                                            | 3.4 kB    00:00
base/7/x86_64/filelists_db                                         | 6.9 MB    00:01
epel/x86_64/filelists              59% [----------      | 526 kB/s | 6.1 MB    00:07 ETA
 * epel: del mirrors extreme-ix.org
 * extras: centos.excellmedia.net
 * updates: centos.excellmedia.net
base                                                               | 3.6 kB    00:00
extras                                                             | 3.4 kB    00:00
updates                                                            | 3.4 kB    00:00
base/7/x86_64/filelists_db                                         | 6.9 MB    00:00
epel/x86_64/filelists                                              | 10 MB     00:23
extras/7/x86_64/filelists_db                                       | 524 kB    00:00
updates/7/x86_64/filelists_db                                      | 1.5 MB    00:00
net-tools-2.0-0.22.20131004git.el7.x86_64 : Basic networking tools
Repo        : base
Matched from:
Filename    : /sbin/ifconfig


net-tools-2.0-0.22.20131004git.el7.x86_64 : Basic networking tools
Repo        : @base
Matched from:
Filename    : /sbin/ifconfig

[root@localhost ~]#
```

In this example, we are searching for all the package names that include files or commands named `ifconfig`. As we can see, we have one hit in the `net-tools` RPM package where a binary or command exists in `/bin/ifconfig`.

Now, to install a software package, use the `yum install` command, providing the package name as an argument. Here, in this example, we install the Apache HTTP server package:

```
There are unfinished transactions remaining. You might consider running yum-comp
lete-transaction, or "yum-complete-transaction --cleanup-only" and "yum history
redo last", first to finish them. If those don't work you'll have to try removin
g/installing packages by hand (maybe package-cleanup can help).
The program yum-complete-transaction is found in the yum-utils package.
--> Running transaction check
---> Package httpd.x86_64 0:2.4.6-80.el7.centos will be installed
--> Finished Dependency Resolution

Dependencies Resolved

================================================================================
 Package        Arch          Version                   Repository      Size
================================================================================
Installing:
 httpd          x86_64        2.4.6-80.el7.centos        base           2.7 M

Transaction Summary
================================================================================
Install  1 Package

Total download size: 2.7 M
Installed size: 9.4 M
Downloading packages:
httpd-2.4.6-80.el7.centos. 71% [===========      ] 1.5 MB/s | 1.9 MB   00:00 ETA
```

Another interesting command is the `rpm -ql` command followed by the name of the installed software package to get a list of all the files and their exact location in the filesystem that has been installed by this software package. To remove a software package, you can use the `yum remove` command and then the name of the software package you want to remove.

In `Chapter 4`, *Working with the Command Line*, we showed you how to use a third-party repository, called `epl`, to install software such as `htop`, and `iotop` because they are not available from the official CentOS 7 repositories. For example, if you search for the `htop` package, it's not available from official sources:

```
[root@localhost ~]# yum search htop
Loaded plugins: fastestmirror
Loading mirror speeds from cached hostfile
 * base: centos.excellmedia.net
 * epel: del-mirrors.extreme-ix.org
 * extras: centos.excellmedia.net
 * updates: centos.excellmedia.net
============================ N/S matched: htop ============================
htop.x86_64 : Interactive process viewer

  Name and summary matches only, use "search all" for everything.
[root@localhost ~]#
```

So let's install the `epl` repository, as it is available from default package sources. As you can see, the `epl` repository can be installed using the `epl-release` RPM package:

```
Package                Arch          Version       Repository         Size
==========================================================================
Installing:
 epel-release          noarch        7-11          extras             15 k

Transaction Summary
==========================================================================
Install  1 Package

Total download size: 15 k
Installed size: 24 k
Downloading packages:
epel-release-7-11.noarch.rpm                            |  15 kB   00:00
Running transaction check
Running transaction test
Transaction test succeeded
Running transaction
  Installing : epel-release-7-11.noarch                                1/1
  Verifying  : epel-release-7-11.noarch                                1/1

Installed:
  epel-release.noarch 0:7-11

Complete!
[root@localhost ~]#
```

Use the following command to see if the `epl` repository has been successfully installed by retrieving a list of all the available repositories in the system.

We can now find the `htop` package, as it is part of `epl`. Installing other repositories is not so easy, since no RPM packages are available from the official sources, but most third-party repositories can be installed by downloading an external RPM. You will most likely find the repositories on a web page. For example, for the famous `remi` repository, you can first download the official `remi` repository RPM package from the official `remi` website:

```
[root@localhost ~]# cd /tmp
[root@localhost tmp]#
[root@localhost tmp]# wget http://rpms.famillecollet.com/enterprise/remi-release
-7.rpm
--2018-06-28 08:05:48--  http://rpms.famillecollet.com/enterprise/remi-release-7
.rpm
Resolving rpms.famillecollet.com (rpms.famillecollet.com)... 195.154.241.117, 20
01:bc8:33a1:100::1
Connecting to rpms.famillecollet.com (rpms.famillecollet.com)|195.154.241.117|:8
0... connected.
HTTP request sent, awaiting response... 200 OK
Length: 15384 (15K) [application/x-rpm]
Saving to: 'remi-release-7.rpm'

100%[====================================>] 15,384      --.-K/s   in 0s

2018-06-28 08:05:48 (177 MB/s) - 'remi-release-7.rpm' saved [15384/15384]

[root@localhost tmp]# _
```

Next, install this downloaded `remi` repository RPM using the `rpm` command with the capital `Uvh` option:

```
[root@localhost tmp]# rpm -Uvh remi-release-7*.rpm
warning: remi-release-7.rpm: Header V4 DSA/SHA1 Signature, key ID 00f97f56: NOKE
Y
Preparing...                          ################################# [100%]
Updating / installing...
   1:remi-release-7.5-2.el7.remi      ################################# [100%]
[root@localhost tmp]# _
```

Then, you need to enable the `remi` repository by editing the `remi yum config` file. First, open the `remi.repo` file in your `/etc/yum.repos.d` folder. Here, in this file, go to the section `remi`, then go down to the keyword enabled and change it from 0 to 1:

```
# Repository:  http://rpms.remirepo.net/
# Blog:        http://blog.remirepo.net/
# Forum:       http://forum.remirepo.net/

[remi]
name=Remi's RPM repository for Enterprise Linux 7 - $basearch
#baseurl=http://rpms.remirepo.net/enterprise/7/remi/$basearch/
#mirrorlist=https://rpms.remirepo.net/enterprise/7/remi/httpsmirror
mirrorlist=http://cdn.remirepo.net/enterprise/7/remi/mirror
enabled=0
gpgcheck=1
gpgkey=file:///etc/pki/rpm-gpg/RPM-GPG-KEY-remi

[remi-php55]
name=Remi's PHP 5.5 RPM repository for Enterprise Linux 7 - $basearch
#baseurl=http://rpms.remirepo.net/enterprise/7/php55/$basearch/
#mirrorlist=https://rpms.remirepo.net/enterprise/7/php55/httpsmirror
mirrorlist=http://cdn.remirepo.net/enterprise/7/php55/mirror
# NOTICE: common dependencies are in "remi-safe"
enabled=0
gpgcheck=1
gpgkey=file:///etc/pki/rpm-gpg/RPM-GPG-KEY-remi

[remi-php56]
"/etc/yum.repos.d/remi.repo" 71L, 2685C
```

Now save the file. Then you can use your newly installed third-party repository after updating your repositories software packages list. To recheck if the third-party repositories have been installed correctly, you can also use the `yum repolist` command again:

```
[root@localhost ~]# yum update -y
Loaded plugins: fastestmirror
Loading mirror speeds from cached hostfile
 * base: centos.excellmedia.net
 * epel: del-mirrors.extreme-ix.org
 * extras: centos.excellmedia.net
 * remi-safe: rpms.remirepo.net
 * updates: centos.excellmedia.net
remi-safe                                        | 2.9 kB   00:00
remi-safe/primary_db                             | 1.3 MB   00:01
No packages marked for update
[root@localhost ~]#
```

Introduction to services

In this section, we will show you how to work with services in CentOS 7.

Let's open your three VMs, master, client1, and client2, from the previous section of this chapter in three different tabs that are connected together on the same internal subnetwork.

Let's begin by installing a simple networking service. In our example, let's install the Apache2 web server on the master server, as it is very easy to set up and use:

```
Package              Arch              Version                    Repository        Size
================================================================================
Installing:
 httpd               x86_64            2.4.6-80.el7.centos        base              2.7 M

Transaction Summary
================================================================================
Install  1 Package

Total download size: 2.7 M
Installed size: 9.4 M
Downloading packages:
httpd-2.4.6-80.el7.centos.x86_64.rpm                          | 2.7 MB   00:00
Running transaction check
Running transaction test
Transaction test succeeded
Running transaction
  Installing : httpd-2.4.6-80.el7.centos.x86_64                            1/1
  Verifying  : httpd-2.4.6-80.el7.centos.x86_64                            1/1

Installed:
  httpd.x86_64 0:2.4.6-80.el7.centos

Complete!
[root@localhost ~]# _
```

Now, following installation of the `httpd` package on CentOS 7, you can manage services using the `systemctl` command, which is part of the `systemd` service.

To get a list of all the units currently available in the system, use the following command: `system ctl list-units`. This will open the unit list with less navigation:

```
UNIT                                               LOAD   ACTIVE SUB         DESCRIPTION
proc-sys-fs-binfmt_misc.automount                  loaded active waiting     Arbitrary Executable
sys-devices-pci0000:00-0000:00:01.1-ata1-host0-target0:0:0-0:0:0:0-block-sda-s
sys-devices-pci0000:00-0000:00:01.1-ata1-host0-target0:0:0-0:0:0:0-block-sda-s
sys-devices-pci0000:00-0000:00:01.1-ata1-host0-target0:0:0-0:0:0:0-block-sda.d
sys-devices-pci0000:00-0000:00:01.1-ata2-host1-target1:0:0-1:0:0:0-block-sr0.d
sys-devices-pci0000:00-0000:00:03.0-net-enp0s3.device loaded active plugged
sys-devices-pci0000:00-0000:00:05.0-sound-card0.device loaded active plugged
sys-devices-platform-serial8250-tty-ttyS0.device   loaded active plugged     /sys/
sys-devices-platform-serial8250-tty-ttyS1.device   loaded active plugged     /sys/
sys-devices-platform-serial8250-tty-ttyS2.device   loaded active plugged     /sys/
sys-devices-platform-serial8250-tty-ttyS3.device   loaded active plugged     /sys/
sys-devices-virtual-block-dm\x2d0.device           loaded active plugged     /sys/devices/
sys-devices-virtual-block-dm\x2d1.device           loaded active plugged     /sys/devices/
sys-module-configfs.device                         loaded active plugged     /sys/module/configfs
sys-subsystem-net-devices-enp0s3.device            loaded active plugged     82540EM Gigabi
-.mount                                            loaded active mounted     /
boot.mount                                         loaded active mounted     /boot
dev-hugepages.mount                                loaded active mounted     Huge Pages File System
dev-mqueue.mount                                   loaded active mounted     POSIX Message Queue File Sy
run-user-0.mount                                   loaded active mounted     /run/user/0
sys-kernel-config.mount                            loaded active mounted     Configuration File System
sys-kernel-debug.mount                             loaded active mounted     Debug File System
brandbot.path                                      loaded active waiting     Flexible branding
lines 1-24
```

As you can see, different kinds of unit files are available; for example, one that ends with `device`, one that ends with `mount`, and the service files. Press *q* to quit the navigation. To get a list of all the services currently available in your system, just type `systemctl list-unit-files` and then filter for services by using `--type=service`. In this list, you will see all the available services currently enabled or disabled in your system. As we installed Apache2 Web Server an `httpd services` file that is currently disabled also exists. To get a detailed status of a single service, use the `systemctl` command with the `status` option and the service name; in our example, the `httpd` service:

```
[root@localhost ~]# systemctl status httpd.service
* httpd.service - The Apache HTTP Server
   Loaded: loaded (/usr/lib/systemd/system/httpd.service; disabled; vendor prese
t: disabled)
   Active: active (running) since Thu 2018-06-28 08:15:15 EDT; 3s ago
     Docs: man:httpd(8)
           man:apachectl(8)
 Main PID: 1811 (httpd)
   Status: "Processing requests..."
   CGroup: /system.slice/httpd.service
           ├─1811 /usr/sbin/httpd -DFOREGROUND
           ├─1812 /usr/sbin/httpd -DFOREGROUND
           ├─1813 /usr/sbin/httpd -DFOREGROUND
           ├─1814 /usr/sbin/httpd -DFOREGROUND
           ├─1815 /usr/sbin/httpd -DFOREGROUND
           └─1816 /usr/sbin/httpd -DFOREGROUND

Jun 28 08:15:15 localhost.localdomain systemd[1]: Starting The Apache HTTP Se...
Jun 28 08:15:15 localhost.localdomain httpd[1811]: AH00558: httpd: Could not ...
Jun 28 08:15:15 localhost.localdomain systemd[1]: Started The Apache HTTP Ser...
Hint: Some lines were ellipsized, use -l to show in full.
[root@localhost ~]# _
```

As you can see, following installation of our new Apache HTTP server, the service is not running. By default, there are two different states a `systemd` service can have that are important for us: enabled or disabled, and active or inactive. In our example, the `httpd` service is disabled and inactive by default after installation. Just like any other service, the Apache HTTP server, by default, is disabled and inactive. Enabled means that a service should automatically start every time you start your Linux system, which is also referred to as on boot. Active means that a service is currently running.

To start a service, use the `systemctl start` option and then the name of the service; in our, example, the `httpd.service`. Now recheck the service, using the `status` option again:

```
[root@localhost ~]# systemctl status httpd.service
 httpd.service - The Apache HTTP Server
   Loaded: loaded (/usr/lib/systemd/system/httpd.service; disabled; vendor prese
t: disabled)
   Active: active (running) since Thu 2018-06-28 08:15:15 EDT; 48s ago
     Docs: man:httpd(8)
           man:apachectl(8)
 Main PID: 1811 (httpd)
   Status: "Total requests: 0; Current requests/sec: 0; Current traffic:   0 B/s
ec"
   CGroup: /system.slice/httpd.service
           ├─1811 /usr/sbin/httpd -DFOREGROUND
           ├─1812 /usr/sbin/httpd -DFOREGROUND
           ├─1813 /usr/sbin/httpd -DFOREGROUND
           ├─1814 /usr/sbin/httpd -DFOREGROUND
           ├─1815 /usr/sbin/httpd -DFOREGROUND
           └─1816 /usr/sbin/httpd -DFOREGROUND

Jun 28 08:15:15 localhost.localdomain systemd[1]: Starting The Apache HTTP Se...
Jun 28 08:15:15 localhost.localdomain httpd[1811]: AH00558: httpd: Could not ...
Jun 28 08:15:15 localhost.localdomain systemd[1]: Started The Apache HTTP Ser...
Hint: Some lines were ellipsized, use -l to show in full.
[root@localhost ~]# _
```

As you can see, it's now running. Also, you can see two other very important things in the output here. First, you can see that a service can consist of several processes. In our example, the httpd service consists of six different HTTP processes. The other important thing is that the `systemctl status` command will output the last lines of messages generated by the service when it is started up. Such lines of useful text generated by a process are also called a log and can give us useful information about the running behavior of a service. Still, our service is disabled. To enable it, use the `systemctl enable` option. Now view the status again:

```
Jun 28 08:15:15 localhost.localdomain systemd[1]: Started The Apache HTTP Ser...
Hint: Some lines were ellipsized, use -l to show in full.
[root@localhost ~]# systemctl status httpd.service
■ httpd.service - The Apache HTTP Server
   Loaded: loaded (/usr/lib/systemd/system/httpd.service; disabled; vendor prese
t: disabled)
   Active: active (running) since Thu 2018-06-28 08:15:15 EDT; 2min 4s ago
     Docs: man:httpd(8)
           man:apachectl(8)
 Main PID: 1811 (httpd)
   Status: "Total requests: 0; Current requests/sec: 0; Current traffic:    0 B/s
ec"
   CGroup: /system.slice/httpd.service
           ├─1811 /usr/sbin/httpd -DFOREGROUND
           ├─1812 /usr/sbin/httpd -DFOREGROUND
           ├─1813 /usr/sbin/httpd -DFOREGROUND
           ├─1814 /usr/sbin/httpd -DFOREGROUND
           ├─1815 /usr/sbin/httpd -DFOREGROUND
           └─1816 /usr/sbin/httpd -DFOREGROUND

Jun 28 08:15:15 localhost.localdomain systemd[1]: Starting The Apache HTTP Se...
Jun 28 08:15:15 localhost.localdomain httpd[1811]: AH00558: httpd: Could not ...
Jun 28 08:15:15 localhost.localdomain systemd[1]: Started The Apache HTTP Ser...
Hint: Some lines were ellipsized, use -l to show in full.
[root@localhost ~]#
```

You can see now that it's also enabled, so this service will automatically start up every time we restart our server. To stop a currently running service, use the `systemctl stop` option. We will see that it's inactive again.

It's important to note that starting or stopping will not influence the service's disabled or enabled server boot behavior. Here, this service is still enabled while it's not running. This is also true for the other way around. Disabling or enabling a service will not start or stop it.

To disable a service, use the `systemctl disable` option. Then, again, start the service up. Now, to test if our HTTP server is working and can host and deliver web content, let's first create a standard home page for our server. The standard home page for our server is the `index.html` file in the `/var/www/html` folder. Now, incorporate the following HTML content, which is a greeting message from our server:

```
<html>
<head></head>
<body>
Hello from Master Server
</body>
</html>
```

Save and exit the file. Now, to access our home page from our new web server on the master server where this web server is located, use `wget`:

```
[root@localhost www]# wget -qO- http://localhost
<html>
<head></head>
<body>
Hello from the Master Server
</body>
</html>
[root@localhost www]#
```

As you can see, we can properly access the home page locally from our master server. Now, what happens if you stop the web service and try again to access our web page? You will see that the web page is not accessible any more. Restart the web server. Now, let's test if we can access our new web server from another machine in our local network. Just go to the client1 tab and test if the web server is accessible through the network. You will see that it is not.

Basic system troubleshooting and firewalling

In this section, we will continue our work on the Apache2 Web Server we started in the last section, so as to make it accessible for other computers in our subnetwork. Also, we will give you a brief introduction to Linux firewalls in CentOS 7.

As briefly mentioned in the first section of this chapter, a network connection is always made through a combination of an IP address and the port, which together is called a socket address. Now, every Linux network service, such as a mail or web server, must be connected to an IP address and the port so that we can establish a connection to it at all from a different computer in the network or from the same local one:

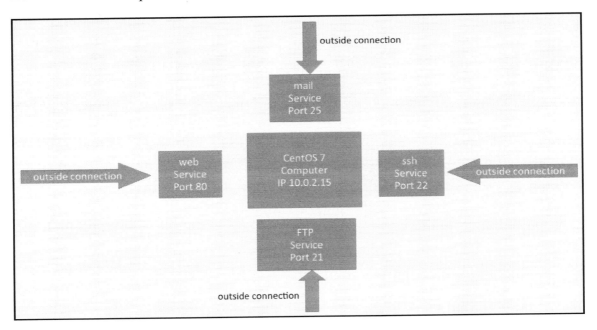

When we are talking about network communication, we often refer to this as "a service is listening to IP address a port b". For example, our web server is listening on port 80 of the IP address 10.0.2.15, the mail service is listening on port 24, the web service is listening on port 80 of the IP address 10.0.2.15, and the FTP service is listening on port 21 of IP address 10.0.2.15.

But maybe you are wondering which IP address does a service use for communication if we have configured multiple network interfaces on our system, all with a different IP address? The answer to this is simple. Most networking services on any Linux system listen to all available network interfaces for network connections by default after installation. For almost all standard services, you can also change this to listen only to a specific network interface, or network connection, or subnetwork, or even ranges of networks:

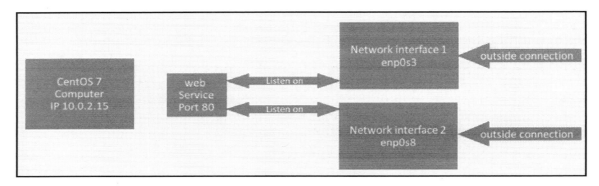

Some even only listen to a localhost by default after installation, as these often are very critical services where system administrators need to change the listening address intentionally as a measurement of responsibility to make them aware of the risks.

So let's say you have a Linux server that is running several networking services and each is listening on a different port. A firewall is a tool for managing connections to your computer. In Linux, the standard firewall is called **firewalld**. This firewall can protect your system against unwanted network connections from outside your system, for example, if some intruder is trying to break into your system and steal data. It does so by managing your incoming network ports for communication. By default, `firewalld` closes all incoming network ports except the port 22 for SSH connections. Otherwise, you would not be able to remotely connect to your machine:

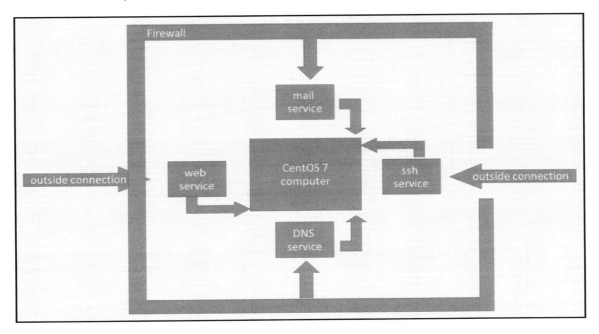

So if you want to have some kind of network communication, you have to explicitly tell the firewall to do so. You can open or close individual ports or ranges of ports, and so on. This helps a lot in managing security on your server, but it's important to note that, by default, firewalld does not restrict any local network communication within a system, so the localhost network connection is always working and is not blocked by the firewall. Also, it's very important to know that firewalld, by default, is an incoming firewall only, which means it does not block any outgoing connections at all:

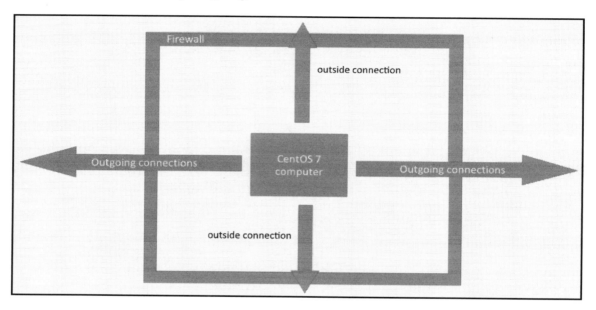

In order to fix this problem, we need to know how we can troubleshoot a system service. So, first go back to our master server where this web server is running. To find out if something is wrong with your service, there are always at least three places where to look. The first thing we should do is to check the `systemctl status` output, as we have done before. As you can see, the service is currently running and the final current lines of output of the service also look `OK`:

```
[root@localhost www]# systemctl status httpd.service
 httpd.service - The Apache HTTP Server
   Loaded: loaded (/usr/lib/systemd/system/httpd.service; disabled; vendor prese
t: disabled)
   Active: active (running) since Thu 2018-06-28 08:15:15 EDT; 9min ago
     Docs: man:httpd(8)
           man:apachectl(8)
 Main PID: 1811 (httpd)
   Status: "Total requests: 2; Current requests/sec: 0; Current traffic:    0 B/s
ec"
   CGroup: /system.slice/httpd.service
           ├─1811 /usr/sbin/httpd -DFOREGROUND
           ├─1812 /usr/sbin/httpd -DFOREGROUND
           ├─1813 /usr/sbin/httpd -DFOREGROUND
           ├─1814 /usr/sbin/httpd -DFOREGROUND
           ├─1815 /usr/sbin/httpd -DFOREGROUND
           └─1816 /usr/sbin/httpd -DFOREGROUND

Jun 28 08:15:15 localhost.localdomain systemd[1]: Starting The Apache HTTP Se...
Jun 28 08:15:15 localhost.localdomain httpd[1811]: AH00558: httpd: Could not ...
Jun 28 08:15:15 localhost.localdomain systemd[1]: Started The Apache HTTP Ser...
Hint: Some lines were ellipsized, use -l to show in full.
[root@localhost www]#
```

Sometimes, here in this output, you will find error messages or warnings if a service is not functioning normally.

Sometimes, the last two lines of the log output for a service are not enough, so the second place to look for if you need to troubleshoot your service, is the journalctl command. If you use the journalctl command with the -u flag, you can filter log messages for your service of choice; in our example, the httpd service:

```
[root@localhost www]# journalctl -u httpd.service
-- Logs begin at Thu 2018-06-28 07:50:38 EDT, end at Thu 2018-06-28 08:15:15 EDT
Jun 28 08:15:15 localhost.localdomain systemd[1]: Starting The Apache HTTP Serve
Jun 28 08:15:15 localhost.localdomain httpd[1811]: AH00558: httpd: Could not rel
Jun 28 08:15:15 localhost.localdomain systemd[1]: Started The Apache HTTP Server
lines 1-4/4 (END)
```

Here, in our example, no suspicious log output can be found in `journald`, which is the service that writes all the log messages of all the services running into a centralized database. The journal log for the Apache HTTP Server looks normal.

So, the third place where we can have a look for troubleshooting services is the `rsyslog` log file, which is located at `/var/log/messages`. Open this file and go to the end of it, pressing capital *G*:

```
Jun 28 08:00:48 localhost yum[1329]: Installed: mailcap-2.1.41-2.el7.noarch
Jun 28 08:00:48 localhost yum[1329]: Installed: httpd-tools-2.4.6-80.el7.centos.
x86_64
Jun 28 08:00:49 localhost systemd: Reloading.
Jun 28 08:00:49 localhost yum[1329]: Installed: httpd-2.4.6-80.el7.centos.x86_64
Jun 28 08:01:02 localhost systemd: Started Session 2 of user root.
Jun 28 08:01:02 localhost systemd: Starting Session 2 of user root.
Jun 28 08:01:43 localhost yum[1425]: Erased: httpd-2.4.6-80.el7.centos.x86_64
Jun 28 08:01:43 localhost systemd: Reloading.
Jun 28 08:02:01 localhost systemd: Reloading.
Jun 28 08:02:01 localhost yum[1446]: Installed: httpd-2.4.6-80.el7.centos.x86_64
Jun 28 08:04:09 localhost yum[1542]: Erased: epel-release-7-11.noarch
Jun 28 08:04:24 localhost yum[1544]: Installed: epel-release-7-11.noarch
Jun 28 08:05:53 localhost systemd: Starting Cleanup of Temporary Directories...
Jun 28 08:05:53 localhost systemd: Started Cleanup of Temporary Directories.
Jun 28 08:11:53 localhost yum[1687]: Erased: httpd-2.4.6-80.el7.centos.x86_64
Jun 28 08:11:53 localhost systemd: Reloading.
Jun 28 08:12:29 localhost systemd: Reloading.
Jun 28 08:12:29 localhost yum[1707]: Installed: httpd-2.4.6-80.el7.centos.x86_64
Jun 28 08:15:15 localhost systemd: Starting The Apache HTTP Server...
Jun 28 08:15:15 localhost httpd: AH00558: httpd: Could not reliably determine th
e server's fully qualified domain name, using localhost.localdomain. Set the 'Se
rverName' directive globally to suppress this message
Jun 28 08:15:15 localhost systemd: Started The Apache HTTP Server.
[root@localhost www]#
```

Here also, nothing really suspicious has been logged to the `rsyslog` file.

Some services, such as our Apache HTTP Web Server, provide their own log files for troubleshooting or getting info about the service.

Please note that there is no standardized directory where a service outputs its own log files, but some services write their log files into a subdirectory under the `/var/log` file directory. Here, you can find two log files. One is the `access_log`, which logs user access to our web server (for example, the files on the server that have been downloaded). The other is the `error_log` file, which logs all kinds of errors that this service may encounter. So, first have a look at the `access_log` file:

```
[root@localhost httpd]# less access_log
127.0.0.1 - - [28/Jun/2018:08:21:10 -0400] "GET / HTTP/1.1" 403 4897 "-" "Wget/1
.14 (linux-gnu)"
127.0.0.1 - - [28/Jun/2018:08:23:34 -0400] "GET / HTTP/1.1" 200 73 "-" "Wget/1.1
4 (linux-gnu)"
access_log (END)
```

This looks very normal. Now, also open the error_log file. Jump to the end using capital G:

```
[root@localhost httpd]# less error_log
[Thu Jun 28 08:15:15.305301 2018] [core:notice] [pid 1811] SELinux policy enable
d; httpd running as context system_u:system_r:httpd_t:s0
[Thu Jun 28 08:15:15.306911 2018] [suexec:notice] [pid 1811] AH01232: suEXEC mec
hanism enabled (wrapper: /usr/sbin/suexec)
AH00558: httpd: Could not reliably determine the server's fully qualified domain
 name, using localhost.localdomain. Set the 'ServerName' directive globally to s
uppress this message
[Thu Jun 28 08:15:15.314374 2018] [auth_digest:notice] [pid 1811] AH01757: gener
ating secret for digest authentication ...
[Thu Jun 28 08:15:15.315119 2018] [lbmethod_heartbeat:notice] [pid 1811] AH02282
: No slotmem from mod_heartmonitor
[Thu Jun 28 08:15:15.316853 2018] [mpm_prefork:notice] [pid 1811] AH00163: Apach
e/2.4.6 (CentOS) configured -- resuming normal operations
[Thu Jun 28 08:15:15.316874 2018] [core:notice] [pid 1811] AH00094: Command line
: '/usr/sbin/httpd -D FOREGROUND'
[Thu Jun 28 08:21:10.524529 2018] [autoindex:error] [pid 1816] [client 127.0.0.1
:52593] AH01276: Cannot serve directory /var/www/html/: No matching DirectoryInd
ex (index.html) found, and server-generated directory index forbidden by Options
 directive
error_log (END)
```

Here, no special error messages can be found.

The solution to the problem of why nobody outside of our server can access the Apache HTTP Web Server instead of CentOS 7 is that a very restrictive firewall is active that blocks almost any incoming network connection.

You can view the currently allowed firewall rules by typing `firewall-cmd --list-all`. On CentOS 7, the standard firewall is called firewalld:

```
[root@localhost httpd]# cd /var/log/httpd/
[root@localhost httpd]# ls
access_log   error_log
[root@localhost httpd]# firewall-cmd --list-all
public
  target: default
  icmp-block-inversion: no
  interfaces:
  sources:
  services: dhcpv6-client ssh
  ports:
  protocols:
  masquerade: no
  forward-ports:
  source-ports:
  icmp-blocks:
  rich rules:

[root@localhost httpd]#
```

As you can see here, only the SSH service is allowed by default to communicate with our server. Firewalld is mainly protecting all incoming network connections. Outgoing connections from our server to other servers are not restricted or limited; that's the reason why we can access our web server from the localhost, but not from any other host.

To fix this problem, we can open the HTTP service, also known as opening port 80, in our firewall. So that we can do that permanently, use the following two commands: `firewall-cmd --permanent --add-service`, and then `http`. So that the changes can be applied, next reload the firewall rules. Finally, let's see if the HTTP service is now enabled in the firewall:

```
[root@localhost httpd]# firewall-cmd --permanent --add-service http
success
[root@localhost httpd]# firewall-cmd --reload
success
[root@localhost httpd]# firewall-cmd --list-all
public
  target: default
  icmp-block-inversion: no
  interfaces:
  sources:
  services: dhcpv6-client ssh http
  ports:
  protocols:
  masquerade: no
  forward-ports:
  source-ports:
  icmp-blocks:
  rich rules:

[root@localhost httpd]# _
```

As you can see, it works.

Finally, let's test if we can make remote connections to our Apache Web Server from another server. Go to client1 and repeat the wget command:

```
[root@client1 olip]# wget -qO- http://master
[root@client1 olip]# wget -qO- http://master
<html>
<head></head>
<body>
Hello from Master Server
</body>
</html>
```

Yes, it works! You are now able to access your web server in your network.

Until now, we haven't talked about how to remove a service from the firewall. To remove the HTTP service or port from the firewall configuration, use the following firewall command syntax, firewall-cmd --permanent --remove-service.

Then the service of choice; in our example, the `http` service. Similar to adding a service, you also have to reload the firewall here. Let's recheck our firewall settings:

```
[root@localhost httpd]# firewall-cmd --list-all
public
  target: default
  icmp-block-inversion: no
  interfaces:
  sources:
  services: dhcpv6-client ssh http
  ports:
  protocols:
  masquerade: no
  forward-ports:
  source-ports:
  icmp-blocks:
  rich rules:

[root@localhost httpd]#
```

As you can see, HTTP port has been closed.

Finally, a very useful feature of the firewalld service is to open individual port numbers without providing a service name. This is very useful if you need to open a port where no service file, such as the HTTP, is available. For example, to open port `12345`, use the TCP protocol. Let's show the new firewall configuration after we have reloaded the firewall:

```
[root@localhost ~]# firewall-cmd --permanent --add-port=12345/tcp
Warning: ALREADY_ENABLED: 12345:tcp
success
[root@localhost ~]# firewall-cmd --reload
success
[root@localhost ~]# firewall-cmd --list-all
public
  target: default
  icmp-block-inversion: no
  interfaces:
  sources:
  services: dhcpv6-client ssh http
  ports: 12345/tcp
  protocols:
  masquerade: no
  forward-ports:
  source-ports:
  icmp-blocks:
  rich rules:

[root@localhost ~]#
```

As you can see, the port `12345` is now open using the TCP protocol. Instead of TCP, you can also use the UDP protocol. Now, to close the port `12345` using the TCP protocol, use the following command. Here, also reload the firewall configuration. Let's perform a recheck:

```
[root@localhost ~]# firewall-cmd --permanent --remove-port=12345/tcp
success
[root@localhost ~]# firewall-cmd --reload
success
[root@localhost ~]# firewall-cmd --list-all
public
  target: default
  icmp-block-inversion: no
  interfaces:
  sources:
  services: dhcpv6-client ssh http
  ports:
  protocols:
  masquerade: no
  forward-ports:
  source-ports:
  icmp-blocks:
  rich rules:

[root@localhost ~]#
```

Let's summarize what we have learned so far:

1. If it is a service-related problem, first have a look at the `systemctl` output for the service.
2. If the problem persists, next look at the `journalctl` output for the service.
3. If it is a general system problem, or you cannot fix your service problems with the `systemctl` and `journalctl` outputs, next have a look at the `/var/log-messages rsyslog` output file.
4. Also, some services provide special log file locations outside of `journald` or the `rsyslog` file, so also have a look there. But you must be aware that not every service or program has such a special log file directory or output.
5. Finally, we gave you a brief introduction to the firewalld service using predefined service files, such as the HTTP, and also we showed you how to work with individual ports that are not defined by service files. In the next chapter, we will show you advanced file permissions.

Introducing ACLs

In this section, we will give you a brief introduction to how ACLs, or access control lists, work.

Linux has some special file and folder permissions, namely the ACLs, setuid, setgid, and sticky bit. If you look at the file in the filesystem, such as a new file that only the root user has access to, currently we are logged in as olip:

```
[root@localhost ~]# # acl, setuid, setgidm sticky bit
[root@localhost ~]# su -c 'touch /tmp/new-file'
[root@localhost ~]# su -c 'chmod 700 /tmp/new-file'
[root@localhost ~]# ls -l /tmp/new-file
-rwx------. 1 root root 0 Jun 28 08:51 /tmp/new-file
[root@localhost ~]# whoami
root
[root@localhost ~]# echo "Write content to the file" >> /tmp/new-file
```

As you can see, the olip user has no write access on that file. Maybe you have already asked yourself this question: how can you give permissions to a file or folder to individual users who are not the file or group owner, in our example root? The only way is to use the others group, but this is not individual as all users who are not the file or group owner fall into this category. But here, we want to set single user permissions; for example, for the olip user.

Access control lists, or ACLs, is a system that extends our normal file access control under Linux with its simple ownership and permission model. With ACLs you can define file or folder permissions on a single user or group-level basis. To work with ACLs, use the getfacl and setfacl commands.

For example, to display ACLs, use the getfacl command and then the filename where you want to show permissions:

```
[olip@localhost root]$ # getfacl, setfacl
[olip@localhost root]$ getfacl /tmp/new-file
getfacl: Removing leading '/' from absolute path names
# file: tmp/new-file
# owner: root
# group: root
user::rwx
group::---
other::---

[olip@localhost root]$
```

Here, as you can see, no ACLs have currently been set on this file. As with normal file permissions, if we want to change something, we need to log in as root. Now, to set ACLs, for example, for the `olip` user, use the following command. If you remember Chapter 3, *The Linux Filesystem*, this should be self-explanatory:

```
[olip@localhost root]$ su
Password:
[root@localhost ~]# setfacl -m user:olip:rwx /tmp/new-file
[root@localhost ~]# getfacl /tmp/new-file
getfacl: Removing leading '/' from absolute path names
# file: tmp/new-file
# owner: root
# group: root
user::rwx
user:olip:rwx
group::---
mask::rwx
other::---

[root@localhost ~]#
```

To display the ACL, again view the ACL of this file. If you compare the `getfacl` command output before and after, you will see that we now have single user permissions for the `olup` user: `read`, `write`, and `execute`. Now, the `olip` user should be able to write to this file:

```
[root@localhost ~]# echo "Write content to the file" >> /tmp/new-file
[root@localhost ~]#
```

Success; the ACLs are working as expected.

You can also set ACLs on a group-level basis. Here, instead of using the user, we will use the group identifier. To remove a single ACL, use the -x flag. You can also see if a file has an ACL set by the marked plus in the output of the `ls -l` command:

```
[root@localhost tmp]# getfacl /tmp/new-file
getfacl: Removing leading '/' from absolute path names
# file: tmp/new-file
# owner: root
# group: root
user::rwx
user:olip:rwx
group::---
group:it_department:r--
mask::rwx
other::---

[root@localhost tmp]# setfacl -x group:it_department /tmp/new-file
[root@localhost tmp]# getfacl /tmp/new-file
getfacl: Removing leading '/' from absolute path names
# file: tmp/new-file
# owner: root
# group: root
user::rwx
user:olip:rwx
group::---
mask::rwx
other::---

[root@localhost tmp]# _
# file: tmp/new-file
# owner: root
# group: root
user::rwx
user:olip:rwx
group::---
group:it_department:r--
mask::rwx
other::---

[root@localhost tmp]# setfacl -x group:it_department /tmp/new-file
[root@localhost tmp]# getfacl /tmp/new-file
getfacl: Removing leading '/' from absolute path names
# file: tmp/new-file
# owner: root
# group: root
user::rwx
user:olip:rwx
group::---
mask::rwx
other::---

[root@localhost tmp]# ls -l /tmp/new-file
-rwxrwx---+ 1 root root 52 Jun 28 08:57 /tmp/new-file
[root@localhost tmp]# _
```

setuid, setgid and sticky bit

In this section, we will show you everything you need to know about the special file permission flags, setid, setgid, and the sticky bit.

setuid

Now let's talk about setuid, setgid, and the sticky bit. As we work with users, groups, and file permissions, let's first log in as root.

First, let's create a new user, group, and the copy of the whoami command locally to see what's going on with the setuid flag:

```
[root@localhost tmp]# su
[root@localhost tmp]# adduser awesome_user
[root@localhost tmp]# groupadd awesome_group
[root@localhost tmp]# cp /usr/bin/whoami /home/olip/whoami-local
[root@localhost tmp]#
```

Next, let's change the file owner and group owner of this command to awesome_user and awesome_group:

```
[root@localhost tmp]# chown awesome_user:awesome_group /home/olip/whoami-local
```

Setting the setuid, setgid, and the sticky bit can also be done using octal notations. You already know about them from the file permissions chapter. These special permissions can be represented by one single additional bit in the file permission string, using the following code:

```
[root@localhost tmp]# # setuid=4, setgid=2, sticky bit=1
```

The setuid has the number 4, the setgid the number 2, and the sticky bit the number 1. Similar to the files' simple read, write, and execute permissions, here you can also add combinations of special permissions to a file:

```
[root@localhost tmp]# # setuid=4, setgid=2, sticky bit=1
[root@localhost tmp]# # setuid + setgid = 4 + 2 = 6
[root@localhost tmp]# # setuid + setgid = 2 + 1 = 3
[root@localhost tmp]# # sticky bit + setuid = 5
[root@localhost tmp]#
```

If you want to set both setuid and setgid flags, you need to add up the 4 and the 2, which totals 6, or setgid and sticky bit are represented by the 3, or sticky bit and setuid are represented by the 5.

Now, how do we set the special permission information? It can be set using an additional number in the chmod command. You already know that it takes three numbers to define permissions for the user, group, and others. To display special permissions on the file, you can use the ls -l command, but this is very hard to read and it's more easy to use the getfacl command, which not only works for ACLs, but also shows flags that are the names for our special permissions. By default, no flag or special permission is defined on any file, as you can see in the output of the getfacl command:

```
[root@localhost tmp]# chmod 755 /home/olip/whoami-local
[root@localhost tmp]# ls -l /home/olip/whoami-local
-rwxr-xr-x. 1 awesome_user awesome_group 28984 Jun 28 09:06 /home/olip/whoami-lo
cal
[root@localhost tmp]#
```

Now, to add a special permission flag to a file, or, in other words, set the `setuid`, `setgid`, or `sticky bit`, you can use the `chmod` command with four numbers instead of three, where the first leading number defines the special permission. For example, if you use a 2 as the leading first number for the `chmod` command, you will set the set group ID flag, which is shown in the flags line. If we have an s at the second position, it's the set group ID:

```
[root@localhost tmp]# chmod 2755 /home/olip/whoami-local
[root@localhost tmp]#
[root@localhost tmp]# getfacl /home/olip/whoami-local
getfacl: Removing leading '/' from absolute path names
# file: home/olip/whoami-local
# owner: awesome_user
# group: awesome_group
# flags: -s-
user::rwx
group::r-x
other::r-x

[root@localhost tmp]#
```

Now, to set the `setuid` flag, use number 4 as your first number in the `chmod` command. Recheck using the `getfacl` command. Here, in the flags line, the first leftmost character has been set to an s:

```
[root@localhost tmp]# chmod 4755 /home/olip/whoami-local
[root@localhost tmp]# getfacl /home/olip/whoami-local
getfacl: Removing leading '/' from absolute path names
# file: home/olip/whoami-local
# owner: awesome_user
# group: awesome_group
# flags: s--
user::rwx
group::r-x
other::r-x

[root@localhost tmp]#
```

Now, adding a combination of special file permission flags (for example, number 6, which is a combination of setuid and setgid, or 4 plus 2, equals 6), is shown in the following way in the getfacl output:

```
[root@localhost tmp]# # setuid + setgid = 4 + 2 = 6
[root@localhost tmp]#
[root@localhost tmp]# getfacl /home/olip/whoami-local
getfacl: Removing leading '/' from absolute path names
# file: home/olip/whoami-local
# owner: awesome_user
# group: awesome_group
# flags: s--
user::rwx
group::r-x
other::r-x

[root@localhost tmp]#
```

The first leftmost flag is the setuid flag, and the second flag is the setgid flag. To set all three permission types, setuid, setgid, and sticky bit, use getfacl (path):

```
[root@localhost tmp]# chmod 7755 /home/olip/whoami-local
[root@localhost tmp]# getfacl /home/olip/whoami-local
getfacl: Removing leading '/' from absolute path names
# file: home/olip/whoami-local
# owner: awesome_user
# group: awesome_group
# flags: sst
user::rwx
group::r-x
other::r-x

[root@localhost tmp]#
```

Here, you see that all three flags have been set. The short flag for the sticky bit is a t instead of an s.

To remove all special file permissions, just use 0 as the number for the file permission encoding, and just use 0 as the first number for the chmod command:

```
[root@localhost tmp]# chmod 0755 /home/olip/whoami-local
[root@localhost tmp]#
```

Now, let's briefly discuss the setuid permissions. The setuid flag is only important on executable commands and never on a directory or other file types. It is also important to know that it does not work on script files for security reasons, but only on compiled binary executable files.

As already mentioned, each process has an associated user that we refer to as "a user runs a command". Here, in this example, all the processes you see are run by the root user:

```
[root@localhost tmp]# ls -l /etc/passwd
-rw-r--r--. 1 root root 1353 Jun 28 09:06 /etc/passwd
[root@localhost tmp]#
```

Now the setuid permission flag will run a command as the user that is defined as the file owner of that file. This is important and useful for some special commands in the system; for example, commands that must be run as the root user because they access protected filesystem files or folders, but must also be executable for normal users. Take, for example, the passwd command. It accesses and writes to files such as the etc/passwd file, which is only writable for root, so this command must be run as root, but normal users also need to change their passwords on the passwd command:

```
[root@localhost tmp]# exit
exit
[root@localhost tmp]# whoami
root
[root@localhost tmp]# /home/olip/whoami-local
root
[root@localhost tmp]#
```

Now, let's exit the root user to test the setuid flag with a normal user account.

Let's recheck if we are really the `olip` user. Now, without setting the `setuid` flag on a file, if we execute our local `whoami` command, it will print out our username, as we are the user who started it:

```
[root@localhost tmp]# su -c 'chmod 4555 /home/olip/whoami-local'
[root@localhost tmp]# getfacl /home/olip/whoami-local
getfacl: Removing leading '/' from absolute path names
# file: home/olip/whoami-local
# owner: awesome_user
# group: awesome_group
# flags: s--
user::r-x
group::r-x
other::r-x

[root@localhost tmp]# /home/olip/whoami-local
awesome_user
[root@localhost tmp]# _
```

Now, what happens if we set the `setuid` permission on that command and execute it again? First, let's view the permission flags. We will see that the `setuid` flag has been successfully set on that file. Now, let's execute a command again:

```
[root@localhost tmp]# su -c 'chmod 2755 /home/olip/whoami-local'
[root@localhost tmp]# getfacl /home/olip/whoami-local
getfacl: Removing leading '/' from absolute path names
# file: home/olip/whoami-local
# owner: awesome_user
# group: awesome_group
# flags: -s-
user::rwx
group::r-x
other::r-x

[root@localhost tmp]#
```

As you can see, the `setuid` flag works as expected. We run our command as the `olip` user but the file owner, `awesome_user`, was used during the execution of the process.

setgid

Now, let's learn about the `setgid` permission. This flag has two different meanings, which is important to know about and should be memorized. When set on a file, it has the same effect as the `setuid` permission, but here it will execute a command with the rights of the group owner instead of the file owner.

To set the `setgid` flag on the file, use the number 2 in the `chmod` command:

```
[root@localhost tmp]# mkdir project_folder
[root@localhost tmp]# su -c 'chown :awesome_group project_folder'
[root@localhost tmp]# touch project_folder/filea
[root@localhost tmp]# ls -l project_folder/filea
-rw-r--r--. 1 root root 0 Jun 28 09:25 project_folder/filea
[root@localhost tmp]# su -c 'chmod 2777 project_folder'
[root@localhost tmp]# touch project_folder/fileb
[root@localhost tmp]# ls -l project_folder/
total 0
-rw-r--r--. 1 root root         0 Jun 28 09:25 filea
-rw-r--r--. 1 root awesome_group 0 Jun 28 09:26 fileb
[root@localhost tmp]# _
```

The second meaning of the `setgid` flag is very important and should be memorized because it can be a typical use case. If you set the `setgid` on a folder instead of a file, every new file, or folder, or subfolder created within this folder will automatically get the group permissions of the folder where you set the `setgid` flag. This works for all the files included recursively. This can become very important because normally the group permissions of new files created automatically get assigned by the creator of the file.

So if you want to separate locations in your filesystems for collaborations or group work where you can put in shared files for anyone belonging to a special group, setgid is a very powerful feature. This is like a shared folder you may know about from other operating systems. So if you want to separate your filesystems into locations for collaborations or group work, where anybody who is belonging to a special group can create documents that automatically can be fully accessed by other persons of that same group, just set a setgid flag on a folder.

To test this:

1. Create a new folder under the username olip.
2. Now, change the group ownership to awesome_group. Now, if a user creates a new file in this folder, it will have the group ownership of that user.
3. Now, let's set the setgid flag on that folder and see what happens.
4. Let's create a new file under the username olip in that folder where we set the setgid flag:

```
[root@localhost tmp]# getfacl /tmp/
getfacl: Removing leading '/' from absolute path names
# file: tmp/
# owner: root
# group: root
# flags: --t
user::rwx
group::rwx
other::rwx

[root@localhost tmp]# _
```

As you can see, any new file created in this folder now gets the group ownership of the folder, which is awesome_group. So our setgid flag is working properly.

sticky bit

`sticky bit` only has an effect on directories and not on files. If `sticky bit` is set on a folder, only the owner of a specific file, folder, or subfolder created in that directory is allowed to delete it. There are some special cases where this is useful, for example, in the `/tmp` directory, where anybody should be allowed to see anything, but quite often processes create and rely on data stored in that folder, so it would be very bad if someone other than the creator of the process could be able to delete files from other users.

So let's test this out:

```
[root@localhost tmp]# getfacl /tmp/
getfacl: Removing leading '/' from absolute path names
# file: tmp/
# owner: root
# group: root
# flags: --t
user::rwx
group::rwx
other::rwx
[root@localhost tmp]# touch /tmp/file-of-user-awesome
[root@localhost tmp]# rm /tmp/file-of-user-awesome
rm: remove regular empty file '/tmp/file-of-user-awesome'? y
[root@localhost tmp]# rm /tmp/file-of-user-olip
rm: remove regular empty file '/tmp/file-of-user-olip'? y
[root@localhost tmp]#
```

As you can see, `sticky bit` has been set on the /tmp directory, so let's create a new file with the `olip` user in the /tmp directory. Now, let's look in with `awesome_user`. As no password has been set, let's set one for it. Now, `awesome_user` will also create a new file in the /tmp directory. Now, let's try to delete our own file, which works. Now, let's try to delete the file of the `olip` user; this does not work, so `sticky bit` is working as expected:

```
[olip@master ~]$ getfacl /tmp/
getfacl: Removing leading '/' from absolute path names
# file: tmp/
# owner: root
# group: root
# flags: --t
user::rwx
group::rwx
other::rwx

[olip@master ~]$ touch /tmp/file-of-user-olip
[olip@master ~]$ su -c 'passwd awesome_user'
Password:
Changing password for user awesome_user.
New password:
BAD PASSWORD: The password is shorter than 8 characters
Retype new password:
passwd: all authentication tokens updated successfully.
[olip@master ~]$ su awesome_user
Password:
[awesome_user@master olip]$ touch /tmp/file-of-user-awesome
[awesome_user@master olip]$ rm /tmp/file-of-user-awesome
[awesome_user@master olip]$ rm /tmp/file-of-user-olip
rm: remove write-protected regular empty file '/tmp/file-of-user-olip'? y
rm: cannot remove '/tmp/file-of-user-olip': Operation not permitted
[awesome_user@master olip]$
```

Summary

In this chapter, we gave you a brief introduction to special file permission flags in Linux. The `setuid` flag works only on commands and not on scripts, and lets a program execute as the user defined as the file owner instead of the user who is running that program. The `setgid` flag has two special meanings. The first is for commands and the other for folders. If you set it on a command, it will work like the `setuid` flag, but will run it as the group ownership of that file instead of the file owner of that file. The second meaning is if you set it on a folder, the group owner of the folder where you set `setgid` will automatically be assigned to every new file you created within that folder. Within a directory where `sticky bit` has been set, only the file owner can delete his own files

Other Books You May Enjoy

If you enjoyed this book, you may be interested in these other books by Packt:

Mastering Linux Shell Scripting - Second Edition
Mokhtar Ebrahim, Andrew Mallett

ISBN: 978-1-78899-055-4

- Make, execute, and debug your first Bash script
- Create interactive scripts that prompt for user input
- Foster menu structures for operators with little command-line experience
- Develop scripts that dynamically edit web configuration files to produce a new virtual host
- Write scripts that use AWK to search and reports on log files
- Draft effective scripts using functions as building blocks, reducing maintenance and build time
- Make informed choices by comparing different script languages such as Python with BASH

Mastering Linux Security and Hardening
Donald A. Tevault

ISBN: 978-1-78862-030-7

- Use various techniques to prevent intruders from accessing sensitive data
- Prevent intruders from planting malware, and detect whether malware has been planted
- Prevent insiders from accessing data that they aren't authorized to access
- Do quick checks to see whether a computer is running network services that it doesn't need to run
- Learn security techniques that are common to all Linux distros, and some that are distro-specific

Leave a review - let other readers know what you think

Please share your thoughts on this book with others by leaving a review on the site that you bought it from. If you purchased the book from Amazon, please leave us an honest review on this book's Amazon page. This is vital so that other potential readers can see and use your unbiased opinion to make purchasing decisions, we can understand what our customers think about our products, and our authors can see your feedback on the title that they have worked with Packt to create. It will only take a few minutes of your time, but is valuable to other potential customers, our authors, and Packt. Thank you!

Index